THE CASE FOR ISRAEL

THE CASE FOR
ISRAEL

BY

FRANK GERVASI

Foreword by Abba Eban

THE VIKING PRESS
New York

To the memory of
Sarah,
mother of Georgia and Helen, Robert and Murray,
with love

ACKNOWLEDGMENTS

It is impossible to thank by name the many persons who helped me write *The Case for Israel*. The sources are duly acknowledged in the footnotes, text, and Bibliography. I owe personal thanks, however, to Dr. Paul Friedman, Hebrew scholar and eminent psychiatrist, who provided valuable information and insight into the problem of anti-Semitism; to Mrs. Doris Gottlieb, a diligent researcher in Biblical history; and to Jonas Silverstone, friend and counselor, for moral support. My professional research assistant was Craig Karpel, and to him too my thanks, as well as to Robert Billow, who helped reduce to manageable dimensions the material on the refugees, and to Lillian Georgick, secretary, for uncomplainingly typing and retyping the manuscript.

—F.G.

CONTENTS

Bibliography, *185*

Appendices

MAPS

FOREWORD

BY ABBA EBAN

Foreign Minister of Israel

"THE CASE FOR ISRAEL" APPEARS AT A TIME WHEN WORLD ATTEN-
tion is focused on the Middle East. Here, in this region, at the
crossroads of three great continents, a human drama has un-
folded which has few parallels in the annals of nations. A very
old people has reconstituted its patrimony on the soil of its
ancient homeland after twenty centuries of dispersion. Reviving
its sovereignty through the investment of arduous and often
agonizing effort, Israel has re-created itself, reasserted its intrinsic
unity, and revived its culture.

Israel, on the threshold of its freedom twenty years ago, never
contemplated the savage belligerency it was destined to face on
the part of its Arab neighbors. Thrice in two decades that belligerency has erupted into Arab attempts to subdue Israel and
destroy its independence and integrity. Thrice that design has
been brought to nought by the determined stand of the people
of Israel, but always at great cost.

The patient pursuit of peace remains the cornerstone of Israel's policies. For twenty years Israel has been conducting a soliloquy of peace with its neighbors, hopeful that a day would soon dawn when monologue would be replaced by dialogue. That this will come about is inevitable. It is the deep conviction of Israel that, when it does, a new and great chapter will open for the Middle East as a whole. The dominant theme will be human cooperation, mutual enrichment, and constructive development for the benefit of all the peoples in the region.

It is against this background that *The Case for Israel* should be read and studied.

INTRODUCTION

ISRAEL REVISITED

JERUSALEM. "Ten measures of beauty came into the world," says an old Hebrew proverb. "Jerusalem received nine measures, and the rest of the world one." I fully subscribe to the ancient words. I find more quiet beauty here than in the Rome of my ancestors and feel with this brownish-pink city a kinship that baffles me. I am not Jewish. Yet, as I look eastward from the broad terrace of the King David Hotel at what was yesterday the edge of the New City toward the splendid wall that Suleiman I built around the Old City, I exult as a Jew does that Jerusalem is whole again. Gone is what I knew on previous visits as a no man's land of barbed-wire barricades and deadly mines that separated the two halves of the same city—gone is the valley of hate that separated two peoples. The wire, the mines, and the rubble have been bulldozed into history, and the Old City is revealed in all its millennial glory, breathtakingly beautiful at sunset and sunrise, dancingly vibrant as though alive in the clear, sweet air of early morning or early evening, dramatic as a magnificent stage set for a Verdi opera in the light of the big, fat moons of late summer.

From what I saw and heard during my few days' stay there—including one night in a modern, well-run, though slightly war-scarred, Arab hotel on Mount Scopus—it seemed to me inconceivable that the unity of Jerusalem should ever again be disturbed. The busloads of Israelis whom I saw pouring into the Old City every day, the thousands of all ages who daily went to the Wailing Wall to pray, were drawn by forces nobler than sheer possessiveness or mere curiosity. They shone in the face of a helpless old woman as she was carried in a litter to pray at the wall. What glowed in that old person's face was fulfillment of lifelong yearnings, and convinced me more than Mayor Teddy Kollek's multi-million-dollar publicly subscribed Reconstruction and Restoration Fund, important though it is, that the City of David and Solomon would remain united as the capital of Israel.

I found the Israelis well aware that possession of Jerusalem carries with it heavy responsibilities toward Christians and Moslems. But while they might consider permitting the holy places themselves to come under the jurisdiction of their respective faiths, perhaps even to the extent of allowing extraterritoriality to guardians and staffs, the Israelis will never yield sovereignty over Jerusalem to the Arabs, whose principal holy city is Mecca in any case. As a Christian, I could not help but be touched by the reverence shown at the Holy Sepulcher by streams of Israeli visitors. It occurred to me that perhaps in Jewish hands, the Christian holy places might be rescued from their present, often depressing surroundings and be made to emerge in the nobler settings which they deserve. The place where tradition says Jesus Christ was entombed in the Church of the Holy Sepulcher is reachable only through a maze of squalid foul-smelling bazaars, called suqs.

Jerusalem, under Jewish administration again for the first time since the Romans leveled it 1897 years ago, is being administered in the ecumenical spirit preached by the Rome of Pope John XXIII and his successor, Paul VI. Probably never before has an administration paid such close heed to the exigencies of the city's universality; neither Byzantines nor ancient Romans—and certainly not Crusaders or Moslems—ever showed such concern for the rights and traditions of other religions. Under recent Jordanian administration, Israeli Moslems were refused access to their holy places in the Old City—among them the Mosque of Omar, under whose gilded dome sits the rock from which Mohammed leaped into heaven on his favorite horse. Now they come freely in busloads from Nazareth and Galilee and the Gaza Strip. Of course, the Jordanians also forbade the Old City to Israel's Christian Arabs, except at Christmastime and Easter. When I visited the Holy Sepulcher, its small space was crowded with Christian Arabs, while a party of Israelis awaited their turn through the low, narrow entrance to the place.

Some Arabs have refused to cooperate with the Jewish authorities in Old Jerusalem, I learned, but resistance is not nearly as widespread as newspaper headlines back home have indicated. Each of two "strikes" by Arab shopkeepers who closed their places of business to protest annexation of the Old City by Israel lasted only a few hours. Commerce, the great leveler, is daily at work in the Old City, and it will not be long before Arab stocks of souvenir baubles, worry beads, and carved olivewood trinkets will be replenished from Israeli factories.

When I left Jerusalem at the end of August, Jews and Arabs were mingling freely and peacefully in the Old City, and unless the Arabs wore traditional dress—*gallabeah* and tarboosh, or turban—it was difficult to tell them apart. But for their uniforms, the Arab-speaking young Israeli soldiers of Yemenite origin who patrolled the winding cobbled streets and fetid suqs might have been Arabs. Closing days for shops and businesses had been worked out in the commercial area: Fridays for Moslems, Saturdays for Jews, Sundays for Christians. Arab businessmen grumbled about the higher Israeli taxes which they would have to pay. But, as the man who sold me an inexpensive rosary put it, "If there is peace, business will be good, and taxes won't matter."

GAZA STRIP. Eight miles south of Ashkelon, and only forty miles from Tel Aviv, green orchards and fields of ripening corn yielded to flat, dun-colored desert, and I was back in the Gaza Strip. I had not seen the area since that gloomy, rainy night in March 1957 when the Israelis evacuated it to make way for United Nations Emergency Forces (UNEF) troops and wondered what I would find after the war that came three months short of ten years later. I was prepared for the worst. There had been sharp fighting in the Strip, and I expected to see what I have seen too often as a reporter of wars—gnawed buildings, smashed homes, torn roads, burned-out vehicles, broken weapons. Inwardly, I braced myself. I have seen enough of war and war's aftermath in Spain, Africa, Italy, Greece, France, and Germany never to want to see another war or what war leaves in its wake in terms of destruction and human suffering.

On the grubby landscape on the left a few Bedouins were camped here and there, their goat-hair tents raised like huge, misshapen umbrellas against the sting of the noonday sun and the cold of desert nights. Ragged, skinny-legged children played in the muck of a goat corral, and women fanned camel-dung fires under gasoline-can stoves. Off to the right, perched on the dunes this side of the faraway, clean-looking Mediterranean, was a refugee camp, its tin-roofed, concrete huts arranged in rows like a poor man's Levittown. I caught glimpses of small gardens, and from a distance of less than half a mile the refugees' village looked far more livable than the mud-walled, windowless, hovels where Gaza's "native" inhabitants lived. I had visited that very village back in 1957 and saw no point in revisiting it now. I wanted to see Gaza proper, and Rafa and Khan Yunis.

Ragged surrender flags still fluttered from the rooftops of the clusters of low nondescript houses on the way to Gaza proper. I looked for signs of fighting, but saw remarkably few. Some buildings were pock-marked around windows and doorways from machine-gun and rifle fire where the Israelis had replied to snipers' bullets, but there were no signs of wanton shooting. This was confirmed later when I learned that civilian casualties in the Strip had been amazingly low. The area's inhabitants—approximately 450,000, of whom a doubtful 315,000 [1] were classed as refugees—live in three main towns, eight refugee camps, in innumerable scattered farmhouses, and in groups of dwellings in fractional villages. Not one of the refugee camps was hit. Damage to civilian property in Gaza, Rafa, and Khan Yunis, as in the countryside as a whole, was minimal. Writer Martha Gellhorn, who spent a month checking Arab reports of civilian casualties with local civil authorities, hospitals, and the refugees themselves, estimated the total Arab civilian death toll of the six-day war on all fronts at fewer than two hundred, and in the Gaza area at no more than ten. What I saw in Gaza and later in the towns of the Israeli-occupied west bank of the Jordan confirmed her findings. If war can ever be called "civilized," the Israelis fought a civilized war last June, judging by the respect they showed for all but strictly military targets.

The road rolled smoothly, broadly on to Gaza. The Egyptians had widened and resurfaced it only recently, the sole improvement, it developed, that they made during their nineteen-year tenure in the Strip. Scores of Arabs, some in *gallabeahs*, but most wearing trousers and Western-style shirts, wielded picks and shovels along the wayside, deepening the drainage ditches and repairing occasional potholes left by tank tracks. As always,

[1] United Nations Relief and Welfare Administration (UNRWA) officials said their latest census listed 315,000 refugees in the Strip, but Israeli authorities said that the rolls were padded, and that the true figure probably was closer to 270,000.

unemployment was high in the Strip—approximately 40 per cent among the regular inhabitants, and maybe as much as 80 per cent among the refugees. The road repairs, though largely unnecessary, were creating employment until the Israelis found other solutions to the area's staggering economic problems.

The Egyptians, for whom the Gaza Strip was merely a *fedayeen* base and a repository for fourth-rate administrators, left behind them economic chaos. The Strip's economy is largely based on the export of low-grade citrus fruit. Last year's crop of 1.8 million cases fetched about 10 million dollars. The Egyptian occupation authorities allowed the exporters to bring in 75 per cent of their revenue in the form of luxury goods, which became the backbone of the Strip's main industry—smuggling. Imported perfumes, cosmetics, lingerie, fancy canned goods, flashlights, neckties, knit goods, cheap cutlery, and chinaware were smuggled into Egypt and brought in around 15 million dollars. The inhabitants have been doing a brisk business selling their goods to eager Israeli tourists who are swarming all over the occupied territories, but the boom is bound to be short-lived. The Israeli government has no intention of allowing the merchants to replenish their stocks of unessentials. However, it is permitting Gaza citrus exporters to travel to Europe to negotiate new contracts in their regular Soviet-bloc markets.

Gaza had changed for the worse since I last saw it. It was noisier, more squalid if possible, and considerably more run-down, after being treated for twenty years by the Egyptians as a virtual concentration camp. Its inhabitants were never granted Egyptian citizenship, enjoyed no freedom of movement and were subject to Egyptian military law. A shiny new Seven-Up bottling plant and a citrus-fruit processing factory were inoperative. As before, the only really respectable public building in the place was the brown, blocklike three-storied combination jail and administrative center built by the British back in Mandate days. Now, as in 1956–1957, it was being used as Military Gov-

ernment and Civilian Administration headquarters by the Israelis. And there, in an upper-story office redolent of disin-
fectant, I talked at length with Mordekhai Shnerson, a foreign-
office official and former Ambassador to Tokyo who had been
turned into a civil administrator in the emergency.

He said the Egyptians had wanted to keep the Gaza Strip as
a "horrible example" and had done nothing to develop the area's
economy. Not even handicrafts were encouraged. The population
was unwilling to cooperate at first, for those who collaborated
with the Israelis after the Sinai campaign of 1956 had been mis-
treated, imprisoned, even tortured, when the Egyptians returned
in March 1957. But things were improving. The area's five hospitals were functioning with the few doctors and nurses who
stayed behind when the Egyptians left, and the public services
are fully restored, administered by local officials under Israeli
supervision.

On Gaza's main street, a wide, crowded, dusty thoroughfare,
crowds of boys in faded denim nightshirts hawked everything
from cheap fountain pens with phony American trademarks and
"feelthy peectures" from Hungary to pencils made in Red China
and plastic toy pistols from Czechoslovakia. Shops were open
and full of sleazy goods as various as any in an old-time neigh-
borhood notions shop. Oriental music blared monotonously
from cafés, where countermen brewed cups of sickly-sweet Turkish coffee. There were no women in sight; mid-town Gaza
seemed to be populated entirely by men in tarbooshes, some
wearing Western clothes, most of them in blue, white, or striped
nightgowns. Khaki-clad Israeli soldiers, armed but not ostenta-
tiously so, weaved in and out, ignoring and being ignored, but
quietly watchful. No Arab town is ever quite as entrancing as
Hollywood would have one believe, and Gaza, notwithstanding
Crusaders and Saladins and as gory and romantic a history as
may be found anywhere along this much-fought-over slab of
Mediterranean real estate, is no exception.

The United Nations Relief and Welfare Administration was feeding the refugees, and the Israelis were feeding the rest. Sanitary and health conditions were appalling, with tuberculosis, trachoma, dysentery, and typhoid at menacing levels. This, however, was not true in the refugee camps where the UNRWA people had matters under control. The refugees were the best-cared-for people in the Strip, judging both health and diet. The efficient, thorough way in which the Israelis were going about normalizing Gaza, and the Strip as a whole, indicated they meant to stay.

In a possible move to facilitate a population shift from this obviously overpopulated 130 square miles of sand and rock, the Israeli authorities are allowing Strip Arabs to travel freely in their own vehicles to Hebron and the west bank. This may be a subtle attempt to stimulate emigration from the poor soil of the Gaza Strip to the richer lands which the Israelis occupy along the Jordan. Hundreds make the trip daily, but there was no indication whether the emigration was permanent. The Israelis call the movement tourism, but the outward flow of Gaza residents might well be the beginning of a resettlement process.

KHAN YUNIS. The center of attraction for Israeli tourists here was the local school where Arab tots were taught their three Rs —and hatred of Israel—by Nasser's teachers. Two schoolrooms on the ground floor of the reddish-brown stucco building were devoted to the most hideous art exhibit I have ever seen. The walls of both rooms were covered with "paintings" by grade-school children aged twelve to fifteen years. One depicted a Jewish soldier being crushed under an Egyptian boot, and the child artist had not spared the red of his paintbox. Another showed Jews being slaughtered within an enclosed area that suggested a ghetto; the killers were armed, uniformed youths with machine guns, and the central figure was a crazed Arab boy who waved a bloody dagger and all too hideously had obviously been drinking blood. Of the thirty-odd examples in the exhibit, half were devoted to glorifying Nasser, who was immortalized in one crude painting as a sort of Arab Augustus, in flowing Roman robes, a laurel wreath around his noble brow, an olive branch in one hand and an upright sword in the other. Behind him were ranged the flags of the Arab states, and at his feet groveled Jews, begging mercy. Charming.

WEST BANK. This was terrain that I had not seen since 1940, when it was still part of Palestine—the great, kidney-shaped bulge of land north and south of Jerusalem and west of the Jordan River, within which lie Hebron, Bethlehem, Jericho, Ramallah, Nablus, and Jenin. Mountainous, though by Alpine standards merely rugged, and as deforested as goats and Arabs can render any country, it is much like parts of Sicily—raw, rugged, but with sweet green valleys. Well-tilled but not intensively so, the countryside cannot have changed much since the Prophets walked its trails, and the shepherds and goatherds of the Bible pastured their flocks on its slopes. Certainly, it had changed little in twenty-seven years.

Bethlehem was so crowded with Israeli tourists and Arab visitors from Gaza that it was impossible to find parking space in the area outside the Church of the Nativity—the Jews came to visit the tomb of Rachel, the Arabs to be reunited with friends and relatives and, perhaps, find work and new homes in less crowded circumstances than those prevailing in the Strip.

The road that winds northward from Jerusalem passes through Ramallah, high (about three thousand feet) on the Judean massif. It was once a summer resort for well-to-do merchants from Jerusalem, and if it remains in Israeli hands as seems eminently possible, given its nearness to the Jewish capital and its strategic importance, Ramallah has a bright future as a tourist center. Squarely built of grayish-white stone with a pinkish glow, the town, though close to the recent fighting, was intact, a gleam-

ing monument to the skill of Israeli strategists and the crafts-
manship of Arab masons. Arabs build in cubes—and decorate
with domes and arches—fitting stone to stone with a cunning
that I thought only Italians possessed. One house in a row of
fine homes was King Hussein's residence when he visited these
parts and now was heavily guarded by Israeli soldiers.

Nablus, once the Hebrew city of Schechem, now a populous
but rather run-down, undistinguished community of thirty thousand, was in full cry, radios blaring Oriental music, idle-seeming
Arabs sitting at their cafés, sucking at hookahs, sipping coffee,
playing checkers, and taking little notice of Israeli passersby.
Every foot of ground hereabouts is related to Biblical times and
personages—near Nablus may be found Jacob's well and Joseph's
tomb.

Then Jenin, the ancient Ein-Ganim of Hebrew times. It lies
at the foot of the hills of Samaria where they dip into the Jezreel
valley. Its name means Spring of Gardens, but it will take years
of expert farming to make it live up to its name. Like Nablus
and Ramallah, the town was unmarked by war, for the military
surgery with which the Israelis isolated the great kidney from
the rest of the Hashemite Kingdom was swift and sure. The
"incisions" occurred farther west—at Tulkarem, Latrun, and
Kalkilya, which King Hussein's Arab Legion had heavily fortified. In smashing through the defenses, the Israelis also damaged the towns. But again, the civilian casualties were astound-
ingly low.

"But a human life is a human life," said an Israeli intelligence
officer with whom I discussed the matter of civilian casualties.
"We never look at a smashed or seriously damaged house without wondering what happened to the people who lived there."

Several refugee villages lay off the road, partly depopulated—
some of their occupants having fled eastward into Jordan proper
when the fighting started. Many who wish to return have been
allowed to do so, though not those who had been among Ahmed

Shukairy's Palestine Liberation Organization fifth columnists and guerrillas.

The refugees' re-entry was held up for about six weeks because the processing forms had STATE OF ISRAEL printed across the top. Jordan refused to accept the blanks. But a compromise was worked out with Red Cross help. The new forms say HASHEMITE KINGDOM OF JORDAN in the upper left-hand corner, STATE OF ISRAEL in the upper right-hand corner, and INTERNATIONAL RED CROSS in the center. Jordan's acceptance of the new forms probably was motivated by its desire to get rid of the refugees. However, acceptance, for whatever motive, constituted cooperation, and something more—something akin to Jordanian recognition of the fact that Israel exists.

Anyhow, here was proof that, working together, Arabs and Jews could solve a problem.

It occurred to me, as I rode through the west bank on my way to Afula and the Golan Heights in Syria, that one of the major consequences of the Israeli victory might be a final settlement of the Arab refugee problem. An entirely new situation has been created—Israelis and the bulk of the refugees are all living within the same frontiers. They are face to face at last on their own land, in a position to strip their problem clean of poisonous propaganda and external pressures. Indications have come from a number of Arab mayors of west-bank cities and towns that their people have had enough of war and uncertainty and want now to get on with building rural roads, schools, hospitals and improving their farms with the use of tractors, irrigation systems, and fertilizers.

Many west-bank Arabs already have visited relatives and friends in the prosperous Israeli Arab villages, and seen that life with the Israelis is not as bad as the hate-propagandists had painted it. However, one could not know, so soon after the war, and after nineteen years of Nasserian brainwashing, how accurately the local Arab leaders reflected the peoples' true feelings and intentions—or their own. The Israelis were proceeding cautiously, feeling their way, and backing up their hopes with practical moves, such as appropriation of the equivalent of two and a half million dollars for road-construction projects to help the area's farmers speed their produce to market.

GOLAN HEIGHTS. It seemed to me a large fraction of the entire population of Israel was there with me, in automobiles and busses, or on motor scooters, bicycles, and horse-drawn buckboards, crowding the narrow, winding dirt track leading up the escarpment to Baniyas, then on to Saoura, Mannsoura, and Quneitra. As far as Baniyas, the traffic was bumper to bumper, through areas still drearily festooned with barbed wire and ribbon markers warning of mines. Those who rode the air-conditioned buses were lucky, for the dust rose in thick, almost viscous clouds.

Most stopped at Baniyas, where the stream of the same name makes large, cool green pools before the waters reunite to flow into the beloved Jordan, which nourishes half of Israel's northern farms. An enterprising soda-pop merchant had set up a refreshment stand in an abandoned shack under some scrubby trees grayish-brown with dust. He did the kind of business one might expect—he was taking in money so fast he was using cookpots for cashboxes. Armed with soda pop, families resumed the long, hot drive to see every inch of the difficult terrain their army had conquered, and to confirm what they already knew: that never again would Syrian guns fire down on their homes and fields in the valley below. They bought fruit from friendly Druse villagers, and picnicked by the roadside wherever places had been cleared of mines.

Many remained at Baniyas, to feast their eyes on the waters which the Syrians had tried so long and so hard to deny them; hundreds took off shoes and stockings to wade in the pools, happy as ducks. Others went on to Quneitra, stopping on the way to inspect the bunkers, pillboxes, revetments, and trenches which the Syrians had built à la Maginot. The evidence of hard, deadly —even desperate—combat was everywhere. War leaves behind the look and smell of death, even when the field has been cleared of dead and maimed men and only dead and maimed weapons remain, and of these there was an abundance along the brownish-red mountains above Qiryat Shemona, Dan, Kefar Szold, La-havot Habashan, Gonen, Notera, Gadot, and a score of other kibbutzim and settlements north of the Sea of Galilee, secure now for the first time in nearly twenty years.

There were many obvious differences between the Israel of the summer of 1967 and the Israel of many previous visits. But the difference that mattered above more cars on the broadened highways, the sharply modern skyscraper hotels and public build-ings of metropolitan Tel Aviv, the greening Negev, and the many other physical signs of growth and progress was the change that ordeal and triumph had wrought in the Israelis themselves. Although not yet at peace with their neighbors, they were at peace with one another, a nation free of the inner strifes and conflicts that characterize other societies, including our own. "Alienation" is an alien word in Israel.

There is kinship between Israelis of diverse cultural back-grounds. Though some Israelis of Sephardic Oriental origin might complain, for instance, that Ashkenazi Europeans hold the better jobs, they admit, when pressed, that had they re-mained in Yemen, Egypt, Iraq, or their other lands of origin, their sons and daughters would not now be attending college and preparing themselves for a better life. What contention exists between the comparative newcomers and the old-timers might erupt in debate but never in violence.

Similarly, the elderly are not ostracized by the young in a land where the family unit remains the basic ingredient of society, and there are no quarrels between rich and poor, quite probably

because the gap between the two is smaller than in most societies, and is nearly nonexistent by comparison with any other
Middle Eastern society. Israel has its hippies, cranks, crooks,
soreheads, and extremists, for Jews are people, with the failings
and idiosyncrasies common to all peoples. Theirs is hardly the
Utopian society the ultra-Zionists would have one believe, but
neither is it the harsh theocracy that anti-Zionists paint it.

There is plenty of disunity, for the Israelis are a quarrelsome
lot, stiff-necked and stubborn. But their protests take the forms
democracy provides: angry letters to the editors of a host of
newspapers representing every hue of the political spectrum
from left to right; sharp debates in the Knesset, their parliament; and ballots at election time.

What seems most to characterize the Israelis at this particular
juncture in their development is a sense of security that derives
not only from their recent victory but from the deep knowledge
that in any national emergency they can rely completely on one
another. They give, it seemed to me, new meaning to the word
"patriotism," for theirs is a loyalty to a common welfare rather
than to symbols, and each cares as much as the next fellow about
defending that welfare.

I have never found it difficult to uphold the Israelis' side in
their long, unsought quarrel with the Arabs. I sincerely believed
that they were in the right in seeking to retrieve their nationhood and in defending it in 1948 and 1956. I found their case
stronger than ever in 1967, particularly after having visited Egypt
and Syria extensively in 1957, and Egypt again in 1958 and 1959.
I honestly tried to see the Arabs' side of the story, but when in
both Cairo and Damascus I heard Israel described *ad nauseam*
as "a cancer that must be cut out of the flesh of the Middle
East," and in the United Nations later heard the Jewish state
compared to Nazi Germany for defending itself against promised annihilation, the compulsion to rise to Israel's defense
became irresistible.

What follows, then, is the case for Israel, as seen by a non-Jew who sympathizes wholeheartedly with the Arab peoples' longings for the schools, hospitals, good government, jobs, and better lives that centuries have denied them, but who cannot abide their leaders' maniacal notion that Israel and its people must disappear from the map of the Middle East. By renouncing war as a doctrine and recognizing the reality of Israel's legitimate permanency in the region, the Arabs can take the first essential steps toward achieving those human goals which for so long have been beyond their reach.

It is my great hope, shared, I know, by millions, that the Arabs will find their way to peace with their Semitic cousins, and with it to the better life so long denied them.

THE CASE FOR ISRAEL

1

EMBATTLED ZION

For as the body without the spirit is dead, so faith without works is dead also.

—James II, 26

ISRAEL, A YOUNG COUNTRY WITH OLD ROOTS, IS AN UNPRECEDENTED phenomenon in nation-making. Its emergence in 1948 was a triumph of the human spirit, proving faith can indeed move mountains. Never has a people clung so long to a dream of national identity, achieved it as uniquely as have the Jews in Israel, or paid so dearly for the privilege. Never has a people been obliged to defend its nationhood so continuously, or at such great cost to itself and its enemies.

The state was born of a human tragedy so colossal that it defies description or historical comparison; it emerged after six million of the world's fifteen million Jews were massacred during the twentieth-century madness we knew as Hitlerism. The survivors have fashioned themselves into something new on the face of the earth, a classless society of free men in which no one is really rich or really poor, and the individual rights of citizens—

vacuum has existed in this area since the demise of the British and French empires after World War II, and the Russians are trying to fill it. That the region has not succumbed to the westward thrust of Soviet imperialism is an important by-product of the Jews' struggle to survive as a sovereign people.

Had the Arabs rather than the Jews won in June 1967, the Middle East today would be a constellation of Soviet satellites, for it would have been essentially a Russian, not an Arab, triumph. It would have compensated impressively for Soviet failures in Berlin, Cuba, the Congo, and Ghana; enabled Moscow to tighten its grip on its more self-assertive European satellites like Poland and Romania; and re-established the U.S.S.R. as the godhead of world Communism with predictable consequences: an end to peaceful coexistence, a return to a Soviet policy of revolutionary struggle against "capitalist imperialism," and eventual atomic confrontation with the free world. Far worse, from the human standpoint, an Arab victory last June would have meant a massacre of Jews comparable in monstrousness only to the Hitlerian holocaust which preceded the state's birth. As we shall see from documents captured by the Israelis in June, Arab units had been instructed to *destroy* not only Jewish cities, towns, and villages but their populations as well.

The Russian military presence as an Arab ally was already well established by 1956, as was evidenced by a desert littered with Soviet guns and armor after General Moshe Dayan swept southward through Sinai. Puzzled by what then still seemed an odd alliance of Communists and avowedly anti-Communist Arabs, I asked a highly placed intelligence officer of the Israeli General Staff, an Arabist of international repute, to explain it. He found nothing strange in the partnership.

"Rightly or wrongly," he said, "the Arabs hate the West, which, to them, means British and French colonialism. In Arab eyes, Israel represents Western concepts of culture and civilization. Ergo, the Arabs hate Israel. Since they have made it their primary object in life to eject the West from their midst, they are determined to destroy Israel. Arabs do not think in ideological terms. It is folly to believe, as some Western diplomats do, that because Egypt's President Gamal Abdel Nasser is anti-Communist, he can be weaned away from Moscow. Nasser and the Kremlin have an identical objective: the expulsion of the West from the Arab lands. Hence they are allies, and we Israelis are their common enemy."

For Israel, defense of its existence through three wars, with ceaseless raids by *fedayeen*—specially trained guerrillas—between each, has been costlier in lives and money than so small a state should be called upon to bear. The dead and totally disabled are counted in the thousands.[2] Incalculable, however, is the cumulative cost in actual cash of armaments, of productivity lost as a result of guerrilla harassment and periodic mobilizations, and of potential revenues unearned because of the prolonged Arab boycott against nations trading with Israel. Only the generous assistance of friendly nations and of Jews residing abroad in free societies has enabled Israel to advance economically—help it could do without if the state could live in peace.

However costly to Israel, war has been costlier still to its enemies. Estimates of the direct damage suffered in June 1967 by the Egyptians alone start at $1,500,000,000, roughly the value of the Russian planes, tanks, guns, and missiles smashed or captured by the Israelis in Sinai. In addition, by jamming the Suez Canal with sunken ships, Egypt deprived itself of transit fees totaling about $600,000 a day. Gone too, for Syria and Jordan as well as Egypt, were the receipts of a lucrative tourist trade. War not only smashed the enemies' armies, but also seriously weakened the already feeble economies of Israel's principal enemies.

Moreover, when the fighting ended on June 11, Israel held

[2] An estimated 5000 were killed in the 1947–1948 war of independence, and 170 in the Sinai campaign. Jewish casualties in the recent fighting included, as of July 5, 1967, about 750 dead and 1700 "permanently disabled." The dead and wounded resulting from raids on Jewish settlements run into the hundreds.

Egypt's Sinai Peninsula, including the east bank of the Suez Canal and the vital Strait of Tiran,[3] strategic high positions in Syria above the Sea of Galilee in the north, Jordanian territory west of the Jordan River, and the Jordanian-occupied part of Jerusalem ruled by the Arabs since their invasion in 1945.

After defeats of the magnitude of those sustained in 1948, 1956, and 1967, reasonable men have reached the obvious conclusion: Israel is in the Middle East to stay, hence better acceptance and peace than rejection and war. But Arab leaders are not reasonable men.

The Arab outlook is conditioned principally by the all-exclusive nature of the Moslem religion as interpreted, or misinterpreted, by its present-day priests, the mullahs. "Allah is great," calls the muezzin from his slender minaret at nightfall. "I bear witness that there is no God but Allah, that Mohammed is the Lord's messenger." This is taken to mean that the world belongs to the faithful, and that the infidel is an enemy to be exterminated. Yet, as in the Jewish Torah and the Christian Bible, from both of which it derives, the Koran teaches love of one's neighbor, even of one's enemy. "It is the highest virtue," said the Prophet, "to seek out him who had repulsed you, to forgive him who had offended you."

Arab leaders like Nasser, however, prefer to lean on Mohammed's more chauvinistic sayings, such as "Death means Paradise, victory means pillage, and defeat means only the chance to try again." Beset by economic and social problems beyond their ability to solve, they resort to demagoguery to stay in power. It is easier to shout "Araby for the Arabs!" and demand the return to Palestine of several hundred thousand refugees who fled when Israel was created than it is to build schools, hospitals, and decent housing. Most Arabs remain untouched either by the ideas or the technology of the twentieth century, but many thirst for

[3] Gateway between the Gulf of Aqaba and the Red Sea and as indispensable to Israeli maritime commerce as the Panama Canal is to American traffic with the Orient.

a better life for themselves and their children. But their cries for schooling, decent homes, bread, and shoes are answered by their leaders with vague promises of a better tomorrow when all Islam is "united," "free of Western imperialism," and "purged of Jews."

The facts are that Arab unity is chimerical except when war on Israel is invoked; that "Western imperialism" ceased to exist in the area with the departure of the British and French after World War II; and that the Jewish people's claims to Palestine predate those of the Arabs by centuries.

The complex drama being played out in the Holy Land bulges with psychological, cultural, and historical complications. However, the drama is based on one main premise, namely that the Jews have no right being where they are. Palestine, the Arabs claim, is theirs by right of prior possession. It is an argument which many decent people rightly concerned with the humanitarian aspects of the problem of the Palestinian refugees accept as gospel. It happens to be false, or, at best, only partly true. Fanatic faith, said Thomas Moore in "Lalla Rookh," "once wedded fast to some dear falsehood, hugs it to the last." There is no greater falsehood in history than that the Arabs are the sole, legitimate heirs to the lands of an Israel that once was Palestine and before that was Canaan.

2

THE PROMISED HOMELAND: ITS BIBLICAL ROOTS

*And I give to thee and thy seed after thee, the land of
thy sojourning, all the land of Canaan for an everlast-
ing possession.*
                    —God's Promise to Abraham, Genesis XVII, 8

THE STORY OF THE JEWS' RELATIONSHIP TO PALESTINE IS AS OLD
as recorded history. Some of it is legend, but legend supported
by the Bible, "the most authentic and longest written record of
any nation except China," [1] and confirmed by contemporary
archaeological discoveries.

Jewish history begins some four thousand years ago in Ur of
the Chaldees, ancient Mesopotamia (now Iraq), home of the
Semitic tribes known as "Ibrim," or Hebrews, meaning people
from "beyond the river," the Euphrates. Their patriarch was
Abraham, forefather of the Hebrews through Isaac, his son by

[1] Walter Clay Lowdermilk, *Palestine, Land of Promise*, New York:
Harper and Brothers, 1944.

his wife, Sarah, and of the Arabs through Ishmael, his son by Hagar, Sarah's servant. Thus Arabs and Jews descend from and venerate a common ancestor—the Arabs remembering Abraham as the "Friend of God," [2] the Jews honoring him as their father and the founder of monotheism.

For it was Abraham who, in Mesopotamia's spiritual squalor of idolatry and polytheism, conceived the single God of Judaism, a concept that many centuries later would animate Christianity, and, later still, Mohammedanism. During the period of Abraham's soul-searching in Ur, Jehovah urged him to leave the country and lead his people "unto the Land which I shall show thee." Abraham obeyed, and led the Hebrews southwestward into Canaan, then a "land of milk and honey" only by contrast with the desert. South of the cool, green hills above Galilee, the Promised Land was barren, pitted with caves, veined with the dry beds of dead streams, and blotched with salt swamps. Its few Bedouin inhabitants eked out a living tending goats and camels, and serving the caravan routes linking Cairo and Damascus. Thus began the Hebrews' simultaneous search for spiritual and national identity. The quest would occupy them through four millennia and culminate in the present struggle which, given the ancient consanguinity of the combatants, is less war than civil war and why Moshe Dayan says, "This is between the Arabs and us and nobody else." [3]

To understand the Hebrews' yearnings for God and nationhood is to understand the mystique of Judaism and the justice of their claim to survival as a people in their own land, pro-

[2] Biblical data and archaeological findings place Abraham's tomb about two miles north of Hebron, at Haram Ramet el Kalil, Arabic for "Sanctuary of the Hill of the Friend of God," a spot venerated by the Arabs. Legend has it that Abraham bought the plot originally as a burial place for Sarah and like the Jews who bought land from the Arabs after him paid an exorbitant price: four hundred silver shekels, a fortune (see Genesis XXIII).

[3] As quoted by Curtis G. Pepper in "Hawk of Israel," *The New York Times Magazine*, July 9, 1967.

tected by their own laws within those of the international community. As with other peoples, the Jews' strivings for a homeland derive from mankind's deep-rooted urge to ensure perpetuation of himself in terms of family, the social unit whereof the nation is merely a larger expression. Apart from imperishable ideas and enduring works of art, nations are probably the only true immortality man achieves. He begins dying the moment he is born, but the societies he creates live on. They may be destroyed, even obliterated for long periods, but somehow, in one form or another, they re-emerge, for nations are creatures not only of human minds and hands, but of the human spirit.

In the third generation of Hebrew residence in Canaan, Abraham's grandson Joseph, son of Jacob, was sold into slavery and taken into Egypt. There Joseph prospered and rose to become viceroy and there, when famine struck Canaan, he was joined by his brothers and their father. Jacob and his children settled in a valley of the Middle Nile as herders and farmers, for in Canaan they had learned to raise grain. Under the Hyksos kings of Egypt, themselves almost certainly of Semitic origin, the Hebrews lived peacefully until about 1580 B.C., when the Hyksos dynasty fell.

The new pharaoh "knew not Joseph" or his kin, and Jacob and his people sank into serfdom. Misfortune shared, however, forged the Hebrews into a nation. Even before they were allowed to leave Egypt, they owned all the attributes of nationhood—a common origin, language, and desire for national identity, and above all a common God. Because his descendants now called Jacob "Israel," one who "prevails with God," Egypt's Hebrews became known as "the Children of Israel," and another thousand years would pass before they would be known as Jews.

Deliverance from persecution and enslavement came with Moses, who would become the Israelites' political leader as well as spiritual redeemer. Raised in the court of a pharaoh as a royal prince, Moses saw his people threatened with extinction, reidentified himself with them, and led them out of Egypt in the

Exodus. Their goal was the Promised Land which throughout their trials in Egypt held the forefront of their prayers and aspirations.

The Exodus into Sinai, where Moses and the Hebrews wandered for forty years, was one of the watersheds of Jewish history. From it flowed that climactic moment on bleak Mount Sinai when the Children of Israel hearkened to the Ten Commandments. It was undoubtedly the most significantly seminal event in history, the emergence of a code of ethics governing man's relationship to his fellow man and to his God that would not only inspire and shape two other great faiths, but would serve as the basic law of what we fondly call "Western civilization."

In a pagan world that encouraged free rein to passions, Moses taught not to slay one's enemy but to feed him and give him drink. He who hates, he said, is on the side of him who sheds blood. Remembering the days of his own people's Egyptian exile, Moses allowed the stranger to share their laws and customs. Most astonishing of all, especially to those aristocrats of ancient liberalism the Greeks, Moses decreed labor a blessing, not a humiliation; he gave equal rights to the slave, awarded him a sabbath as a day of rest, and invited him to table and the festivals. Formulated with earnestness, boldness, and resolute logic, these laws for human conduct, the product of an insignificant Hebrew tribe of nomads and herdsmen, remain forever imbedded in the conscience of civilized man. Some fifteen hundred years after Moses another Jew, by trade a carpenter and by avocation a prophet, universalized Jewish moral law by offering it to the world. His name was Jesus of Nazareth.

After the revelation on Mount Sinai, Moses lived only long enough to lead his people to the edge of Canaan, and, following his death sometime in the middle of the second millennium before Christ, it fell to Joshua to lead the Children of Israel into the Promised Land.

The Jewish conquest of Canaan was devised and executed by Joshua, personal attendant and chief of staff to Moses. He struck only after he and eleven other spies had infiltrated Canaan and studied the land, its people, and their defenses. The Jordan was forded north of the Dead Sea; the key city of Jericho was taken by storm, and after a series of brilliant victories, the Israelites commanded the plains and the central hill country. The conquered land was divided among the tribes and for three centuries, under rulers they called Judges, the Israelites settled down to a life of farming, husbandry, and trading.

As the danger from older enemies diminished—the Canaanites, Ammonites, and Moabites on the Hebrew side of the Jordan and the Edomites across the river—the Israelites grew stronger, and their sovereignty was undisputed. But soon a new and common danger materialized. Seafarers from Crete and the Aegean Islands, driven away from Egypt in 1194 B.C., fell upon the rich coastal plain of Canaan. Armed with the iron weapons they had invented, they established themselves without difficulty against the slings and stone-tipped arms of the Jews and founded a confederation of five cities: Gath, Gaza, Ashkelon, Ashdod, and Ekron, place names in current newspaper headlines.

The newcomers were the Philistines. From their city fortresses they conquered all Israeli-held territory, and the Israelites became their tributaries. The Philistine domination gave the country its name, Palestine, a corruption of Philistinia, "land of the Philistines." Unified against a common foe under Saul, chosen by Samuel, last and greatest of the Judges, to be their first king, the Children of Israel started a war of liberation which, in the broadest sense, persists to this day. Saul and his sons were killed in battle before the king could entirely rid the homeland of the well-entrenched invaders, and he was succeeded by a young farmer's son from Judah named David, who, as a page at Saul's court, had become famous for daring commando-type raids against the enemy and for having bested Goliath, the Philistine champion.

During David's thirty-three-year reign a number of events occurred, a knowledge of which is essential to an understanding of the Jewish people's claims to the land and holy places they hold today as a result of the military and political actions of the summer of 1967. The Philistines were finally and utterly shattered (and subsequently absorbed into various Semitic tribes) and the subjugation of the central hill country and coastal towns was completed. Edom, the bleakness east of the Jordan River—an area that later arbitrarily became Trans-Jordan and later still became Hashemite Jordan—was also conquered and joined to Canaan.

In David's time, what had been a loose and frequently quarrelsome confederation of Hebrew states, became a peaceful, tightly knit, strong nation. Most important of all, however, was the establishment of Jerusalem, a former Jebusite stronghold artfully designed to dominate the central land mass, as the spiritual and political capital of the unified Kingdom of David.

In the long, splendid, but spendthrift reign of David's son and successor, Solomon, occurred another event of far-reaching significance in Jewish history: construction of the Great Temple on the hill called Zion, a spot superbly chosen by David before his death. The Temple anchored Judaism to Jerusalem, the Holy City remaining ever afterward the focus of Jewish yearnings for re-emergence as a nation with Zion as the center of Hebrew government and worship. Down through the ages, wherever they found themselves, Jews daily repeated in prayer and thought, hymn and psalm, the same solemn oath: "If I forget thee, O Jerusalem, let my right hand forget its cunning."

The Hebrews never forgot. Jerusalem remained the lodestar of their national and spiritual aspirations through two centuries of division that saw the conquest of the Northern Kingdom by Sargon the Assyrian (and the disappearance of its people from history) and the creation in the south of the new, strong Kingdom of Judah. From then on the Hebrews were known as "Yehudi," or "men of Judah," hence "Jews" and synonymous with the earlier "Children of Israel." Today, "Israeli" signifies citizenship in the State of Israel common to Jew, Moslem, and Christian, whereas "Jew" denotes Jewish religious affiliation.[4]

Thus, sovereign Jewish states, governed first by Judges, then by kings, existed in Palestine until the Babylonian conquest of 586 B.C. Nebuchadnezzar broke into Solomon's Temple, destroyed the golden vessels, burned everything else, and carried the people of Judah off into captivity. Again, misfortune had a salutary effect, and the Jews, released by Cyrus, conqueror of Babylon, emerged from exile within a half century a more unified people than ever before under Ezra and Nehemiah. They enjoyed self-government during a long period of Persian and Greek overlordship, then regained full sovereignty in 143 B.C. with the Maccabean war of liberation.

Jewish autonomy continued even after the Roman conquest and the destruction of the Temple in 70 A.D. It did not end until the suppression of the Jews' rebellion against Roman rule about sixty years later when the Great Dispersion began in 137 A.D. In some 1500 years of direct pre-Christian relationship to Palestine—not counting the continuity of settlements left there when the Hebrews departed from Canaan for Egypt—history establishes about nine centuries of complete Jewish sovereignty in the Holy Land and approximately five of self-government. It is not surprising, therefore, to find in the State of Israel's Declaration of Independence, of May 14, 1948, these opening words: "In the Land of Israel the Jewish people came into being. In this land was shaped their spiritual, religious, and national character. Here they lived in sovereign independence. Here they created a culture of national and universal import, and gave to the world the eternal Book of Books."

The annals of the Jews after the year 137 A.D. are a chronicle of continuous devotion to their homeland and repeated en-

[4] L. I. Rabinowitz, *The Land and the People, a Brief History*, Jerusalem, 1964.

deavors to return. During their dispersion, they never renounced their claim to Palestine, and in all countries repeated the ancient vow: "If I forget thee, O Jerusalem . . ."

Palestine continued as a Roman, then a Byzantine province, until the first Arab conquest in 634 A.D. The country's mixed population of Jews, Greeks, and Syrians was forcibly converted to Islam and obliged to speak Arabic. The Arabs, however, never settled the country but ruled it as foreign conquerors for a little more than four centuries, yielding in 1071 to the Seljuks. Then followed two centuries of fragmentary rule by the Crusaders, the Mameluke domination that began in 1291 and ended in 1517, and the Ottoman occupation that lasted until 1917, when the Turks were driven out by the Western Allies of World War I.

To the Turks, Palestine was simply a remote, unproductive part of their Empire. However, recognizing Jewish skill in agriculture and, in effect, Jewish rights in Palestine, they permitted the beginning of resettlement of Jews (mainly from Russia) in 1881.

During the long interval of Arab, Seljuk, Christian, Mameluke, and Ottoman overlordship, Palestine never became a national homeland for any people, or even existed as a geopolitical fact. Conquered and reconquered fourteen times in thirteen centuries, each conqueror merely absorbed Palestine as occupied territory and ruled it from without, each leaving its legacy in soldiers and slaves whose descendants shared no ethnic or cultural identity. Successive conquerors meant famine as well as massacre, and the population of Palestine was catastrophically reduced. By 1881 the inhabitants totaled barely 300,000, the Jews among them numbering a scant 25,000 compared to the 2,000,000 of Roman times.

Between the time the Great Dispersion began and resettlement started, the land itself sank back into an oblivion of

malarial swamp in the wet north and eroded soil in the dry
south. Desolation was universal. Mark Twain saw it in 1867
and was appalled. In *Innocents Abroad* he wrote:

> There is not a solitary village throughout its whole ex-
> tent, not for thirty miles in either direction [near Merom].
> There are two or three small clusters of Bedouin tents, but
> not a single permanent habitation. One may ride ten miles,
> hereabouts, and not see ten human beings. To this region
> one of the prophecies is applied: "I will bring the land into
> desolation; and your enemies which dwell therein shall be
> astonished at it . . ." No man can stand here by deserted
> Ain Mellahah and say the prophecy has not been fulfilled.
>
> Grey lizards, those heirs of ruin, of sepulchers and desola-
> tion, glided in and out among the rocks or lay still and
> sunned themselves. Where prosperity has reigned and
> fallen; where glory has flamed and gone out; where gladness
> was and sorrow is; where the pomp of life has been, and
> silence and death brood in its high places, there this reptile
> makes his home, and mocks at human vanity.

But although many of Palestine's two million Jews left after
the Roman conquest to become a nation scattered among nations, considerable numbers maintained a foothold in the country. At no time, not even during the worst period of famine and
massacre, did they totally abandon the land. In mountain villages such as Peki'in in Galilee, in the Holy Cities of Safad and
Jerusalem, and in Roman Tiberias, present-day inhabitants can
trace residence and property ownership directly and flawlessly
back to ancient Hebrew antecedents.

For the Bible is not the only proof of the Jews' claim to Palestine. It exists in recorded deeds demonstrating Jewish ownership in fee simple of great tracts of land bought from various
owners, and converted from marsh and desert into orchards and
gardens. And it also exists in a massive body of international law
envisioning and sanctioning the creation in Palestine of a Jewish
national homeland.

3

THE DEVELOPMENT OF
JEWISH SOVEREIGNTY

*His Majesty's Government views with favor the estab-
lishment in Palestine of a national home for the Jewish
people . . .*
—Balfour Declaration, November 2, 1917

IN THE CONTINUING DIALOGUE BETWEEN JEWS AND GOD THAT
began in ancient Ur of the Chaldees, the prayer "Bring us back
to Zion, Thy city in gladness . . ." remained a constant of Jewish religious ritual and thought throughout the Diaspora. But
the Messianic dream of a return to the Holy Land was not translated into political action until the advent of Zionism late in the
last century. The founder of what quickly became a movement
that energized the eventual creation of a Jewish state was Theodor Herzl, a lawyer-journalist son of a wealthy family of so-
called assimilated Jews from Budapest.

Some rich or merely well-to-do European Jewish families living in societies that tolerated them in politics, law, medicine,
literature, art, and science prayed faithfully for a return to Zion

but did little about it. Attainment of full civil rights in the communities within which they lived, not in a homeland of their own, had become the nineteenth-century goal of this category of Diaspora Jews. Basking in the sunlight of ostensible freedom and equality, the Messianic vision of Jewish nationhood faded before a more dazzling one of humanity united in accordance with the libertarian and egalitarian ideals of the French Revolution. But events—and Theodor Herzl—recalled them to their ancient mission as a people and as a civilization.

Some Western European Jews had gone as far as total loss of Jewish identity; even the less extreme stripped Judaism of its "national" content, avowing it to be merely a faith, or form of worship. But in Eastern Europe, where the great masses of Jewry still lived, the old loyalties held their ground, entrenched by adamant religious allegiance. The hope of ultimate return to Zion retained its aura of mystery and miracle, and it soon became evident it would be achieved not by divine intervention, but human effort. The need for action as a dynamic ally of passive prayer was made tragically clear by the shocking pogroms in Russia in 1881 and the vicious anti-Jewish Czarist "May Laws" confining the Jews to the towns and villages of the pale, in Poland, then part of the Russian Empire.

A large-scale emigration began. By 1900, some six hundred thousand Jews, mostly Russian, had landed in the United States. Others went to Britain, South Africa, Australia, and Western Europe. But one small band of idealists forever shook the dust and degradations of exile from their feet and settled in Palestine. They were known as *Bilu*,[1] pioneer farmers constituting the vanguard of the First Aliya, or "first homecoming" to the land that would become Israel. Enthusiastic, but untrained, they and other would-be farmers who followed them went through hard times, until Baron Edmond de Rothschild came to their rescue.

[1] Word made up of the initial Hebrew letters of the Biblical verse (Isaiah III, 5): *Beit Yaàkov Lechu Veneilcha*—"House of Jacob, come, let us go!"

But the Great Return had begun. Organizations were formed overseas under the auspices of the Hovevei Zion ("Lovers of Zion") to promote the reversion of Jews not only to the land to repopulate it, but to its very soil to wrest it from Mark Twain's lizards. It was at this point that Herzl entered Jewish history.

A brilliant essayist and writer of boudoir comedies, Herzl was the Paris correspondent of the Vienna *Neue Freie Presse* at the time of the trial in 1894 of Captain Alfred Dreyfus, an Alsatian Jew in the French army, charged with espionage for Germany. In Europe, reaction against liberalism had started and with it, modern anti-Semitism, that virulent form of anti-Jewishness which holds Jews to be racially inferior, alien, and unassimilable. Despite evidence of his innocence, Dreyfus was found guilty of treason. His appeal denied, it was plain he was a victim of the new, increasingly popular doctrine of anti-Semitism which would assume unspeakable horror under Hitler.

It came to the "assimilated" Herzl like a Mosaic revelation that emancipation and assimilation were not solutions to the problems Jews faced, but dangerous delusions that could only end in calamity. As long as Jews remained a minority, prisoners of circumstances and policies they could not control, discrimination or worse would be their ever-recurring lot. The answer, he saw, was fulfillment of the age-old Jewish yearnings. The Jews must return to Palestine and establish an independent state guaranteed by international law. They must become masters of their own fate, in their own house, where they would be free to live in accordance with their own traditions. Herzl articulated his ideas, tantamount to reidentification with his people, in clear, concise, challenging form in *Der Judenstaat* (*The Jewish State*).

To be sure, Herzl's idea was not new. It was inherent and fundamental in Judaism since God and Abraham began their dialogue in Mesopotamia. It had been the theme of the Prophets, the "rod and staff" of Jewry through agonizing exile, and the stuff of prayer and hymnal for nearly four centuries. It was re-enunciated in 1862 by Moses Hess in *Rome and Jerusalem*, and so vividly in 1881 by Leo Pinsker in his *Auto-Emancipation* that Herzl admitted he would not have written his own book had he read Pinsker first.

What Herzl did was to restore to primacy and influence a concept which, except for a brief eighteenth–nineteenth-century eclipse, had swayed Jewish thought since the time of Abraham. Herzl's contribution lay in formulating in concrete terms what had been only an evanescent dream. He, who had personified a theory which he now wholeheartedly dismissed, now preached that God helps only those who help themselves and that the return to Zion would not come about by divine intervention.

Herzl was a rare blend of visionary, realist, and statesman. The Jewish masses came to adore him. In 1897, under his stimulus, the World Zionist Movement came into being at the First Zionist Congress in Basel, Switzerland, devoted to "the creation for the Jewish people of a home in the Land of Israel secured by public law." [2]

Except for its uniquely Jewish Messianic overtones, Zionist nationalism closely resembled in origins and objectives the nationalist movements that burgeoned in post-Napoleonic Europe. The scene of Bonaparte's final military defeat was still cluttered with the debris of battle when his conquerors [3] assembled at the Congress of Vienna in June 1815 to restore to their European thrones the reactionary kings and princes he had toppled. The signatories of the Holy Alliance turned the clock back

[2] Herzl wore himself out in the cause and died in 1904 at the age of forty-four. In his diary, after that First Congress, are the prophetic words: "I have founded the Jewish State. If I were to say so today, people would laugh at me. But in five years' time—certainly in fifty years, it will be seen that I was right."

The State of Israel was born (or reborn) by a majority vote of the General Assembly of the United Nations on November 29, 1947, almost fifty years after Herzl wrote those words.

[3] Austria, Russia, Prussia, and Britain.

to feudalism, vowing to crush democracy wherever it challenged their absolute power. The result was revolutions and counter-revolutions, rebellions and suppressions of unprecedented violence and persistence.

From the 1820s onward, Europeans clamored and fought for the social justice and economic progress promised by the French Revolution and partly realized under Napoleon, but only as dependencies of the French Empire. Now they wanted sweeping constitutional reforms guaranteeing individual liberties within free, independent nations, and Jews everywhere were in the forefront of the struggle. The nation-making process found Jews fighting side by side with Spaniards for constitutional rights, with Frenchmen against restoration of the Bourbon dynasty, with Greeks to overthrow the Turks, and with Italians and Germans for unity and nationhood.

Jewish nationalism came of age midway between the beginning of the nationalist movements of the middle decades of the nineteenth century and the reawakening of nationalist forces in Asia and Africa in the middle of the twentieth. Like the Europeans, and later the Asians and Africans, the Jews—a "midway people" as Eastern in origin as they are Western culturally—were motivated by identical needs for self-determination.

The Jews were not the only people whose independence was obliterated by foreign conquerors, whose national frontiers had disappeared from the map, and who yearned to re-emerge. The phenomenon is recurrent, as in the case of the Italians. For nearly fourteen hundred years—from the fall of Rome in the fifth century to the *Risorgimento* [4] in the nineteenth—Italy remained partitioned into a baker's dozen of tiny kingdoms and principalities ruled by foreign and domestic despots. Like the

---

[4] The *Risorgimento*, meaning "Resurrection" (of an Italian nation), is the name given to the long revolutionary process that began early in the nineteenth century and ended with the creation of the modern Italian state in 1870 through the efforts of Giuseppe Mazzini, Camillo Cavour, and Giuseppe Garibaldi. Jews participated actively as both fighters and supporters.

Jews, the Italians shared common ancestry, historical experience, cultural mold, and religious affiliation; like the Jews, the Italians clung for centuries to dreams of unity and freedom, realizing them only after a protracted national struggle.

The Italians, however, had a tremendous advantage over the Jews in their drive for freedom and national identity—they all lived in their native lands, while the Jews were scattered over the face of the earth in other people's countries. The revival of a Jewish nation, unlike the rebirth of an Italian state, required a multitudinous return to the land of origin.

In Herzl's plan for the making of a Jewish nation, the return to Zion was not to be by Jews singly or in small groups, unprepared for the tasks that awaited them, but in a massive movement of farmers, laborers, managers, businessmen, mechanics, engineers, doctors, technicians, intellectuals, scholars, teachers—a cross section of the manpower and skills needed for the building of a homeland.

What Herzl proposed was a voluntary exodus, not for Jews to wander in another Mosaic wilderness, but to make a sovereign state whose voice would be heard in world councils. The audacity of Herzl's concept outraged the wealthy, comfortable assimilationists of his time but lifted the spirit of the less fortunate ghetto Jews of Eastern Europe who saw in him a new David.

The first waves of immigrants went to Palestine before the turn of the century. They were for the most part young idealists, many of them students, impelled by strong ideological motives to transform themselves into farmers and builders. By a process of trial and error, they concluded that collective endeavor was preferable to individual effort. Thus were started the *kibbutzim* —collectives—and later, the *moshavim*—cooperatives. The newcomers settled on Palestine's sand dunes and swamps, linking up with fellow Jews who had been the stewards of uninterrupted Jewish settlement in the country for nearly two thousand years.

Palestine, then still under Turkish domination, had returned to the desert, its mountains long since denuded of forests, its ancient terraces destroyed, its soil eroded. The partnership of land and farmer that constitutes the "rock foundation of our civilization" [5] had long been broken. The early settlers lovingly restored it.

In time, scientific farmers and irrigation experts arrived to hasten development of the country's agriculture, for nations rise or fall upon their food supply. Then came builders of factories and cities, educators and thinkers, and waves of young people starry-eyed with dreams of a future as free men and women in their own land—and ready to help defend it.

By 1914, on the eve of World War I, the Jewish population had risen to about one hundred thousand, of whom half lived in Jerusalem, forming a majority of the city's population. Large numbers of Jews also resided in Safad, Tiberias, and Hebron. About twelve thousand settled on the land, living in fifty agricultural villages and farming approximately one hundred thousand acres, mostly land bought for gold from Arab or Turkish owners.

The outbreak of war halted work on building the national homeland and threatened to extinguish Zionism. Turkey disappointed the British by entering the war on the side of Germany instead of joining the Allies, presaging disaster for Britons and Jews. With Palestine in enemy hands, Britain's imperial lifeline through the Suez Canal was threatened, and Palestine's Jews were in mortal danger. Zionist settlers with Allied citizenship were deported by the thousands, others were compelled to adopt Turkish citizenship, and a number suspected of Allied sympathies were hanged.

British campaigns were mounted in Palestine and Iraq to knock Turkey out of the war as quickly as possible. Before military operations started, however, the British made political overtures to Arabs and Jews projecting creation of eventual independent Arab and Jewish states in the Middle East. The British indicated that they were favorably disposed toward Zionist aspi-

[5] Lowdermilk, *op. cit.*

rations to redress historic wrongs done to the Jewish people. Before long, Jewish volunteers were fighting and dying with British "Tommies" at Gallipoli.

As the war progressed, British sympathy was translated into political action with the famous Balfour Declaration of November 2, 1917. Addressed to Lord Rothschild and signed by British Foreign Secretary Arthur James Balfour, the Declaration expressed Britain's official "sympathy with the cause of the Zionists" and added:

> His Majesty's Government views with favor the establishment in Palestine of a national home for the Jewish people and will use its best endeavors to facilitate achievement of this object, it being clearly understood that nothing shall be done which may prejudice the civil and religious rights of existing non-Jewish communities in Palestine, or the rights and political status enjoyed by Jews in any other country.

It was an expression of traditional English sympathy for the historic rights of the Jews, of gratitude to the Jewish people for their support in the war against Germany, and to Dr. Chaim Weizmann.[6] This ardent Zionist and brilliant chemist had helped Britain overcome a critical shortage of high explosives by devising a formula for producing cordite, previously manufactured with chemicals imported from Germany. The explosive unquestionably helped the British win the war, and when Dr. Weizmann approached cabinet ministers on the question of a national home for his people, he found them receptive.

The Jews were jubilant. They regarded the Declaration as a contract binding victorious Britain to support the foundation of a Jewish state on Jewish land liberated from a foreign enemy. Balfour's position was promptly ratified by the United States and by the French and Italian governments. Four years later the newly formed League of Nations approved the establishment of

[6] Later first president of the state of Israel.

a national homeland for the Jews as outlined by Balfour and conferred the administration of Palestine upon Britain as a mandate. According to the terms of the League's mandate system, a contribution of President Woodrow Wilson,[7] Britain's government of Palestine was to be a "temporary arrangement whose ultimate aim was emancipation and independence of the territory."

With the publication of the Balfour Declaration, Jewish volunteers for service in Palestine were recruited in Britain and incorporated into the regular British forces as the Thirty-eighth Battalion, Royal Fusiliers. It sailed for Palestine early in 1918, followed by the Thirty-ninth and Fortieth Battalions. With American entry into the war, the movement to form Jewish battalions spread to the United States, where 2700 Jewish volunteers were enrolled in the three battalions. In Palestine itself, another entire battalion was raised and supplied locally. The Thirty-eighth and Thirty-ninth Fusiliers,[8] though composed of volunteers, fought as regulars in General Edmund ("The Bull") Allenby's decisive 1918 campaign against the Turks.

"Bull" Allenby arrived in Palestine at a crucial moment in the Allied effort to knock Turkey out of the war. Jerusalem and Damascus remained in enemy hands. The threat to Suez continued. In fact, the Allies were losing the war until Allenby, fresh from having stopped the Germans in France at Vimy Ridge, was rushed to the Middle East.

As indicated earlier in this chapter, the British, in order to summon support against the Turks, promised postwar fulfillment of both Jewish and Arab nationalist aspirations. It seems

[7] Woodrow Wilson was not the first American President to express sympathy for the return of the Jewish people to their homeland. John Adams, second President of the United States, wrote to the pioneer American Zionist, Major Mordecai Manuel Noah, in 1818: "I really wish the Jews again in Judaea, and an Independent Nation."

[8] The Thirty-ninth Fusiliers numbered in its ranks Izhak Ben-Zvi and David ("The Little Lion") Ben-Gurion, later president and prime minister, respectively, of the state of Israel.

relevant at this point to sketch in briefly how the Arabs were persuaded to fight against their Turkish overlords and coreligionists and, without drawing invidious comparisons, to assess the extent of the Arab contribution to the Allied war effort in the Middle East.

What fighting the Arabs did for more than two years after the outbreak of war in 1914 was as regulars in the ranks of the Turkish army. This was understandable. The Sultan of Turkey was titular head of all Islam, and master of the holy Moslem cities of Mecca and Medina with power to declare *jihad* against all infidels, including the British overlords of partly Moslem India. Mindful of this, the British tried hard to induce Turkey to come into the war against Germany. Failing, they proceeded to try to persuade the Arabs to change sides. It proved a long, difficult, costly process.

It was not until Captain (later Colonel) T. E. Lawrence persuaded Sherif Husein ibn-Ali, Hashemite Emir of Mecca, to abandon the Turco-German cause in 1916 that anything remotely approximating an Arab revolt occurred. Simultaneously with Sherif Husein's conversion to the Allied cause, an Arab uprising took place in Syria. Whether it was a bona fide expression of Arab nationalism or merely an outbreak inspired by Husein with the help of British gold remains, however, a moot question. The evidence is considerable that Husein was not seeking Arab "freedom" and "independence" from Ottoman rule quite as much as he sought aggrandizement of his own Hashemite fortunes.

According to the late British General Sir Archibald Wavell, who served as a colonel in the Palestine campaign, Husein "had conceived the idea of a revival of an Arab Empire to include Arabia, Iraq, Palestine, and Syria," [9] a concept approved in principle in an agreement negotiated with the Emir by Sir Arthur Henry McMahon, High Commissioner for Egypt. The agreement, Wavell wrote, was "subject to certain limitations to satisfy

[9] *The Palestine Campaigns*, London: Constable and Company, 1928.

French claims to a special interest in the future of Syria." [10]

The military consequence of the Husein-McMahon deal was creation of an army of Arab irregulars commanded by Husein's son, the Emir Faisal, with Lawrence as his lieutenant and adviser. Faisal's force was nominally 10,000 strong but its size, like the importance of Lawrence's exploits, was grossly exaggerated. Only 1800 Arabs participated in Lawrence's most famous coup, the capture of Aqaba in the summer of 1917, and a scant 600 took part in Allenby's campaign the following year. [11]

The revolt in the desert boiled down to a series of damaging but hardly decisive raids on Turkish supply trains along the Hejaz railway running from Medina to Damascus, and the destruction of a few Turkish outposts in Arabia. Lawrence's harassment of Turkish communications undoubtedly helped Allenby's over-all strategy but it was Allenby, not Lawrence, who won the British war in the Arab lands.

The revolt cost the British exchequer the equivalent in gold of $20,000,000. [12] Lawrence was supplied $2,000,000 in gold sovereigns for his operations, which included bribing desert tribesmen to participate in the fighting. Actual payments to Arab leaders totaled about $5,000,000, always in gold. Despite the heavy outlay, the revolt was not very active when Allenby arrived in Palestine, and stalemate prevailed along the entire front. "The Bull" reanimated the area with his vitality and skill, captured Beersheba in a brilliant cavalry operation, cut off the Turks at Gaza, took Damascus, and kept a promise to capture Jerusalem by Christmas. The Holy City fell December 9, 1918, and Allenby's Jewish troops prayed at the Wailing Wall with the liberated Jewish population of the Old City in a scene that

[10] France's "special interests" were defined in the Sykes-Picot Treaty of 1916, which divided Araby into two spheres of influence, the French predominating in Syria and Lebanon, the British in all the rest. In it, the two powers double-crossed the Arabs and, in effect, the Jews.

[11] Bertram Thomas, *The Arabs*, London: Thornton Butterworth Ltd., 1937.

[12] Thomas, *op. cit.*

would be repeated under different circumstances forty-nine years later.

Events moved swiftly after the Turkish surrender. Allied promises to the Arabs bore fruit with the creation of independent states in Egypt, Saudi Arabia, Yemen, Iraq, Syria, Lebanon, and the utterly unexpected formation of the Kingdom of Transjordan. It was not the Arab Empire Husein had envisioned with McMahon, but it was vastly more than the Jews received. The Allies' pledges to them were territorially and politically whittled down in a continuing process of British indecision.

Palestine, as defined by maps of the period and as mandated to Britain by the League of Nations, spanned the Jordan River and covered 45,000 square miles, an area approximately the size of Pennsylvania. In 1921, nearly four-fifths of the territory that was to have been the Jewish homeland of the Balfour Declaration was handed over to the Emir Abdullah ibn-Husein, Husein's second son. What remained of Palestine was now about the size of Maryland—10,000 square miles. The area in which the Arab states gained independence comprised 1,342,900 square miles, a territory five times the size of Texas.

The decision to create Transjordan was made in Jerusalem at a conference that included Winston Churchill, then Lloyd George's Secretary of State for War and Near Eastern Affairs, Sir Herbert Samuel, the newly appointed British High Commissioner, and the Emir Abdullah, fetched to the meeting by Colonel Lawrence, indefatigable Arabophile and intriguer. Churchill represented a Tory government that stood in mortal fear of the Russian Revolution, then in full cry, and was anxious to solidify Britain's position with the Arabs. Samuel, although Jewish, was more eager to serve his government than his coreligionists. Lawrence was his usual persuasive self and Abdullah was, from his point of view, a man with a genuine grievance. The matter was settled in half an hour: Churchill lopped Transjordan from Palestine, and a kingdom of Hashemite Bedouins from distant Hejaz, with no prior claim whatever on the land of Palestine, was created.

Transjordan, later known as Jordan, materialized from the failure of the British to honor at the peace conference the wartime pledge to the Arabs incorporated in the Husein-McMahon agreement. If the McMahon promise had been respected, the Emir Faisal would have been the head of an extensive Arab state with its capital in Damascus, and Abdullah would have been made King of Iraq, their father Husein retaining the throne of Hejaz, along with titular leadership of Islam. But when Faisal entered Damascus to claim his throne in the summer of 1920, the French were there before him in accordance with the nefarious Sykes-Picot Treaty, and forcibly expelled him. Faisal became King of Iraq. Abdullah threatened holy war against the French.

The Arabs exposed British perfidy during the peace conference by making public the secret exchange of letters between McMahon and Husein. The publication was a diplomatic bombshell. Lloyd George dispatched Churchill to Jerusalem to calm down the Jews with assurances the Balfour Declaration would be respected, placate the Arabs with honeyed words about the inviolability of their rights in Palestine, and find a throne for the irate Abdullah. Churchill succeeded only partly in the first two missions, but completely in the third. Abdullah got his consolation prize—the kingship of Transjordan.

It was later learned that McMahon had expressly excluded from his agreement with Husein all of Palestine on both sides of the Jordan.[13] But nobody listened—or cared. The arrangement with Abdullah, grandfather of the present king of Jordan, was upheld. The 35,000 square miles of sparsely settled territory was subtracted from the territory promised in the Balfour Declaration. Jordan has existed ever since as a subsidized ward of Britain and, more recently, of Britain *and* the United States.

[13] See Appendix.

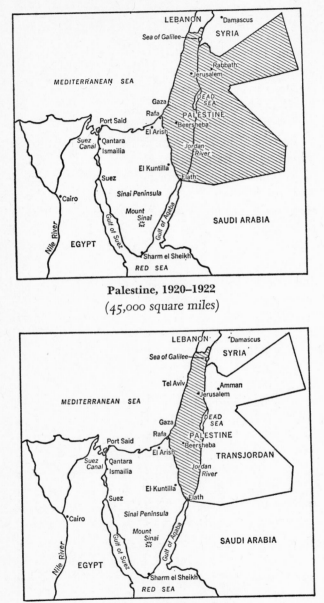

Palestine, 1920–1922
(45,000 square miles)

Palestine, 1922–1948
(10,000 square miles)

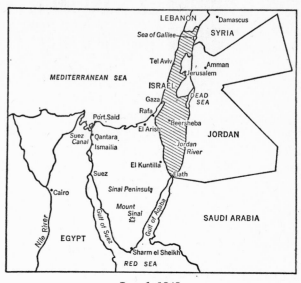

Israel, 1948
(8000 square miles)
The area of Arab sovereignty is 3,533,107 square miles.

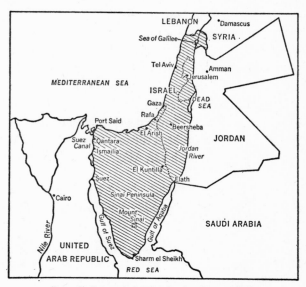

Israeli-Occupied Territory, June 1967
(Dotted lines show Israel's former borders)

Until 1920, Arab hostility to Jewish national independence had not crystallized. On the contrary. Early the previous year, at the Paris Peace Conference, the Emir Faisal announced full acceptance of the Balfour Declaration. As chief of the Arab delegation to the Conference he signed, with Dr. Weizmann, who represented the World Zionist Organization, an agreement [14] confirming that "all such measures shall be adopted as will afford the fullest guarantee of carrying into effect" the policy enunciated by the British government in respect to establishment in Palestine of a national home for the Jewish people. It was a remarkable document. One of its clauses said, in part:

> All necessary measures shall be taken to encourage and stimulate immigration of Jews into Palestine on a large scale . . . through closer settlement and intensive cultivation of the soil. In taking such measures the Arab peasant and tenant farmers shall be protected in their rights, and shall be assisted in forwarding their economic development.

Faisal was a true Arab,[15] a truly great Arab leader, and a man of vision. He was keenly aware of the benefits that would accrue to his people from sharing the rights and privileges of a democratic Jewish state in Palestine. He was also alive to the probable deviousness of Franco-British diplomacy. He and his father, Husein, expected cooperation between Britain, the League's mandatory power in Palestine, and France, the mandatory in Syria, for social and economic development of the whole of the Middle East. But he doubted the intentions of the Great Powers, for in his agreement with Dr. Weizmann Faisal stipulated:

> If the Arabs are established as I have asked in my manifesto of January 4 (1919) addressed to the British Secretary

[14] See Appendix.
[15] The Egyptians who sway Islam today as self-appointed spokesmen of Arab nationalism are not true Arabs, ironically enough, but of Ethiopian Copt origin.

of State for Foreign Affairs,[16] I will carry out what is written in this agreement. If changes are made, I cannot be answerable for failing to carry out this agreement.

While Faisal was writing those words, France was betraying the Arabs in Syria and Lebanon as completely as Britain was welshing on her promises to the Jews in Palestine. They were doing what Faisal had foreseen, maneuvering to rule a divided Arab world, fomenting dissension by playing upon the cupidities and ambitions of local sheiks and mullahs.

Two months after signing his agreement with Dr. Weizmann, Faisal wrote a personal letter to Felix Frankfurter, later justice of the United States Supreme Court, a letter memorable for its humanity toward the Jews and the statesmanship it reflected. The letter,[17] dated March 3, 1919, and addressed to Mr. Frankfurter as an American member of the Zionist delegation to the peace conference, said, in part:

I want to take this opportunity of my first contact with American Zionists to tell you what I have often been able to say to Dr. Weizmann in Arabia and Europe.

We feel that the Arabs and Jews are cousins in race, having suffered similar oppressions at the hands of powers stronger than themselves, and by a happy coincidence have been able to take the first steps toward the attainment of their national ideals together.

We Arabs, especially the educated among us, look with the deepest sympathy on the Zionist movement. Our deputation here in Paris is fully acquainted with the proposals [i.e., for a Jewish state on both sides of the Jordan] sub-

[16] The manifesto to which Faisal referred envisioned creation of an independent Arab state encompassing Arabia, Iraq, Lebanon, and Syria along the lines of the Husein-McMahon agreement, explicity excluding Palestine and certain areas, including Mersina and Alexandretta, allegedly of strategic importance to the French, as a Mediterranean naval power. See Appendix for additional details.

[17] See Appendix for the full text.

mitted yesterday by the Zionist Organization to the Peace Conference. We will do our best . . . to help them through: we will wish the Jews a most hearty welcome home. Dr. Weizmann has been a great helper in our cause, and I hope the Arabs may soon be in a position to make the Jews some return for their kindness. . . .

After his enthronement as King of Iraq, Faisal's voice rarely was heard on behalf of his Jewish cousins. Long before his death in 1933, the fanatics of Arab nationalism had taken over the leadership of Islam. Political ambition seized Arab leaders, who did not hesitate to arouse envies and hatreds or exploit religious fanaticism.

Jewish claims to sovereignty in Palestine were clearly established by history since the twelfth century before Christ. They were recognized by the Balfour Declaration, accepted by responsible leaders like Faisal, supported by McMahon and, finally, legalized by the League of Nations Mandate which, in effect, transferred title to the Holy Land from the Ottoman Empire to the mandatory power as a trustee of the League. But the mandatory—Britain—was too busy expanding an empire in the Middle East, and ensuring itself the lion's share of the area's vast oil resources to worry too much about keeping promises to the Jews. The oil wells were owned by Arabs, not by Jews.

From the moment of the establishment of the Mandate in 1922 until it ended twenty-six years later, Britain hindered rather than helped Jewish efforts at building their homeland, and often was guilty of the grossest violations of her mandated powers. The indecisiveness of British policy throughout the life of the Mandate was frustrating to the Zionists, but they hung grimly on, fighting their long, uphill fight toward nationhood. They strengthened their hold on the homeland in the most practicable manner possible—huge purchases of land from the small, wealthy class of Arab and Turkish effendis, landowners.

By the end of 1935 the Jewish National Fund had bought approximately 250,000 acres of land, mostly scraggy desert, for a fantastic $21,010,400—about $84 an acre for property not worth one-tenth the amount.

Many effendi sellers were absentee landholders living luxuriously in Cairo or Beirut while their fellaheen earned coolie wages, living in mud huts, sleeping with their animals, burning camel dung for fuel, and dying before they reached the age of thirty-five. The effendis profited handsomely from the Jewish land purchases, but so did the fellaheen, who, for the first time in their lives, were paid decent wages by their Jewish employers and treated as equals in Jewish hospitals when they came for treatment of trachoma, rickets, tuberculosis, and all the intestinal diseases known to man.

The bought land was soon drained if swamp, irrigated if desert and was blooming with fruit trees and other crops. But even as the Zionists set about conquering their homeland with plow and hoe they were obliged to defend it with rifle and grenade. The fighting began in the early 1920s and continues to this day in Arab violation of a mass of legal instruments of unquestionable validity in any court of justice except, apparently, a court ruled by great-power or super-power interests.

4

THE MANDATE YEARS:
TROUBLE AND TOIL

Nobody can live longer in peace than his neighbor pleases.

—Thomas Fuller, Gnomologia, 1632

THERE WAS PEACE IN THE HOLY LAND FOR TWO YEARS AFTER THE war ended. Jews and Arabs went about their business, buying and selling each other's goods and services, haggling over prices in the suqs as they had been doing for generations—and as they did again the moment the opportunity arose when Jerusalem was reunited in the summer of 1967.

For two years it seemed that the Arabs had accepted the facts of history. They sold acreage to the Zionists and did not appear to be much attached to the land: there was little evidence of Arab good stewardship of the soil, an important basis of the country-love called patriotism. Except for the improvements the Zionists made, Palestine remained much as it had been for centuries—a fertile coastal plain, patches of green where Jewish hands had rebuilt ancient terracings against erosion, then rock and dun-colored desert, the Dead Sea like a great, greasy blue puddle, and the mountains of Moab silvery purple in the distance.

There were 400,000 Arabs and only 100,000 Jews. Yet because of its aridity and barrenness, the country remained an area of Arab emigration, not immigration. East of the Jordan, beyond Jericho, the population was largely nomadic, rarely settling down long enough to draw a crop from the unwilling earth. There was no land hunger, nor were the Arabs being overwhelmed by Jewish numbers. Palestine was a big country then, reaching from the Mediterranean to well beyond the Moab Mountains, with room enough for ten times its 500,000 people. Palestine represented less than 3 per cent of the total area the Arabs had access to as a result of the Allied conquest of the Ottoman Empire.[1]

The attitude of the Arabs toward the Jewish national movement from its inception had been one of almost unanimous approval. Wrote Farid Kassab, a famous Syrian author: "The Jews of the Orient are at home. This land is their only fatherland. They don't know any other." Leading sheiks expressed themselves as pleased with the advent of the Jews, for they considered that with them had come *barakat*, blessing.

Throughout Arabia the chiefs, thanks to Faisal, were distinctly pro-Zionist, and in Palestine the peasantry welcomed Jewish settlements near their villages. Land acquisition was easy. Commercial intercourse between Arabs and Jews was constant and steady. Anti-Zionist elements, if they existed, kept silent.

The Arab nationalist movement itself—small, inexperienced, and suspect among the Levantine population, who continued to regard itself as Ottoman subjects—looked to the strong, influential Zionist Organization for sympathy and assistance.

[1] With the truncation of Palestine that created Transjordan, the area allotted the Jews was further reduced to eight-tenths of 1 per cent of the liberated territory of the Middle East in which the Arabs achieved statehood. The Jewish area became one-half of 1 per cent of the whole with partition by the United Nations in 1947.

Jews were living and working in peace in Arab communities from Casablanca to Istanbul, Aden to Karachi. They were the traders, merchants, cobblers, tailors, goldsmiths, carpenters, accountants, physicians—even lawyers—in cities and towns in the Moroccos, Algeria, Tunisia, Tripolitania, Egypt, and the whole of the Middle East and Asia. They were useful citizens and appreciated as such.

Then, suddenly, in Palestine, in the spring of 1920, the Arab welcome to Zionists turned to hostility. Murder, rape, and pillage ravaged the Jewish quarter of Jerusalem, and the social, political, and economic life of hundreds of thousands of Jews living in Oriental societies was placed in jeopardy.

Minor but ominous incidents, in the wake of the intensive Arab nationalist propaganda which followed the crowning of Faisal in Iraq, had caused Zionists to warn the Palestine government of impending major trouble. It responded by ordering the population disarmed, enforcing the order only in so far as Jews were concerned.

The April 1920 riots broke like a clap of thunder. Misled by the naïveté of their leaders, the Jews awoke from dreams of a Third Commonwealth to scenes horribly like those from which they had fled in Russia. The Arab action was perfectly timed. Moslem crowds had gathered in Jerusalem for the Nebi Moussa festival, in honor of the Prophet Moses. A frenzy of chants and dances roused them into a dangerous emotional state bordering on delirium. Anti-Jewish rumors of the wildest sort were circulated. The crowd was rapidly going berserk. Agitators harangued the churning mass, urging them forward against the Jews. Noting hesitancy, the rabblerousers shouted: "The government is with us!"

The stage had been carefully prepared. Jewish policemen had been relieved from duty in the Old City, where most Jews resided. Unopposed and attacking from three different parts of town simultaneously, the mob rushed into the Jewish quarter, brandishing knives and clubs. The slaughter was horrible. Among other manifestations of Arab patriotism, some elderly Jews were locked in a house which was set on fire, and a number of women were raped.

A year later, the blood lust again asserted itself in Jerusalem's narrow streets and in Jaffa. As usual, the riots were carefully timed and prepared. It was the end of April. As before, the Moslems were celebrating Nebi Moussa. Howling creatures worked themselves into a frenzy, much as had happened the year before. The British commander of police was conveniently away, and again the few Jews on the police force had been mysteriously taken off duty for the day.

"Bolsheviki! Bolsheviki!" rose the Arab cry. "The Zionists are flooding the country with Bolsheviki!" The ugly lie had been repeated over and over again for months. The authorities had done nothing to deny the widely circulated accusation that "every Jew is a Bolshevik." The malignant propaganda had been carried on openly under the noses of the administration until it had saturated the minds of every element of Palestine's population. Suddenly, at the height of the festival, mad shouts were heard that the mosques were being "attacked by the Bolsheviks." In Jaffa, the Arabs went on an orgy of murder and pillage unhindered by the police. In many cases, benevolent neutrality was insufficient, and the police demonstrated their patriotism by shooting at Jews, directing the mob, and plundering Jewish shops.

A howling mob, led by uniformed policemen armed with rifles, stormed the Zionist Immigration Depot. Thirteen newly arrived immigrants were butchered amid horrible scenes of rape and looting. Waterfront workmen armed with boat hooks ran through the streets impaling Jews. Respectable-looking middle- and upper-class Arabs rushed into stores and helped themselves to the merchandise. The madness spread. In Tel Aviv the disarmed Jews formed a defense unit and held the "patriots" off with sticks and stones.

On May 5, Petach Tikvah settlement was attacked by hundreds of armed fellaheen from near-by villages. The assault was delivered in military formation. Although outnumbered, the settlers fought with the courage of desperation and managed to beat off the attack. The village Kfar Saba was destroyed, and Rehovoth and Hedera were badly damaged. Arabs ruined fruit orchards, burned homes, and carried off cattle and movable property. Only the fact that almost all Jewish workers and farmers were former soldiers prevented the Jewish national home from being destroyed then and there. The most revolting spectacles occurred. Aged persons and small children were killed and mutilated. Women were dragged out into the open and outraged before being murdered. For several days, bedlam ruled in the land of Moses, Isaiah, and Jesus. Forty Jews were killed and numerous others injured on the first day alone. After that, official censorship made casualty figures a matter of conjecture. The property damage was incalculable—as was the guilt of British officialdom.

British policy could be judged from the case of Shakeer Ali Kishek, a Bedouin chieftain who had led the attack on Petach Tikvah. Arrested, he was immediately released on bail, while Abraham Shapiro, the colony's chief notable and one of the most respected Jewish pioneers in all Palestine, was arrested on unspecified charges and carted off to jail in Jerusalem.

What happened in Jerusalem and Jaffa was something new between the Semitic cousins. It was not classical Arab anti-Jewishness, but, ironically, anti-Semitism, with all its modern connotations of genocide. Anti-Jewishness may be defined as neurotic personal dislike of Jews individually on religious, cultural, social, or aesthetic grounds, a neurosis actually less common among Arabs than other peoples. Anti-Semitism, on the other hand, is mass psychosis, an irrational, illogical force purposefully generated and directed at actual destruction of Jews collectively as a "race." [2]

The man responsible for the riots and killings of 1920–1921, hence the first to employ the techniques of anti-Semitism to political purpose in the Middle East, was the sinister Haj Amin el-Husseini. In a very real sense, he invented genocide before Hitler, whose aide and counselor he later became. If the mindless doctrine of extermination of Jews preached by Arab leaders today can be traced to a single source, that source is unquestionably Husseini, still alive, an unpunished war criminal of the first magnitude.

Born in 1896, or thereabouts, of Egyptian parents, Husseini was educated at Cairo's El Azhar, the world's largest and most influential Moslem university, generative source of the politico-religious fanaticism that characterizes what is generally called Arab nationalism but is really Pan-Arabism, a movement whose aim is to revive the Arab Empire and re-establish the Caliphate,

[2] Born of nineteenth-century nationalism and the economic difficulties resulting from the Industrial Revolution, anti-Semitism became a twentieth-century tool of unscrupulous leaders who, unable to solve national problems by conventional means, shifted the blame for rising unemployment and deepening depression on the Jews, then advocated their extermination as a means of achieving a more favorable political and economic climate. It was a lower-middle-class, white-collar phenomenon. The idea that jobs and property could be had by destroying the Jews who held them appealed strongly to workers and clerks displaced by political and industrial upheaval. Just as the Jews themselves used to load all their sins onto a goat, and then drive it out into the desert to purify themselves (ergo, "scapegoat"), so the ambitious politician loaded national troubles onto the backs of the Jews to deflect mass discontent directed against himself or his regime. Perhaps the best early twentieth-century example of the use of anti-Semitism for political ends was Czarist Russia. Hard-pressed Czar Nicholas II commissioned an unprincipled monk named Sergei Nilus to forge a set of documents entitled the "Protocols of Zion" purporting to prove that a group of Jews known as the Elders of Zion planned conquering the world. The Czar sought to convince Russian peasants that their abysmal poverty and squalor was not the fault of their ruler, but of a vast, mysterious Jewish conspiracy. The *Protocols*, published in 1903, may have helped the Czar justify his pogroms but failed to persuade the masses, for they soon destroyed him. However, the *Protocols* served the purposes of anti-Semitism abroad even after they were exposed as a cruel fake.

and whose current self-appointed high priest is Gamal Abdel Nasser.

During the war, Husseini served briefly as an officer in the Turkish army, and in 1920 was appointed by the British high commissioner as mufti of Jerusalem, religious head of the Moslem community in part of Palestine. It became immediately evident he was using his ostensibly spiritual office for political purposes, but the authorities made no move to oust him until the disturbances were unmistakably traced to him. Before he could be arrested, however, Husseini fled to Transjordan. Tried in absentia, he was sentenced to fifteen years' imprisonment, but his Arab supporters threatened further violence. The high commissioner amnestied him, and appeasement of the Arabs was established as the leitmotiv of British administration for the duration of the Mandate.

Of medium height, with pointed ears and a close-cropped, scraggly round beard, Husseini was not an imposing or impressive man, but he soon became a powerful figure in Palestine's political life. He was not in any sense an Arab patriot. He considered Western concepts of nationalism, which the feeble Arab national movement had borrowed, as obsolete nonsense. His ideal was an Arab world within which none but True Believers should survive.

With his pardon, Husseini, a common felon restored to society not by a court of law but by a stroke of the high commissioner's pen, returned to Jerusalem to become one of the key men in the administration of Palestine's affairs. Despite the opposition of the Moslem High Council, whose members regarded him as an unsavory personage, Husseini was reappointed grand mufti for life. The Council rejected his appointment, but was overruled by the high commissioner. The 1921 Jerusalem riots and the Jaffa massacre were as clearly Husseini's work as the 1920 disturbances had been, but none dared touch the grand mufti now.

The following year Husseini was made president of the Supreme Moslem Council in an election in which three rivals far better qualified than he received more votes but were "persuaded" by the high commissioner to step aside in favor of the rehabilitated criminal. In his new position, Husseini acquired complete control over religious charities with annual incomes in excess of five hundred thousand dollars. Previously rigidly audited by Turkish government representatives from Istanbul, the funds now were free of any outside supervision of any kind.

Soon after, the grand mufti was elevated to the presidency of the Sharia—the religious courts—which added temporal powers to his spiritual prerogatives, with authority to appoint preachers in all mosques, and to discipline them if they stepped out of line. He drew a handsome salary from public funds, ran a staff of two hundred fifty assistants, and supervised the work of some six hundred employees of the charitable institutions. He organized them all into a tightly controlled organization of politico-religious activists to sabotage the British Mandate and kill the Jewish national homeland in its infancy.

Aware of the grand mufti's grand design, the Jews lived with a hoe in one hand and a gun in the other. A phantom militia came into being—an army without uniforms, that had no band and never paraded, drilled secretly by night behind the wind-sculptured dunes at the desert's edge and by day plied the plows, hammers, picks, and shovels that were building a nation. Its officers and noncoms, and many of its troops, were the demobilized men of the Zion Mule Corps that had fought at Gallipoli, of the Thirty-eighth and Thirty-ninth Fusiliers who had marched with Allenby on Jerusalem, and the Fortieth Battalion raised in Palestine as the war was ending. It was called the Haganah, meaning "Defense," and materialized none too soon.

For eight years there was comparative peace. There were small clashes, but nothing serious. Arab villagers made money selling fruit and vegetables to Jerusalem, Tel Aviv, and Haifa; Arab landowners profited by selling land to incoming settlers; Arabs used electricity brought in by Jews, gladly shared the water from Jewish irrigation ditches, and were treated free or at nominal cost in Hadassah hospitals.

The grand mufti's propaganda machine tried to instill in Palestine's Arabs the idea that the Jews would soon overrun the land, become the dominant commercial class, and reduce the fellaheen to slavery. Husseini's political appeal fell on deaf ears. The rich landowners were getting richer, the shopkeeper class was enjoying prosperity trading with the Jews, and the fellaheen, their lot visibly improving wherever they came into contact with the hard-working, ingenious Jews, knew what they were being told was false. On the whole, Palestine's Arabs reacted to the mufti's politics with vast indifference.

During the eight years after the 1921 troubles, about eighty thousand immigrants arrived, mostly from Russia and Poland, some from Romania, Lithuania, Germany, British Empire countries—and the United States. Others came from Bulgaria, Czechoslovakia, and the Yemen. Operating on the accepted, and utterly false, theory that Palestine's absorptive capacity had "limited potentialities," [3] the British set twice-yearly quotas. Many prospective immigrants were denied entry permits. This began working great hardship on Jews living in Moslem communities abroad, where Arab propagandists were starting to echo the anti-Semitism of Haj Amin el-Husseini.

Meanwhile, with economic and living conditions in Palestine rapidly improving, Arabs began coming from Lebanon, Syria, Egypt, and Sinai. They were not native Palestinians, for the most part, but immigrants who had heard about Jewish schools, hospitals, artesian wells, irrigation systems, and the availability of jobs in orchards and factories at wages a man could live on and if he chose, support several wives. The Arab population doubled,

[3] Thomas, *op. cit.*

to eight hundred thousand, by 1929. The British established no quotas for Arab immigration.

A lower Jewish birth rate and a higher Arab fertility further complicated matters. The Zionists asked the British to increase their immigration quotas, or there would be no chance to save Jews from Europe. Plainly, the national home concept of the Balfour Declaration was not being implemented. The British listened politely, but did nothing. In Germany, after having dictated *Mein Kampf* to Rudolf Hess in a Landsberg jail, a man named Hitler was wooing Krupp and other Ruhr industrialists for support in impending presidential elections.[4]

That storm however, was still only a distant rumbling to all but those honest German democrats and the Jews who lived in the Second Reich. For the Jewish residents of Palestine, another Arab storm was brewing. Husseini had changed tactics. Having failed to arouse Palestinian Arabs politically, he appealed now to their religious prejudices and sensibilities. The new tempest broke in the hot, dry summer of 1929.

The trouble had started in Jerusalem the year before, during the Jewish High Holidays. The traditional Jewish division of the sexes during Orthodox worship was only irregularly observed at the Wailing Wall because there was no structure on the ground. The practice of erecting a portable linen screen had lapsed since the 1920–1921 riots, but on the two days of Rosh Hashana 1928 it was revived. After the New Year services, the screen was removed. On Yom Kippur, the Day of Atonement, it was brought in again. Excited Arabs visited Edward Keith-Roach, governor of Jerusalem, and asserted that the Jews had

---

[4] Although unsuccessful in the 1932 elections, when he stood against Hindenburg, Hitler was made chancellor in January 1933 on the advice of Papen, who finally believed that Hitler could best be brought to heels inside the cabinet. Hitler, however, soon dispensed with constitutional restraints, ruthlessly crushed all opposition in the 1934 "purge," and by August was master of Germany.

"violated Arab rights and upset the status quo at the Wailing Wall by the introduction of a portable screen!" They told the governor that unless the screen was removed, they would take matters into their own hands.

Keith-Roach went to the Wall during the *Neilah*, closing service of the most sacred day of worship of the Jewish year, and demanded removal of the screen. Naturally, the request was refused, whereupon Keith-Roach sent English police to remove the screen. This was the beginning of a train of incidents that convinced many Arabs that the mandatory supported their antagonism toward the Jews and led them to believe the British would offer no resistance to violence against Jews.

On the afternoon of *Tishah b'ab*, August 15, 1929, the Black Feast commemorating the destruction of the first and second Temples, Jewish boys and girls marched to the Wailing Wall to protest infringements on Jewish rights of worship. There were no incidents and no arrests. The next day, word spread that following prayers, a Moslem demonstration would be held, and about two thousand Arabs poured toward the Wailing Wall. Three Jews there at the time were attacked. Two were saved by an Arab policeman; the third stood his ground. He was badly beaten, prayer books were ripped and burned, Jewish prayer slips were torn from the crevices of the Wall and burned. The British, who had guarded the Jewish demonstration of the previous day as if it had been a violent mob, sent no police to the Wall that Friday, and issued a statement saying, "Three Jews were at the Wall at the time of the Moslem visit. Reports that the worshipers were assaulted are without foundation."

Tension reigned throughout Palestine in the wake of these incidents. Among the Arabs, wild rumors were current that the Jews were contemplating an assault on the Mohammedan holy places. Frequent attacks on Jews took place in Jerusalem and the situation had become alarming to everyone.

On Saturday, August 17, a young Sephardic Jew named Abraham Mizrachi was stabbed by Arabs in Jerusalem and died of his wounds three days later. The British demanded that he be buried secretly, at night. The boy's horrified parents refused. The funeral was arranged for Wednesday morning, August 21. Two thousand Jews joined the procession. When a small group of young people began urging the procession along one of the main streets forbidden to the procession, the police—British and Arab—reacted by beating the mourners and pursuing them as they fled. The pallbearers had to leave the coffin in the street. Twenty Jews were wounded. A British statement passed off the incident as "minor," and the Arabs' belief that the government was "with them" became a certainty. The mufti's propaganda machine went to work.

The Young Moslem Association of Haifa published a proclamation saying, "The Jews have ancient aspirations regarding our Mosque El Akzah in Jerusalem. These aspirations find expression in their coming to the Wailing Wall and mourning for the Kingdom and palace of Solomon. At El Burak [the Wailing Wall, a place sacred to Arabs as well as Jews] they offend Moslem honor, and curse the Prophet and the Moslem religion."

Another of the mufti's newspapers falsely reported that the Jews had thrown three bombs into the Omar Mosque of Jerusalem and destroyed it. Rumors were loosed that Jerusalem Jews had "killed hundreds of Arabs" and had attacked the Mosque of Omar. Everywhere the cry rose "Defend El Burak." The young Arabs of Ramallah formed the "Knights of El Burak" pledged to the defense of El Burak.

On the morning of August 23 about fifteen thousand Arabs came streaming into Jerusalem armed with firearms, swords, daggers, and nabuts—Arab clubs. (The mufti later accounted for the bristling armament as "Moslem love of display.") Around noon trouble began at the Jaffa gate. About two hundred Arabs advanced down the Jaffa Road, brandishing their weapons, shouting "Al daula maana"—the government is with us. The crowd proceeded to the city gardens, wounding a number of Jews before it was dispersed by the police. Then about five hundred armed Arabs came through the gate, and the governor ordered hoses turned on them. The mob was scattered, but not before it had done its work. A young Jewish boy had his head smashed. Two Jewish workers of the English Electrical Company were caught and murdered near the Jaffa Gate.

The Haganah organized the defense of many sections of Jerusalem—Yemin Moshe, the Old City; Meah Shearim, the Bokharian quarter; Romemah; Talpioth; Beth ha-Karem; and Rechavia. The heaviest Jewish losses occurred where the Haganah had been unable to organize defense units. The worst was the attack on the Georgian quarter. The houses were locked, but there were no police. The mob began to throw stones and to fire through the windows. After a time it was reinforced by Arabs whom the Haganah had beaten back elsewhere, and these, with their reports of Arabs killed, roused the mob to new heights of frenzy. The Arabs gained entry into many houses via courtyards and gardens and slaughtered and wounded the occupants. The police did not interfere for two hours.

Motzah is a small settlement near Jerusalem, on the way to Tel Aviv. Close by is the Arab village of Quolonia. That awful Friday the sheik of this village visited Motzah and swore by God and the Koran that he and his men would defend the Jews from all attack. At noon the next day about thirty Arabs came up the valley between the two villages and attacked the houses at the nearest end of the settlement. One house was also a small hotel. The owner, his two young daughters, his son, twenty-two, and two guests, an eighty-five-year-old rabbi and a sixty-year-old man from Tel Aviv, were butchered with knives. After looting the house, the Arabs set fire to it. A Haganah group from Jerusalem arrived too late to stave off the Arab attack, but held the Arabs at bay until the arrival of a British armored car—two hours later.

The day of the outbreak in Jerusalem, the Jews of Hebron were in a high state of alarm. The day before, Aref el Aref, Arab governor of Beersheba, had preached in the mosque. Aref had been tried, along with the mufti, for his part in the riots of 1920 but, unlike Husseini, had been imprisoned for a short term at Acre. The local chief rabbi implored the Arab governor of Hebron to keep the peace. The governor calmed him, lying that British soldiers were "already in the streets in Arab dress, ready to fulfill their duty if the need arose." On Friday afternoon an Arab mob broke into the Yeshiva and killed the only student who had remained there. Again the rabbi appealed to the governor for help. Again he received the same assurances. Bewildered, he turned to the British officer in charge of the police. That gentleman assured the rabbi there would be no violence.

Early Saturday morning the Arab governor disarmed the police—and the massacre began. For two hours the Arab mob raged, breaking into Jewish homes, dragging the occupants into the streets, and killing them. Students, dying, threw themselves across unwounded comrades, smearing them with blood to save them. Yet in all the horror Husseini had unleashed, the Jews were not without Arab friends. Several Arab landlords sheltered Jews and saved them from the slaughter. One Arab housewife wailed at the top of her voice to drown the cries of the Jewish children she was hiding.

The wounded of Hebron huddled in the police station, with neither water nor toilets. They begged to be allowed to telephone or telegraph Jerusalem but were refused. The Arab governor wired the British authorities in Jerusalem: "Hebron all right." Finally the governor allowed the police to have their weapons, and they easily dispersed the mob. Sixty-five Jews had been slaughtered, fifty-eight wounded. Similar scenes occurred in Jaffa, in the Jezreel Valley, and in the southern villages. But the least excusable of all took place six days after the Jerusalem riots in Safed. Now British troops had been mobilized throughout Palestine. The government was fully aware of the seriousness of the disorder within the country. Yet on August 29 another massacre took place without the interference from the government. It was described in an official bulletin of the High Commission as follows:

> Disorders broke out in Safed at about 6:15 p.m. on the 29th. Troops arrived at 8:35 and immediately restored order. There were several casualties and many houses were burned. The Jewish population was promptly removed to a place of safety in the town. Quiet has prevailed in Safed since.

Thus was dismissed the slaughter of fifteen men, women, and children and the wounding of dozens more.

The animosity of Arab extremists retarded but did not prevent determined Zionists from continuing the building of the Jewish national homeland. With the rise of Hitler in 1933 there was a sharp increase in immigration. Nearly 31,000 immigrants entered Palestine that year, 42,350 arrived the following year, and almost 62,000 came in 1935. In addition, about 5000 victims of Nazi persecution annually made their difficult and dangerous way to Palestine and entered "illegally" because the British withheld immigration certificates.

As Nazi-inspired racism advanced through Czechoslovakia, Italy, Romania, Hungary, Yugoslavia, and Poland, the Jews of Palestine organized ways to bring in refugees in spite of the regulations. A traffic in humans sprang up in the Mediterranean. Secret organizations cooperated with profiteers who owned ships flying Greek or Turkish flags. Together they worked out a racket that provided fabulous profits for a few shipowners in Athens and Istanbul and salvation for thousands. Refugees from the Nazi-Fascist areas filtered down to Greek or Turkish ports. There they were loaded like cattle onto waiting vessels, paying as much as four hundred dollars per head for passage in the dark, stinking holds of foul, unseaworthy tubs for a trip normally costing sixty dollars in first-class cabin with bath. The ships sailed as near as they dared to the Palestinian coast at points where small boats from shore met them to take off their human cargo. At first, the British authorities, aware that these people—scared and sick and penniless—had nowhere else to go, closed an eye. But the Arabs screamed disapproval, and the British banned the traffic, making it a criminal offense to transport or aid "illegal" refugees.

A coast-guard patrol was organized, but the shipowners were making too much money to be easily discouraged. They obtained other, even less seaworthy ships and loaded these to the gunwales with passengers. On dark nights, they would beach the ships. There was nothing for the coast guard to do but rescue the refugees as the vessels began breaking up. Men, women, and children—often babies born on board without medical aid—landed in Palestine without passports or any papers of identification. Most of the time they had no money, no clothes. Sometimes they swam ashore.

The influx from Europe, and from Germany in particular, provided the Jewish homeland with much-needed managers, engineers, physicians, chemists, research scientists, and experts of all kinds not only to help increase productivity, but to improve the quality of goods and enable Palestine to compete in world markets. More important, perhaps, eminent scholars arrived to staff Palestine's Hebrew University and the homeland's expanding educational system. With them came economists and men trained in government service to help create the framework of self-government even while Palestine remained a Mandate under British rule.

Husseini and his extremist clique saw what was happening. If the Jews and the nation they were building were to be destroyed, it would have to be done soon. To that end, the mufti entered into a secret alliance with the Nazis: he promised Hitler Arab support in the Middle East in the event of war with England in exchange for German money and weapons.

The British continued to temporize in Palestine, expecting Arabs and Jews would fight themselves to an exhausted standstill. But they miscalculated both the intensity of the mufti's determination to wipe out Jewry and Jewry's capacity to resist and survive.

In 1936, sporadic Arab terrorism became full-scale guerrilla warfare against the government, the Jewish community, and a large segment of the Arab population itself.[5] But the mufti's forces now faced an augmented, well-drilled Haganah. Arab attacks in cities, towns, and villages and on remote settlements met with fierce resistance. The Jews suffered arson, deforestation, and destruction of homes, wells, and pipelines, but thanks to the Haganah, actual Jewish casualties were not heavy.

Zionist policy was to employ the Haganah strictly for defense —but Arab attacks did not go unpunished. A group of Haganah dissidents formed a secret paramilitary striking force known as the Irgun Zvai Leumi. Its aim was to take the war to the Arabs, which it did; force the British to leave Palestine; and declare the country's independence. The Irgun's ranks swelled with every act of Arab terrorism.

Alarmed at the crescendo of violence, the British government appointed the Peel Commission to study the situation in Palestine and recommend a solution. If London had hoped for a whitewash of British administration of the Mandate, it was bitterly disappointed. The Commission noted with pleasure the sharpness of "the contrast between this intensely democratic and highly organized modern community and the old-fashioned Arab world around it," and conceded that nowhere in the world was the spirit of nationalism "more intense than among the Jews in Palestine." Accordingly, the Commission recommended partition of the country into separate Jewish and Arab states.

The Jews realized that acceptance would mean a further

[5] The Husseini clan took advantage of the situation to settle accounts with Arab political opponents, and the mufti's gunmen actually wound up killing more Arabs than Jews.

whittling down of their Balfour boundaries, but saw partition as the only immediate means of opening Palestine's doors to co-religionists fleeing in increasing numbers from the Nazi terror. For the refugees, Palestine was the only hope—nobody else wanted them. Reluctantly, the Zionists accepted the Peel proposal. The Arabs, assuming an "all-or-nothing" attitude, rejected partition outright and stepped up terrorist activities. For three years, the country echoed to the sounds of rifle fire and exploding grenades and mines. The Arabs fully expected that the Axis powers would win the impending war and help them destroy the Jewish community.

Then came the May 1939 British White Paper renouncing the Balfour Declaration and the Mandate on which British authority rested. The document carried the imprimatur of Neville Chamberlain. It constituted an act of appeasement of the forces of evil that rivaled, and in some ways surpassed in its iniquitous consequences, performances at Berchtesgaden and Munich of the previous autumn.

The Chamberlain White Paper seriously proposed that Jewish immigration be limited to fifteen thousand a year for five years, then cease completely. The Jewish population of Palestine was to be frozen at one-third of the total, and within ten years the country was to become an independent state wherein the Jews would have permanent minority status. This as hundreds of thousands of Jews were already being herded into concentration camps . . .

At war's outbreak, Palestine's Arab leaders openly espoused the Axis cause. Britain, fighting now for its national and imperial life, cracked down on Arab anti-Allied activities and rushed troops to Egypt and the Middle East. The mufti fled to Germany, where he became a Nazi propagandist advocating mass extermination of Jews. How he escaped eventual capture and judgment at the hands of the Allies remains one of the unsolved mysteries of World War II.

War or no war, the White Paper was firmly applied against

Palestine's Jews over the strong opposition of British public opinion at home and the verdict of the League of Nations Mandates Commission, which ruled pro-Arab British policy to be in clear violation of the terms of the Mandate. "From the first," a formal inquiry concluded, "one fact forced itself on the notice of the Commission, namely, that the policy set out in the White Paper was not in accordance with the interpretation which in agreement with the Mandatory Power . . . the Commission had always placed upon the Palestine Mandate."

By the time the White Paper became law, however, the outlines of an Israel-to-be were clearly discernible. The Hebrew language, dead for centuries, had been revived so that Jews from many different nations could communicate with one another in their mother tongue, and elevated to equal status with Arabic and English. Postage stamps and coinage were in the three languages. A Hebrew university was in being. Hospitals, clinics, schools were being opened everywhere. Phenomenal progress had been made in agriculture. By the spring of 1939, many tens of thousands of acres of swampland and desert bought by early settlers were thriving farmsteads and citrus groves. The country was exporting oranges at the rate of ten million cases a year, and rapid expansion had occurred in mixed farming, dairying, poultry production, and sheep-breeding. *Kibbutzim* dotted the countryside from the northern edge of the Negev to Galilee. Newly planted trees furred the brown hills below Jerusalem.

Industrial development had kept pace. The Palestine Electric Corporation had harnessed the Yarmuk and Jordan rivers, and its energy production made possible the construction and operation of thousands of new factories: the total rose from 1850 plants in 1922 to more than 5600 by the end of 1938. The range of products broadened from textiles and leather goods to glass, cement, machinery, chemicals, foodstuffs, pharmaceuticals, and cosmetics. Refugees from Holland and Belgium started a lively trade in industrial and polished diamonds.

By 1939 Zionist immigration boosted the Jewish population

to nearly four hundred fifty thousand despite British restrictions. Meanwhile the Arab population, owing to unrestricted immigration from Syria and Transjordan, more than doubled to almost one million.

The White Paper brought Zionist progress almost to a standstill. The phenomenal rural expansion had occurred almost entirely on purchased land, but the new regulations ended all further acquisition—in violation of Article VI of the Mandate, which prescribed "close settlement by Jews on the land, including State land and waste lands not required for public purposes." Prohibited was the transfer of real estate to Jews in the whole of the hill country together with certain areas in the vicinity of Gaza and Beersheba. Jews could still buy property in the Plains of Esdraelon and Jezreel, eastern Galilee, and in the vicinity of Ramleh and Beer Tuvia. But only with the consent of the high commissioner, which, however, was never given. Plainly the policy of the Chamberlain government was to reduce the Jewish homeland to a Jewish ghetto within an Arab Palestine. From that policy flowed the greatest tragedy ever to befall a single people in written history—and the perhaps not-unrelated decline of British power.

The Jews had proved that Palestine's absorptive capacity had been grossly underestimated. Studies by agronomists and economists showed that the country could have absorbed many times its existing population with simultaneous improvement in general economic conditions and health and living standards for Arabs as well as Jews.

Had the country been permitted to equal Massachusetts in population density, western Palestine alone could have accommodated 5,270,000 people. At the time, Belgium sustained 8,159,000 inhabitants on 11,780 square miles, and Holland, lacking almost every essential natural resource except human intelligence, supported 8,500,000 people on an area of only 13,200 square miles. The island of Sicily, smaller than western Palestine and not too dissimilar in its rugged barrenness, held 4,426,000 inhabitants. After an exhaustive survey, one authority put it this way:

> The consecrated genius and vision of the Jews in drain-
> ing swamps and turning sand dunes into orchards and
> poultry farms, in planting millions of trees on rocky hills,
> in building terraces, digging wells, developing irrigation,
> establishing numerous and varied industries and founding
> hospitals and clinics, has brought a greatly increased meas-
> ure of prosperity to Palestine while making possible not
> only the settlement of almost half a million Jews in the last
> twenty-five years [1914–1939] but doubling the Arab popu-
> lation in the same period . . . It is practically impossible
> to estimate what the final absorptive capacity of Greater
> Palestine [on both sides of the Jordan] could be if all its
> unoccupied or underpopulated areas were rejuvenated by
> the same vigor and understanding love of the land as have
> characterized Jewish efforts on a tiny fraction. . . .[6]

It seems evident that if Britain had not deliberately limited the absorptive capacity of Palestine with its White Paper, the country could have taken in enough Jews to have substantially reduced, perhaps even averted, the catastrophe that befell them at the hands of Hitler and his power-crazed clique of anti-Semites. The world had not yet gone to war in the spring of 1939. There was still time to forestall tragedy.

Political and strategical considerations rather than anti-Semitism, as some critics have charged, undoubtedly motivated the Chamberlain government in appeasing the Arabs at the expense of the Jews. Although there were anti-Zionists, Jew-baiters, even a few anti-Semites among those who administered the Mandate, it is absurd to ascribe anti-Semitic motives to the British. Foremost in the minds of the pucka sahibs who planned and executed War Office and Colonial Office wartime policy

[6] Lowdermilk, *op. cit.*

were such matters as the Suez shortcut to Middle East oil, and the badly needed raw materials and manpower of India, Australia, and New Zealand. In their understandable desire to prevent the sun from setting on an empire that girdled the globe, however, the British overestimated the power and sweep of what passed for "Arab nationalism" and tragically underestimated the strength and depth of Jewish nationalism. This was because they failed to understand the magnitude and nature of the threat Nazism and Fascism posed to Judaism, Christianity, and Western civilization itself—a failure in which they were not alone.

It was plain enough to thoughtful men [7] as early as 1934 that what was at stake was the fate of the Judaeo-Christian ethic, democracy's heritage from Moses and Jesus. It was clear Hitler meant to go down in history not merely as another German politician, but as another Christ or Mohammed, the originator of a new True Faith whereof Judaism and Christianity were mortal enemies—as they are today the enemies of a new True Faith whose godheads sit in the Kremlin. The clues to Hitler's vision of himself were numerous enough. "God," said Nazi apostle Dr. Engelka, "has manifested himself not in Jesus Christ but in Adolf Hitler." "Jehovah, whom the Jews worship is the greatest of all criminals," editorialized the Nazi weekly, *Der Stuermer*. "No one," asserted Dr. Alfred Rosenberg, Nazi ideologist, "has the right to find fault with those of our people who have found their Son of God [Hitler] and have thus regained their Eternal Father."

The late Senator Robert Wagner had no doubt as to the direction and extent of the gathering Nazi storm. "If Palestine falls," he warned, "democracy is endangered. It is an essential responsibility of the democratic nations to assure the preservation and success of the Jewish homeland." Senator Wagner was not alone—the list is long of American and British statesmen,

[7] Among the American journalists writing and warning of the danger at the time were William L. Shirer, Leland Stowe, the late Webb Miller, Wallace Duell, and many others.

churchmen, and professors who knew and warned that anti-Semitism was a weapon with which the liberal, democratic world was to be beaten to its knees. But, as William B. Ziff wrote in his excellent *The Rape of Palestine*, "The old love for truth and justice, and the sturdy character which once armored it," had all but worn away. "Its once proud soul," he said, "has been corrupted by gross materialism. It is full of corroding fears, but cannot act to defend itself." [8]

We are faced with much the same situation today in the Middle East: an embattled Jewish people defending their independence virtually alone in an area coveted by the Soviet descendants of Czarist imperialism, ostensibly not anti-Semitic themselves, but encouraging a Pan-Arab surrogate to do their work for them.

Genocide—extermination of the Jewish people in an area where Arabs came as conquerors and never ruled as a nation—is the stated policy of the Arab leadership of today as it was of the Nazi-Fascist godheads of yesterday. Fortunately the Jews are made of steel, tempered in three wars for survival in less than twenty years, but forged before that in 1939 and in World War II.

Fortunately, too, the Israelis are neither "corrupted by gross materialism" nor "full of corroding fears." They left their fears at Dachau and Belsen and Auschwitz, and they know how to defend themselves. They began learning early, in fighting off Husseini's mobsters from 1920 to 1939, and they took their graduate work in self-defense in World War II.

[8] New York: Longmans, Green, 1938.

5

WORLD WAR II
AND THE MAKING
OF ISRAEL

*Thou hast heard, O my soul, the sound of the trumpet,
the alarm of war.*

—Jeremiah IV, 19

THE OUTBREAK OF WORLD WAR II OPENED ANOTHER MOMENTOUS
chapter in Jewish history. In the writing of it, Jewry achieved a
new unity of action and purpose unprecedented in the eighteen
centuries of dispersion.

For the first time since they had fought the Romans in the
first century of the Christian era the Jews—all of them—found
themselves fighting on the same side against a common enemy.
In World War I, they had fought in the ranks of the Allies and
with equal patriotism in the armies of the Kaiser. So it had been
in previous wars while they remained, in the words of Isaiah,
"a nation scattered and peeled . . . meted out and trodden
down."

They were still not a nation when Hitler unleashed his Wehrmacht and Luftwaffe in 1939, but they reacted with a unanimity characteristic of nations in time of crisis. The first victims of Nazi fury perceived in the German assault on Europe not merely a threat to an established order but an attack on civilization itself and rose everywhere to support the Allied cause.

They fought under the flags of their native lands as draftees or conscripts in all the Allied armies, including those of Russia. Ironically, in the light of later Russian support of Arab efforts to annihilate Israel, the Soviet Union's 2,500,000 Jewish citizens supplied the Red Army with some 250,000 troops, of whom 5163 were honored by the high command for gallantry above the call of duty. Jews also fought in guerrilla bands and resistance groups in German-occupied countries, constantly facing double jeopardy as partisans and as Jews. More than 6000 Jewish freedom fighters helped Tito hold the mountains of Yugoslavia against the Nazis through three terrible winters, and thousands more helped democracy survive in Greece, where the Germans made a special effort to exterminate them.

Jewish eagerness to come to grips with the archenemy was particularly evident in Palestine, where the vision of ultimate nationhood, though obscured by events, fortified Jewish determination. When their radios intoned the news from London that Britain had declared war on the Germans that fateful morning of September 3, 1939, more than 130,000 of the country's 450,000 Jews registered for combat service with the British armed forces. There was no such response from Palestine's 1,000,000 Arabs, whose radios were tuned to Rome and Berlin and whose hearts beat for an Axis victory, as Arab hearts did throughout the Middle East.

Hundreds of thousands of Jews were fleeing before the advancing Germans and clamoring for entry into a Palestine barred to them by the White Paper, but the Zionists were determined to fight the war as though the White Paper did not exist.

In London, Dr. Weizmann, as President of the Jewish Agency, proposed formation of a Jewish army to fight under its own flag, but the proposal was rejected by the Chamberlain government.

At first, the Colonial Office would allow only the formation of the so-called Palestinian Pioneers, really work battalions which went to France armed with picks and shovels. However, those who survived Dunkirk returned to England among the best-armed—with weapons taken from Germans they killed in hand-to-hand combat with hastily issued bayonets and grenades. Not until France fell in June 1940, and the specter of defeat loomed hugely over Suez and the Holy Lands, were Jews allowed to enroll in Britain's armed forces as fighting men. Winston Churchill, always friendly to the Zionist cause, had succeeded Chamberlain and begun his "walk with destiny." He denounced the White Paper as a betrayal of British promises to the Jewish people, and, as the war took on breadth and purpose under his leadership, consented to their admission into His Britannic Majesty's armed services. Even then, however, Palestine's Colonial Office bureaucrats ruled that Jewish recruits should not exceed the Arabs in numbers. But the parity principle was quickly dropped, owing to a dearth of Arab volunteers.

As the war progressed and the Axis threat to the strategic heartland of the Mediterranean increased, the British accepted nearly thirty thousand Jewish volunteers. In addition, two thousand young Jewish women joined the Women's Army Auxiliary (ATS) and some three thousand men served with other Allied contingents—Greek, Czech, and Free French—then helping the British maintain their tenuous hold on Egypt. Later, thousands more served in Palestine's Home Guard. Later still, the Churchill government permitted the formation of a special Jewish Brigade Group, which fought with distinction in Egypt's western desert —helping that country preserve its independence. Fighting under its own colors, the brigade subsequently participated in the North African and Italian campaigns that prevented the Mediterranean cradle of Western civilization from becoming its coffin.

Then there was the Haganah, never officially recognized by the authorities as a Jewish defense force, but always available to the British for delicate, dangerous missions behind enemy lines in the Middle East or Europe. After Syria and Lebanon came under pro-Axis Vichy French control following the fall of France, Haganah men, fluent in French and Arabic and familiar with the terrain, set up invaluable intelligence networks in those countries. When the British later decided to occupy Syria, Haganah commandos in civilian clothes risked capture and death as spies to lead the way, mapping enemy positions, sabotaging communications, and harassing the enemy's flanks and rear. Haganah guerrillas subsequently helped the Allies suppress the pro-Axis Rashid Ali revolt in Iraq. Disguised as Arabs, they crossed the frontier ahead of the British forces, and captured and held strategic strongpoints until the invading troops arrived.

Young Haganah parachutists—women as well as men—were frequently dropped into German-occupied territory to establish communications with Jewish underground forces engaged in hiding and smuggling out refugees and escaped Allied prisoners of war. The adventures of these courageous youngsters alone would fill a volume. Among them was Hannah Szenesh, a talented poetess. Hannah was twenty-four years old with luminous blue eyes and a cloud of dark-brown hair. The British officers who trained her as a parachutist fell in love with her to a man. They were sad to see her go when, one moonless night in the spring of 1944, they dropped her into Yugoslavia. Her assignment was to work her way into Hungary and make contact with members of the Hungarian resistance awaiting instructions for smuggling Jewish refugees out of Nazi concentration camps. The Hungarian police tracked her down by monitoring her transmitter. Her last message to Jewish Agency headquarters in Jerusalem was in the form of a poem:

Blessed is the match consumed
in kindling the flame,
Blessed is the flame that burns
in the secret places of the heart.
Glory to the heart stilled
in its beat with pride,
Glory to the match consumed
in kindling the flame.

Hannah was executed in a Hungarian prison courtyard after refusing under torture to give any information.

The extent of British reliance on Jewish loyalty and courage may be judged from the fact that when they were losing the war in 1941–1942, they asked the Haganah to create in Palestine an underground base from which to continue the war in the event the Germans overran the Middle East. An Axis victory seemed imminent at the time: General Rommel's Afrika Korps had driven the brave but badly outnumbered, inadequately armed Desert Rats of the Eighth Army across Egypt to El Alamein, only seventy miles west of Alexandria. At that critical juncture it was on the Jews, not the Arabs, that the British relied to create the sabotage squads, guerrilla forces, and communications systems needed to keep the war going until a counteroffensive could be mounted against the Germans. A training school was set up in a secret, sealed-off area near Haifa, and for nearly a year Jews trained intensively in the complex art of killing to survive. Then came General Montgomery, American tanks and planes, the Battle of El Alamein, and victory.

The contribution of Palestine's Jews to victory in the Middle East and, later, to winning the battle of the Mediterranean, was measurable in industrial as well as spiritual and military terms. Palestine rapidly converted itself into an arsenal of democracy, the only country between Britain and India capable, at the time, of manufacturing and repairing the sophisticated machinery of modern warfare. By the end of 1942, Palestine had created 432 new factories for turning out rifle and machine-gun parts, electronic equipment, drugs, serums, armor plate, harbor machinery, shoes, canned goods, and optical instruments and for repairing tanks, half-tracks, vehicles, and airplane engines. Its plants employed 50,000 skilled workers, and an additional 25,000 Jews worked in military camps and harbors. Although they constituted only 33 per cent of the total population, the Jews contributed 73 per cent of Palestine's volunteers.

On the other hand, the Arabs' military contribution to the Allied cause in Palestine was negligible. The country's 1,000,000 Arabs represented a potential 75,000 to 100,000 recruits, but in four years they produced only 8745 volunteers for the Pioneer Battalions. Elsewhere in the Middle East the Arab effort on behalf of the Allies was even less impressive.

It would be unjust, however, to fault the Arabs as a people for their unheroic performance in World War II. The responsibility for the unrest, rebellions, and frequent sabotage which complicated Allied defense of the area must fall on the shoulders of unscrupulous leaders who exploited nascent Arab nationalism and long-standing Arab grievances against colonial rule to further their own ambitions.

About 80 per cent of the Middle East's wartime population of approximately forty million were illiterate fellaheen living on the edge of starvation, and suffering from parasitic diseases like ancylostomiasis and bilharziasis that rendered them apathetic and incapable of sustained physical or mental effort. Active hostility toward the Allied cause was not, therefore, a mass phenomenon, nor was it directed against democracy, about which the masses knew less than nothing.

Anti-Allied sentiment predominated largely among the literate and semiliterate 20 per cent who constituted the politically conscious classes of Middle Eastern societies. Their antagonism stemmed from a quarter of a century of colonial rule that fell far short of the full independence which they had been promised by the victors of World War I. They were anti-British and anti-French, and pro-Fascist and pro-Nazi, long before World War II. When war came, they were fully prepared to believe nationalist leaders who told them that the Axis would "liberate" them from Franco-British colonialism.

Nowhere was the anticolonialist syndrome more evident than in Egypt. Under the leadership of the pro-German rector of Cairo's influential El Azhar, the Sheik El Maraghi, and his pro-Italian pupil, King Farouk, Egyptian nationalism soon identified itself spiritually with its Nazi and Fascist counterparts, and developed into Pan-Arabism—a movement to create an exclusively Arab union extending across North Africa and Arabia from the Atlantic Ocean to the Gulf of Oman.

Farouk neither believed in nor desired an Allied victory. Only the presence on Egyptian soil of British garrisons to protect Suez in accordance with the Anglo-Egyptian alliance of 1936 prevented him from taking Egypt into the war on the side of the Axis in 1939. He was intensely, almost fanatically, anti-British and appointed a notorious pro-Fascist, Ali Maher Pasha, as his prime minister.

There was considerable evidence during the first years of the war that Farouk, his prime minister, and high-ranking Egyptian general staff officers were leaking Allied defense secrets to the enemy. A true copy of top-secret British plans for defending Suez was found on an Italian officer killed in a patrol action. Several Egyptian staff officers were discovered in a plot to provide Rommel with details of the defenses of the strategic Siwa Oasis. General Aziz el Masri, deposed chief of staff, attempted to join forces with the Iraqi rebel Rashid Ali in May 1941, but his plane crashed in the desert en route. "I still think," one of the plotters later wrote, "that if ill luck had not so dogged our enterprise, we might have struck a quick blow at the British, joined forces with the Axis, and changed the course of events." [1]

[1] Anwar Sadat, later one of Gamal Abdel Nasser's closest collaborators, in *Revolt on the Nile*, Cairo, 1957.

War correspondents accredited to British General Headquarters, Middle East, recall the alacrity with which Arab shopkeepers and café owners in Alexandria took down portraits of Winston Churchill and substituted those of Hitler and Mussolini when Rommel smashed eastward across Egypt to El Alamein. Nor will they ever forget the morning of February 4, 1942, when the British, weary of Faroukian bad faith, moved tanks into the square outside the Royal Palace in Cairo, aimed their guns at the King's apartment, and delivered an ultimatum: dismiss the Italophile Ali Maher or abdicate. The hedonistic monarch loved his crown too well to part with it—and fired Ali Maher.

Egypt steadfastly refused to declare war and became a belligerent only in February 1945, after the Allies had made a declaration of war on the Axis a prerequisite to attendance at the projected United Nations Conference at San Francisco. In passing, it seems relevant to mention that the new, moderately pro-Western prime minister who engineered Egypt's eleventh-hour belligerence was assassinated by a fanatical Pan-Arabist follower of Sheik El Maraghi while reading the royal decree before Parliament. It was the first act of violence of a new extremist trend that under Farouk's misrule would lead to the revolution of 1952 and the rise of Nasser.

In the meantime the British, hoping to make friends with the Arabs, decided to help them realize their dreams of unity. In London, on May 29, 1941, Foreign Secretary Anthony Eden said that His Majesty's Government would give "full support to any scheme" designed to strengthen cultural, economic, and political ties between Arab countries. The product was the Arab League, founded in 1945, with headquarters in Cairo.[2] Although clearly that had not been Eden's or Britain's intention, the League was from the start an instrument of Egyptian policy,

[2] The initial signatories were Egypt, Iraq, Saudi Arabia, Lebanon, Syria, Transjordan, and Yemen. Later the League's charter was signed by Libya, Sudan, Morocco, Tunisia, Kuwait, and Algeria, as they became independent.

whose only objectives were domination of Arab affairs and elimination of the Jewish homeland from the Middle East.

When the war was over, the full extent of the horrors to which European Jews had been submitted was disclosed. At the various death camps located in areas liberated by British and American troops, visitors could see the cattle cars in which men, women, and children were hauled to the camps; the wooden huts where Jews awaited their turn to die in the gas chambers; the furnaces where the bodies were later disposed of; and the offices where the gruesome tallies of the names and numbers of those exterminated were meticulously kept. Even the amounts of gold taken from victims' teeth were neatly registered. At Auschwitz, where 2,300,000 were killed, there were warehouses full of clothing, shorn hair, and valuables taken from Jews when they arrived for Hitler's "final solution of the Jewish question."

The tens of thousands who had somehow survived the gas chambers, typhus, and starvation pleaded to be allowed to go to Palestine. But they had to be told to wait. The Jewish homeland was still closed to them. Still in force was a colonialist policy rendered obsolete by a war that had sounded the death knell of Western imperialism around the world, and Zionists began fighting the White Paper as vigorously as they had fought the Axis.

Hopes rose that Palestine would be opened to the waiting flood of refugees when the Labor Party came to power in England with Clement Attlee as prime minister and Ernest Bevin as foreign secretary. One of the Laborites' election-campaign promises had been to scrap the White Paper. Once in power, however, Bevin did an about-face, arguing that the Arab countries would rise against Britain if the government carried out the unkept pledge of the Balfour Declaration.

British Labor's overwhelming victory in 1945 cheered Zionist socialists. They fully expected the Laborite champions of the underdog and fellow trade-unionists to revoke the odious White Paper and open Palestine to the refugees flowing into the new Allied displaced-persons camps from Eastern and Central Europe. "The British workers will understand our aims," said Ben-Gurion confidently. He was shocked when the Laborites suddenly abandoned the pro-Zionism of their campaign proclamations and speeches.

"Ernie" Bevin, of whom the Zionists expected most, delivered least. In the conduct of Middle East affairs, he followed religiously his Tory predecessors' policy of propping up the area's Arab potentates and feudalistic regimes in hopes of building a *cordon sanitaire* against the new-old bugaboo of Mediterranean politics—Soviet power. Bevin's traditionalist approach demonstrated an almost complete lack of understanding of the changes wrought by the war in the Arabs' attitudes toward Britain, for it assumed, on the one hand, that the Arabs would fight on Britain's side in another world war, and, on the other, that Arab Moslems and Russian atheists had nothing in common. Bevin blindly wooed Arab help in upholding "democratic civilization" in the Middle East, although the only friends democratic civilization had in the area were the Jews. They had fought a war for it, while most of the Arabs had not.

For the next three years, Bevin ignored British and American public opinion, crushed opposition within his own party, and did everything he could to prevent Jews from reaching Palestine and to frustrate establishment of a Jewish state. He began by countering an urgent appeal from President Harry Truman for immediate admission of 100,000 refugees to Palestine with a proposal that an Anglo-American committee of inquiry be created to study the matter. This was obviously a delaying tactic to postpone solution of the refugee problem, but prompt action by the President in naming the American participants expedited creation of the committee, and enabled it to begin functioning early in 1946.

But if Bevin made it doubly difficult for Jews to reach the

safety of Palestine's shores, he proportionately intensified the Zionists' determination to save as many of their people as possible. David Ben-Gurion was just as stubborn as Ernest Bevin, and a good deal more clever. The moment he realized Bevin had no intention of keeping Labor's pro-Zionist campaign promises, Ben-Gurion ordered into operation a long-readied escape route leading from the displaced-persons camps to Palestine. The system worked out by the Zionists for delivering refugees from the displaced-persons camps to waiting ships at small, remote ports along Europe's southern coast was a masterpiece of organization. It operated much like the historic "U.G." of American Civil War days—the Underground Railroad which delivered about seventy-five thousand Southern Negro slaves to safety in the free states and Canada. From certain secret points along the Polish frontier with Germany, the Zionists' route lay through seven countries, via twenty-four clandestine stations, to Mediterranean embarkation points. Guided and protected by Haganah agents, the refugees were smuggled across frontiers, and moved in stages from station to station. Sometimes they were able to travel in trucks or buses with forged documents. Too often they had to crawl along on hands and knees, and climb mountain trails on foot, moving by night and hiding by day, for British spies were everywhere, mapping the refugees' routes, watching the ports, identifying the waiting ships, and passing the information on to Royal Navy patrols in the Mediterranean.

In three years, nearly ninety thousand refugees attempted to cross the Mediterranean to Palestine in sixty-three over-age, weather-beaten, often unseaworthy vessels. Six of the leaky old tubs managed to evade British destroyers and gunboats and reached Palestine's beaches. The other fifty-seven were intercepted and escorted to Haifa, where, within sight of the Promised Land, the refugees were transferred onto other vessels and taken to detention camps on the island of Cyprus. Horror stories concerning the condition of the arrivals and the treatment accorded them by the British filled the front pages of free-world newspapers. But Bevin, unmoved, blindly kept on with his policy.

Laborite Bevin's ultracolonialism in respect to Palestine angered Zionists. He dealt courageously and sympathetically with Indian demands for independence, and sponsored a progressive colonial-development corporation for social and economic improvements in Africa and the West Indies. But the postwar program for Palestine remained the repressive one announced in 1943 which made no allowance for the country's industrial growth, ignored any mention of the Jewish homeland as such, assumed no further immigration beyond the quotas established by the White Paper, and clearly indicated that all projected improvements, mostly on behalf of the Arabs, were to be financed entirely by Jewish taxpayers.

Zionists saw this policy as unacceptably one-sided. It was clearly calculated, Ben-Gurion said, "to do away with Jews as a nation," and use a country created by Jewish money, ingenuity, and hard work as a base for British troops no longer welcome in Egypt, Iraq, and Syria. In the circumstances it was not surprising that some Jews decided to take the law into their own hands. They concluded that the only way to achieve nationhood was to repeat in Palestine what the Americans had done in the 1770s, the Boers in South Africa in the 1890s, and the Sinn Feiners in Ireland in the 1920s—that is, to make it too costly for Britain in men, money, and prestige to continue colonial rule in the Holy Land. Acting on their own, Jewish terrorist groups attacked British army and police posts, inflicting heavy casualties and causing serious damage to military installations. The Jewish Agency disowned the terrorists, but this did not prevent the authorities from reacting against the Agency and the Haganah. Mass arrests, searches, seizures, and curfews became the rule.

The Anglo-American Committee arrived early in 1946 in a Palestine sandbagged, ribbed with barbed wire, and taut with tension. It recommended immediate removal of the White Paper restrictions on immigration and Arab land sales to Jews and reaffirmed President Truman's recommendation for immediate admission of one hundred thousand refugees whom no other country wanted—they were too sick and too poor to qualify for admission anywhere else. But London continued adamant. Britain rejected the Committee's recommendations and acted to smash the growing resistance movement, plainly having learned nothing from the American Revolution, the Boer War, or the Irish Rebellion. Army units raided the *kibbutzim*, confiscated weapons, rounded up some three thousand Haganah men and confined them to detention camps. Troops occupied the Jewish Agency headquarters. A number of prominent Zionist leaders were arrested, but most of the main ones, among them Ben-Gurion, were out of the country at the time.

By jailing Jewish Agency leaders and "kibbutzniks" suspected of Haganah membership, the British hoped to cripple the resistance at a blow. But sabotage continued. Activists demolished British radar installations for tracking incoming refugee ships. Vessels which the Royal Navy intended using to transfer incoming refugees to Cyprus mysteriously blew up in Haifa harbor. Then, in an incident attributable to terrorists, an explosion ripped through one wing of the administration's civil and military headquarters in Jerusalem's King David Hotel, killing some ninety persons, mostly British, but including several Arabs and some Jews.

Meanwhile, the Zionist leadership functioned almost as efficiently behind the barbed wire and iron bars of the detention camps as it had from its offices in Tel Aviv and Jersualem. Communications between jailed Zionists and their superior, Ben-Gurion, then in Paris, were perhaps a bit slower than normal, but practically uninterrupted. The Haganah underground functioned perfectly and the flow of "illegal" immigrants never stopped: 15,259 entered in 1945, 18,760 came in 1946, and 22,098 reached the Promised Land in 1947.

Simultaneously, a large-scale procurement plan was in operation in Palestine to provide the Haganah with weapons and ammunition. Sensing they might soon be obliged to fight to serve their nationhood, the Zionists started up secret small-arms factories and assembly plants. Heavier weapons were purchased in Europe and smuggled into the country under the noses of the Royal Navy and the military authorities.

In February 1947 the British declared the Mandate "unworkable," and laid the problem of the future of Palestine in the lap of the United Nations. Inevitably, another committee was duly appointed. The United Nations Special Committee on Palestine (UNSCOP), composed of representatives from eleven countries,[3] none a major power, traveled to Europe and the Middle East and heard the testimony of the interested parties—Britain, the Jews, and the Arabs. In August 1947, four months after it had begun its labors, the Committee recommended that Palestine be partitioned into independent Jewish and Arab states, that Jerusalem be internationalized under a United Nations trusteeship, and that the three areas be linked in an economic union.

While conducting their investigation in Palestine, UNSCOP's members had an excellent opportunity to study the mandatory power's policy toward Jewish refugees at first hand. One July morning, Royal Navy destroyers patrolling off Haifa sighted and intercepted a weird-looking, high-decked single-stacker making for port. The ship was the *Exodus,* a four-thousand-ton, wooden-hulled vessel built in the mid-1920s for the Chesapeake Bay excursion trade. Aboard her were more than forty-five hundred men, women, and children whom the *Exodus,* after sailing across the Atlantic, had taken aboard in Sète, near Marseille, in southern France.

The story of the *Exodus* is too well known to warrant repetition in detail here. The ship docked at Haifa, the refugees were debarked, herded into stockades, sprayed with DDT, and after

[3] Members included Australia, Canada, Czechoslovakia, Guatemala, India, Iran, the Netherlands, Peru, Sweden, Uruguay, and Yugoslavia.

barely touching Palestinian soil, were re-embarked on three prison ships whose decks were caged in by wire. The reloading completed, the vessels steamed out to sea and presumably headed for Cyprus, the usual destination of intercepted "illegals." The passengers were taken, instead, back to Sète, and ordered to debark. They refused. Then, an ultimatum arrived for the refugees from London: debark in France within forty-eight hours, or be taken to the British-occupied zone of Germany. Eighteen days later the refugees were in Hamburg and once more behind barbed wire in a land they had hoped never to see again. They made it to Palestine about a year later.

The UNSCOP plan as presented to the General Assembly for debate envisioned another cruel truncation of Palestine, the second since the creation of Transjordan in 1921. The 45,000 square miles of the Balfour Declaration's "Pennsylvania" had shrunk to an only slightly larger "Connecticut" of less than 6000 square miles. Quite apart from the proposed reduction in territory, the plan was full of weaknesses: the boundaries were arbitrary and artificial; the provisions for economic union did not envisage further Jewish immigration; Jerusalem was entirely surrounded by Arab territory, physically removed from Jewish Palestine, and without its own outlet to the sea.

But in the General Assembly debate, Rabbi Hillel Silver, as spokesman for Palestine Jewry and the world Zionist movement, accepted a small one-fifth the Balfour loaf as better than none. "If heavy sacrifice is the inescapable condition of a final solution," he said, "if it makes possible the immediate re-establishment of the Jewish State, the ideal for which a people has ceaselessly striven, then the Jewish Agency is prepared to recommend acceptance of the partition solution. This sacrifice would be the Jewish contribution to the solution of a painful problem and would bear witness to the Jewish people's spirit of international cooperation and its desire for peace."

On the other hand, the Arabs opposed the proposal and

threatened war to prevent its being carried out, demonstrating an intransigence that would characterize their attitude thereafter. Egypt's Mahmoud Fawzi declared the partition scheme lay beyond the scope of the United Nations Charter, which, of course, it did not. Iraq's Dr. Fadhil Jamali said his country would not recognize the validity of the United Nations decision. Syria's Adel Arslan stated his government would "never recognize" the proposed partition. Camille Chamoun, later president of Lebanon, called the plan "unjust and inequitable." The Emir Faisal, of Saudi Arabia, said his government would not consider itself bound by the United Nations decision. Yemen's Prince Seif el Islam Abdullah characterized the proposal as "illegal and unworkable" and flatly announced the Arabs "would not agree to it."

The stage was set for the next act in the drama.

6

NOT PEACE
BUT A SCIMITAR

Peace becomes mankind; fury is for beasts.
—Ovid, Ars Amatoria, III

ON NOVEMBER 29, 1947, THE GENERAL ASSEMBLY OF THE UNITED
Nations, meeting at Lake Success, N.Y., adopted by a vote of
thirty-three to thirteen [1] the United Nations Special Committee
on Palestine proposal to partition Palestine into Jewish and
Arab states. The decision was hailed with joy throughout the
free world. In Palestine, Jews embraced each other in the streets
of Tel Aviv and Jerusalem, their eyes glistening with happy

[1] Those in favor: Australia, Belgium, Bolivia, Brazil, Byelorussia,
Canada, Costa Rica, Czechoslovakia, Denmark, Dominican Republic,
Ecuador, France, Guatemala, Haiti, Iceland, Liberia, Luxembourg, Neth-
erlands, New Zealand, Nicaragua, Norway, Panama, Paraguay, Peru,
Philippines, Poland, Sweden, Ukraine, South Africa, Uruguay, U.S.S.R.,
United States, Venezuela. Those against: Afghanistan, Cuba, Egypt,
Greece, India, Iran, Iraq, Lebanon, Pakistan, Saudi Arabia, Syria, Turkey,
Yemen. Those abstaining: Argentina, Chile, China, Colombia, El Sal-
vador, Ethiopia, Honduras, Mexico, United Kingdom, Yugoslavia. Thailand
was absent.

tears. Thirty years of struggle under the British Mandate, fifteen years of heartache over the plight of Jewry in Hitler's Europe, and two thousand years of longing for a homeland had ended. Civilization as represented by a more than two-thirds majority of the members of the United Nations had invested the Jewish people with nationhood—though only in a gerrymandered fragment of the Promised Land.

Halfway round the world from Lake Success, along Jerusalem's King George V Avenue, named for the monarch who had ruled Britain in the time of Balfour and the Declaration, Jews waved their blue-and-white national flag and sang "Hatikvah," then danced the hora. Independence was theirs at last, but no less important, the United Nations had won a great moral victory—Secretary General Trygve Lie called it its "first rounded positive achievement."

Significantly, four British Dominions—Australia, Canada, New Zealand, and South Africa—voted with the majority in ordering partition, in creating a special United Nations Palestine Commission [2] to take over administration of the country, and in requesting Britain to leave the area by February 1, 1948, to make way for the independent Jewish and Arab states. The General Assembly's resolution also called on the British to make available adequate harbor and reception facilities for immediate entry of Jewish immigrants, and appealed to everyone concerned to refrain from any action which might hamper or delay the carrying out of the partition plan.

Bevin, however, announced on December 11, 1947, that the Mandate would not be terminated until May 15 of the following year, and that British evacuation of Palestine would not be completed by August 1. Britain refused to participate in any collective effort to enforce the United Nations resolution, and denied the Palestine Commission facilities to enable it to operate effectively.

[2] Composed of representatives from Bolivia, Czechoslovakia, Denmark, Panama, and the Philippines.

It seems unbelievable, in retrospect, that a country whose record for conscientious administration as an imperial power surpassed that of any since the Roman Empire [3] could behave in such a manner, but it did. In effect, Britain refused to cooperate in carrying out a United Nations decision that did not conform with her own colonial policy. In Palestine the result was anarchy, for the Arabs were encouraged to believe that they could proceed to undo the collective will of the United Nations with impunity—indeed, with British connivance or acquiescence. And they did.

The events of June 1967 had their roots in 1947–1949, years which saw the triumphant emergence of an independent Israel— and the adoption by the Arab states of annihilation as a policy, with war as an instrument thereof. The bloodshed, economic dislocations, refugee problems (Jewish as well as Arab), and political turmoil of the last twenty years are traceable to Arab refusal in 1947 to accept Resolution 181 of the General Assembly of the United Nations, proposing "partition with economic union" for Palestine.

Had the Arabs accepted partition in 1947, an independent Arab Palestine would have been created. Ergo, had they not launched their war of conquest, there would have been no Arab refugee problem. But let us begin at the beginning.

Partition provided for the establishment of a Palestine Arab state to include western Galilee, the hill country of Samaria and Judea—minus Jerusalem—and the coastal plain from Ashdod to the Egyptian frontier. The Jewish state was to comprise eastern Galilee, the Plain of Esdraelon, most of the coastal region, plus the Negev. Thus each state was split into three sections, linked at three points. (See map, page 78.) Jerusalem was to become a United Nations trusteeship of holy places and minorities, with freedom of access and exit to all faiths, and demilitarized. Economic union of the two states and Jerusalem envisioned a com-

[3] Barnet Litvinoff, *Ben-Gurion of Israel*, New York: Praeger, 1954.

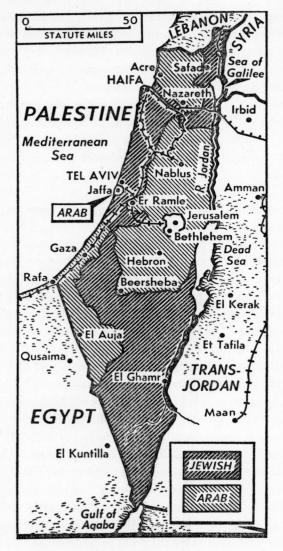

Proposed Jewish and Palestine Arab States
The map of the plan of partition with economic union is
based on the United Nations Palestine partition resolution,
November 29, 1947. *Wide World*

mon currency and joint communications, postal services, seaports and airports, utilities, and developmental agencies.

From the Jewish point of view, the plan offered only minimal satisfaction of long-held dreams. Jerusalem, the Zion of their aspirations, lay within an enclave entirely surrounded by Arab territory, without direct access to the sea. Yet, faced with the urgent need of providing a homeland for the remnants of European Jewry, the Zionists accepted partition. It was not a good solution, but it held the promise of peace.

Partition could not be effected, however, unless both Arabs and Jews wholly accepted the General Assembly's integral resolution. Failure to implement any one of the specific provisions creating the independent Arab and Jewish states, and the Jerusalem enclave, meant failure of the whole. But although the Jews accepted the United Nations decision as their contribution to a peaceful solution of the problem, the Palestine Arabs, represented by their Higher Committee, and supported by the armed intervention of the surrounding Arab states, not only refused to accept the resolution but destroyed it by their attempted conquest of the whole country.

The partition of the territory was to have been a matter between the Palestine Arab community and Palestine Jewry. The Arab states had no claim to even an inch of the land involved, but forty-eight hours after the General Assembly had acted the Arabs moved to frustrate its decision. Convinced that the British armed forces were on their side, eight hundred Arabs from Syria invaded Palestine and attacked Jewish settlements in the north. Another force of approximately the same strength crossed from Transjordan and encamped in Samaria, setting up a local "government" at Nablus. Subsequently, Egyptian troops occupied the Gaza area. Britain did nothing to stop the incursions or expel the invaders.

Occupation of the west-bank area by Transjordanian troops and annexation of the Gaza region by Egyptian soldiers—clear acts of aggression by countries whose sovereignty was not even remotely affected by the United Nations partition proposal—prevented the birth of a Palestine Arab state and the internationalization of Jerusalem. This is a point forgotten, or ignored, by the defenders of Arab claims to Palestine. The result of the dual aggression by Transjordan and Egypt was territorial expansion of both those states at the expense of what would have been a Palestine Arab state and an internationalized Jerusalem.

Both aggressions, furthermore, plainly contravened the will of more than two-thirds of the members of the United Nations and, in so doing, dealt a serious blow to the moral authority of an institution born of history's costliest, most destructive, deadliest war. In the demolition of the first important United Nations step toward preservation of the world's hard-won peace, the Axis won through its wartime Arab friends a posthumous political victory. It succeeded in doing in peacetime what it had failed to do in war—breaking the unity of the Allies.

In a very real sense, what followed was a continuation of Hitler's war against the United Nations, Judaism, Christianity, and democracy itself, directed by the same Haj Amin el-Husseini who, only twenty-four hours before Germany surrendered, in consideration of gold monies paid him to date, had agreed to set up a new Pan-Arab empire to "fight against the common enemy." [4] During his association with Hitler, the not-so-grand mufti had repeatedly suggested "the extermination of European Jewry" as a "comfortable solution to the Palestine problem."

Now he was back from exile and leading what was in effect not only a war against the Jews but also a war against the United Nations and all it represented. His field commander was the notorious brigand Fawzi Bey el Kaukji, who had served with the Turks against the British in World War I, participated in the 1936–1939 disturbances, and spent the World War II years in

[4] Bartley C. Crum, *Behind the Silken Curtain*, New York: Simon and Schuster, 1947.

Nazi Germany. Kaukji began actual military operations in January 1948.

To prevent Jews and Arabs from obtaining the means for mutual annihilation, the United States placed an embargo on arms shipments to the Middle East, and shamed the British into announcing, but not into enforcing, a similar policy. Britain continued to send weapons to the Arab states "in fulfillment of treaty obligations." She had no treaty obligations to Fawzi el Kaukji, but this difficulty was quickly surmounted: the civil administration, in settling up accounts preparatory to departure, handed over to the Supreme Moslem Council a tidy one and a half million dollars—a sum that went straight into the mufti's war chest.[5]

In its first report to the Security Council in February 1948, the United Nations Special Commission on Palestine complained that the administration had declined to establish procedures for transferring its authority to the United Nations representatives, failed to provide port facilities for Jewish immigration, and denied the Commission either the right or the protection to enter Palestine a reasonable time in advance of termination of the Mandate and British evacuation of the country. The report added that "powerful Arab interests, both inside and outside Palestine, are defying the resolution of the General Assembly and are engaged in a deliberate effort to alter by force the settlement envisaged therein." [6]

Arab hostility to partition was not a spontaneous, last-moment emotional reaction to a United Nations decision, but was deliberately planned and organized. Armed invasion as part of what Dr. Hussein Khalidi, acting chairman of the Palestine Arab Higher Committee, later called a "crusade against the Jews" was decided at a secret meeting of the Arab League governments in

[5] Litvinoff, op. cit.

[6] "First Special Report to the Security Council by United Nations Palestine Commission," A/AC 21/9, February 16, 1948.

Sofar, Lebanon, on September 19, more than two months before the General Assembly proposed partition.[7] A training center for a so-called Arab Army of Liberation of five thousand men was established in Damascus. The training was conducted by Syrian officers under the supervision and command of Kaukji.

Actual armed invasion, which began in January, was preceded by systematic Arab attacks in Jerusalem, Jaffa, Haifa, Safad, and Ramleh; ambushes along the Tel Aviv–Jerusalem road and the Haifa–Tel Aviv highway; raids against Jewish settlements in Galilee, the Hebron area, the Sharon, and the Negev; and assaults on the Jewish quarters of the Old City of Jerusalem and the Jaffa outskirts of Tel Aviv. Within a week of the United Nations decision to partition Palestine, 105 Jews were killed and many times that number were wounded.[8]

Arabs shot down Jews as they rode buses home from work in Jerusalem or Haifa, as they tilled their fields in the settlements near Kfar Etzion, as they walked the streets of Beersheba, or as they drove their battered jalopies along the highway between Tel Aviv and Lydda. The toll in Jewish dead mounted daily: five killed here, nine there, fourteen somewhere else. By mid-December the dead numbered more than two hundred.

Spokesman Khalidi attempted to dignify the Arabs' aggression as "holy war," [9] but by any name it was armed insurrection against a majority decision of civilized mankind to grant Arabs and Jews equal self-determination in their own land. It succeeded only in killing partition and, with it, self-determination for Palestine's Arabs. Worse, it set into motion events which twenty years later would culminate in disastrous defeat for the armies of Egypt, Jordan, and Syria. The first shots of the six-day war of the summer of 1967 were fired in the first fortnight of the last December of Jewish statelessness in 1947.

[7] Prof. B. Y. Boutros-Gali, University of Cairo, *The Arab League*, May 15, 1954, p. 411.
[8] *The New York Times*, December 1–13, 1947.
[9] *The New York Times*, December 1, 1947.

The first armed Arab invasion of Palestine occurred January 9, 1948, four months before termination of Britain's Mandate. A strong detachment of Kaukji's irregulars attacked scattered Jewish settlements in Galilee but were driven off by the entrenched settlers. Early the following month Kaukji tried again, this time with a large uniformed force heavily supported by artillery. His objective was to reach the coast and cut the highway between Haifa and Tel Aviv, but he met strong resistance at *kibbutz* Mishmar Ha' Emek, in the Jezreel Valley, where "kibbutzniks" held out until Haganah reinforcements arrived and dispersed the attackers.

These early successes against hireling Kaukji's "Army of Liberation," however, were not indicative of the true state of the Jews' military strength or of their over-all situation. Theoretically, Haganah could field 54,000 men. But of these, 32,000 were men in their late forties and early fifties, too old for anything but guard duty, and 9500 were inexperienced teen-agers too young for field service. Actual fighting men who had had military training numbered only about 12,500, of whom 9500 constituted the regular Haganah defense force and approximately 3000 comprised the Palmach, the elite Haganah corps that had had intensive commando training back when the British organized the Jewish underground that was to have continued the war against the Axis in the event Rommel overran the Middle East.

Weapons, moreover, were in critically short supply. The Haganah's secret workshops had not yet produced sufficient quantities of small arms, mortars, and ammunition to equip an adequate field force. As the fighting increased in intensity and Jewish casualties rose into the hundreds, the Haganah's total arsenal consisted of some 10,500 rifles, mostly of World War I vintage; 3500 submachine guns of various makes; 775 light machine guns and about 160 mediums; 672 one-inch mortars and 84 three-inchers which Haganah officers smilingly referred to as "our heavy artillery." Haganah had no fieldpieces, no armored vehicles of any kind, and its air force consisted of a few Piper Cubs and British trainers assembled from components salvaged from postwar junkheaps and hidden away in secret places in the hills.

The Jews' defensive operations were complicated by the fact that although the British had authorized a Jewish militia, they would not sanction its creation while the Union Jack still floated over Palestine. "Law and order is still an exclusive British responsibility," Bevin declared in London.[10] Haganah members were disarmed and jailed—and sometimes handed over to the Arabs.

Meanwhile Britain's Palestine garrison of one hundred thousand crack troops—an army large enough to have waged successful war against the combined regular armies of all the Arab countries of the Middle East—made no serious effort to put down the Arabs' insurrection against constituted international authority. Consequently, by the end of February, after three months of almost uninterrupted Jewish-Arab fighting, casualties on both sides totaled twenty-five hundred.[11]

Despite the presence in Palestine of British troops in overwhelming numbers, the Arabs managed to occupy hilltops overlooking main highways, and commanding lesser roads leading in and out of Jewish settlements. It became increasingly difficult for the Haganah to supply the scattered *kibbutzim* and villages, and keep communications open between Jerusalem and the coastal cities. By the middle of March, Jerusalem and its large Jewish population were in serious danger of being isolated. The roadway and water conduit from Tel Aviv had been cut, and the sacred city was on a starvation diet, echoed day and night to the sound of mortar and machine-gun fire, and reeked of sewage.

At this juncture, Ben-Gurion the politician became Ben-Gurion the warrior. The "Little Lion" had hailed partition as

[10] Litvinoff, *op. cit.*
[11] George Lenczowski, *The Middle East in World Affairs*, Ithaca, N.Y.: Cornell University Press, 1956.

"a great moral victory of the United Nations, and of international cooperation in the cause of peace, justice, and equality throughout the world." He had hoped Jewish nationhood could be accomplished peacefully, and had counted heavily on "the efforts of the two Great Powers, the United States of America and the Soviet Union" to that end. But with the fate of Jerusalem in the balance, Ben-Gurion knew the time had come to fight. But how, and with what? Grimly he summoned the high command of the Haganah.

The commanders painted a gloomy picture. It would be possible to hold out against local guerrillas, perhaps even defeat them, but if the Arab states invaded en masse to prevent partition, the situation could become grave. The scattered settlements were difficult to defend. It might be wise for the population to withdraw behind redoubts along the coastal area. In any case, the defense of Jerusalem was inadvisable; aside from the obvious difficulties of supply, the city was slated to be internationalized. It seemed bootless to expend the Haganah's limited resources in its defense.

On the diplomatic front, the outlook was equally grim. News of the extent of Arab opposition to partition—and pressure from powerful oil interests—had shaken Washington. On March 18 President Truman had promised Dr. Weizmann full support for Jewish statehood, but the very next day American Ambassador Warren Austen proposed shelving partition in favor of a total United Nations trusteeship over an undivided Palestine. The dispatches from the Jewish delegation at Lake Success advised Ben-Gurion not to proclaim Jewish independence on May 15 as planned. Such action might be construed as defiance of the new American position and preclude Washington's future support. Trusteeship did not necessarily imply abandonment of Zionist hopes; an untimely declaration of independence almost certainly would.

But if thoughts of postponing Jewish independence, or of abandoning Jerusalem, ever crossed Ben-Gurion's mind he never articulated them. He ordered every kibbutz and settlement manned, fortified, supplied, and defended—and Jerusalem held at any cost. Nothing was to be surrendered to the Arab enemy. Suddenly, under Ben-Gurion's leadership, defeat became unthinkable, victory a bright promise. Suddenly no Jewish male was too old to fight or too young to die. Women stepped forward to do men's work and release them for battle; many stepped into the front-line fighting.

In David Ben-Gurion the besieged and bombarded Jews of Palestine found their Churchill.

The Arab ring around Jerusalem tightened during the last two weeks in March. More than 100,000 Jews in the New City, and 1700 in the Jewish quarter of the Old City, were surrounded. Food stocks ran low. There was no running water—the Arabs cut it off as often as it was restored. The Arabs controlled the approaches to Jerusalem and had ambushed numerous Jewish convoys, causing heavy loss of life. As long as they held Kastel, on the heights overlooking the road leading down to Tel Aviv, the enemy retained full command of the situation. A convoy which had taken supplies from Jerusalem to the besieged Etzion group of Jewish villages south of the city, was ambushed on its return journey. In an unequal battle—200 Jews against 3000 Arabs—which lasted until the British decided to intervene, the Jews lost 40 killed and nearly all their vehicles.

The relief of Jerusalem became the first great test of the Haganah's ability to overcome the staggering odds the Jews faced in an undeclared war that had begun as a defense of partition, but in the face of mounting Arab aggression was developing into the Battle for Israel. Light arms began arriving from Czechoslovakia just in time to enable the Haganah to launch a drive to reopen the Tel Aviv–Jerusalem highway early in April. It only partly succeeded, but some food convoys got through, enough to enable the city to fight on, and Jerusalem's ability to "take it" assumed an importance in the Battle for Israel equivalent to London's defiance of the Luftwaffe in the Battle of Britain.

While the Haganah was heavily engaged in attempting to dislodge Arab forces from Kastel, armed Jewish dissidents of the Irgun Zvai Leumi attacked the village of Deir Yassin, long a stronghold of Arab snipers and armed bands. The assault was undertaken without the cooperation or consent of the Haganah. The Irgun killed some two hundred and fifty men, women, and children in a community which, while always a thorn in the side of Jerusalem's defenders, had no great strategic value. It was a dark episode, unworthy of Jewish valor, unreservedly condemned by responsible Jewish authority. Had the State of Israel existed at the time, it would not have happened, but there was as yet no effective control of all armed forces engaged in resisting Arab attacks.[12]

Intensifying their offensive against Jerusalem, the Arabs ambushed a Jewish convoy carrying nurses, doctors, and medical supplies to the Hadassah Medical Center on isolated Mount Scopus. The vehicles were set afire and seventy-seven men and women killed, among them a young scientist engaged to Ben-Gurion's youngest daughter, Renaana. In the Old City, the Jewish position had become desperate, but the citizens remained quietly in homes that Jews had occupied for centuries near the site of the Temple. Efforts to arrange a cease-fire to evacuate them were unsuccessful. The southern part of the New City, particularly the Katamon district, was occupied by Iraqi troops

[12] Menachem Beigin, Irgun leader, subsequently wrote in *The Revolt* (pp. 163–64) that the Haganah had expressly warned his command against the attack. In defending the action, Beigin said that repeated loudspeaker warnings in Arabic advised noncombatants to evacuate the village from which a murderous fire was being directed against the Irgunist irregulars. This was corroborated by a prominent inhabitant of the village, Ahmed Assad, who years later (April 9, 1953) was quoted by *Al Urdun*, a Jordanian newspaper, as saying: "The Jews never intended to hurt the population of the village, but were forced to do so after they met enemy fire from the population, which killed an Irgun commander. The Arab exodus from other villages was not caused by the actual battle, but by exaggerated descriptions spread by Arab leaders to incite them to fight the Jews."

who suddenly appeared in Arab ranks and began harassing adjacent Jewish suburbs. They were expelled by the Haganah, but the Arabs cut off the area's water supply before withdrawing.

The military situation was grave, but Palestine's Jewry charted its own course. Faced with what was rapidly becoming full-scale war in an administrative vacuum being created by Britain's slow but steady withdrawal, the Executive of the Jewish Agency and the Jewish National Council acted to bring order out of the increasing chaos. In a proclamation issued on March 23, the Jewish authorities declared they would oppose any proposal preventing or postponing establishment of a Jewish state, and rejected the scheme for a United Nations trusteeship then being debated at Lake Success as an alternative to partition. They asked that a United Nations commission proceed to Palestine without delay and recognize a Jewish provisional government to help establish authority where only anarchy reigned.

The proclamation announced that a Jewish provisional government would commence functioning no later than May 16 in cooperation with United Nations representatives then already in Palestine, and would meanwhile try to minimize the disruption caused by British withdrawal. The Jews extended the hand of peace to the Arab people, declaring their willingness to cooperate fully with neighboring Arab states and offering to enter into permanent treaty relations with them in the interests of peaceful development of all the countries of the Middle East.

The arrival of additional, and heavier, weapons from Czechoslovakia—fieldpieces and armored vehicles—infused new strength in the Jewish military effort. In Tel Aviv, a force was assembled of 1500 picked men, many armed with rifles and machine guns still greasy with the protective packing in which they had arrived. Scores of vehicles were loaded with provisions. "Armored cars" were improvised by sheathing trucks with heavy sheet metal, and the long forty-five-mile march to Jerusalem began. The Arabs still held the heights of Kastel, whose guns dominated the road where it started its winding climb through

Abu Ghosh into the Judean hills. A Palmach unit operating out of Jerusalem took the heights in a stubborn fight and killed the Arab commander of the Jerusalem front. The convoy from Tel Aviv got through, as did most later convoys by using an improvised "Burma Road" secretly built under the noses of the enemy. Through months of continued ordeal there was no more talk of abandoning the Holy City.

The disintegration of British authority in Palestine became increasingly evident during the month of April as the troops and police withdrew from district after district, leaving behind them deserted blockhouses, munitions dumps, and piles of smoldering documents and records. As army camps, police forts, or landing strips were evacuated they were seized by Jews or Arabs, or bitterly fought over by them, each side now aware that decisive battles lay ahead.

The Jewish military position improved steadily. Haganah forces relieved a four-month siege of the Jewish quarter of Safad, where 2100 Arab guerrillas had taken over two British police fortresses abandoned April 16. In another relief operation the Haganah drove off a Syrian band which had been systematically shelling Jewish settlements on the Tel Aviv–Haifa road, inflicting heavy casualties on the civilian population.

In Haifa, where Arabs earlier had massacred forty-one Jewish oil-refinery workers, Syrian and Iraqi irregulars massed for an attack on the Jewish quarter after British troops under General Hugh C. Stockwell withdrew to the port area preparatory to embarkation. That night, the Haganah swooped down on the Arabs in a four-pronged attack from the heights of Mount Carmel. The Arab commanders deserted, but their troops resisted. Next morning, General Stockwell arranged a cease-fire, and presided over a meeting of Jewish and Arab leaders at which the Jews promised that the city's Arab citizens would not be molested, and could remain peacefully in Haifa provided they deposited their weapons.[13] The general urged them to accept

[13] See Appendix.

the Jewish terms, but the Arabs left to consider the matter. On their return, they said they had orders to evacuate the entire Arab population into Lebanon, which was done with the help of British troop carriers.

What the Arab leaders did not tell the meeting was that they had been instructed to inform Haifa's Arab residents that they would be regarded as renegades if they remained, and that when the British left, an attack in force was planned to "drive the Jews into the sea." Of Haifa's 62,000 Arab residents only about 5000 stayed behind.[14] What was to become the highly publicized "Arab refugee problem," however, was already in full cry.

Jerusalem remained embattled in a siege within a siege. The city itself was cut off from the rest of the country, and the Jewish quarter in the Old City was isolated from the Jewish community in the New City. But convoys, sometimes of several hundred trucks, were getting through with food, medical supplies, and ammunition, and the population bravely fought on. Elsewhere as the Mandate dragged to an end the military situation underwent a sudden, almost spectacular transformation. What happened in Haifa also happened in Tiberias, Rosh Pinna, and other key cities and towns. The Arab armies seemed to melt away, taking with them great numbers of civilians.

Iraqi troops, supported by Arab irregulars, attacked Tel Aviv

---

[14] An account of the incident by a British eyewitness, published in the London *Economist* of October 2, 1948, said: "During the subsequent days the Jewish authorities, who were now in complete control of Haifa (save for limited districts still held by British troops), urged all Arabs to remain in Haifa and guaranteed them protection and security. As far as I know, most of the British civilian residents whose advice was asked by Arab friends told the latter that they would be wise to stay. However, of the 62,000 Arabs who formerly lived in Haifa, not more than 5,000 or 6,000 remained. Various factors influenced their decision to seek safety in flight. There is but little doubt that the most potent of the factors were the announcements made over the air by the Arab Higher Executive urging all Arabs in Haifa to quit. The reason given was that on the final withdrawal of the British, the combined armies of the Arab states would invade Palestine and 'drive the Jews into the sea,' and it was clearly intimated that those Arabs who remained in Haifa and accepted Jewish protection would be regarded as renegades."

from Jaffa, but the Haganah counterattacked on April 29, and two weeks later the Arab city surrendered. There was a seesaw struggle for control of Lydda airport, occupied first by Arabs and then by Jews. On April 27, British troops forced the Jews to withdraw and on their own departure handed the airport over to the Arabs.

So concluded the first round of the Arab offensive against the Jews and the United Nations partition resolution, but it was only a prelude to the main invasion. The Syrian-trained "Army of Liberation" had failed in its main objective, that of seizing control of the greater part of Palestine before the British withdrew, though the Arab Legion had wiped out the isolated Jewish settlements of the Etzion bloc.

Under Arab fire, the Haganah had evolved from a static defense group into an army capable of striking back. It had held Haifa and eastern Galilee and had forced the Arabs to give up their offensive at Jaffa. Arab attempts to break through to the sea had been frustrated.

The Arab offensive had canceled the boundaries set by the partition resolution. The Arab commanders had encouraged mass departures from towns and villages, promising that subsequent early victory would enable the Arab population to return and share the spoils of Jewish defeat. They were responsible for the uprooting of hundreds of thousands of their own people.

Looking ahead, Jewish leaders began forming their own organs of government. The Zionist General Council met in Tel Aviv on April 6 to 12 and set up a National Council consisting of elected representatives of the World Zionist Movement resident in Palestine, executives of the Jewish National Council in Palestine (Vaad Leumi), and representatives of other public bodies. Provision was made to grant representation to the Arabs remaining in the area of the Jewish state. Plans were drawn to float a national loan. Manpower and supply services were organized.

Palestine Jewry was ready to take over.

British rule over Palestine ended officially at midnight on May 14, 1948, a Friday. At 4 p.m. that day, the strains of the Jewish anthem filled the main hall of the Tel Aviv Art Museum, and a small audience of one hundred persons heard David Ben-Gurion, Prime Minister of the newly formed Provisional Government, read the Proclamation of Independence of the Jewish nation as a state to be called Israel. The Proclamation was at once a Bill of Jewish Rights, a statement of ethical principles, and a resolution to serve the world community of peoples. At sundown it would be the Jewish sabbath, so the leader had not waited for the formal termination of the Mandate. Above him as he read the Proclamation hung a portrait of Theodor Herzl.

Israel's Declaration of Independence contained 1027 words, 310 fewer than the one adopted in Philadelphia on July 4, 1776, in a certain earlier rebellion against colonialism.

Eleven minutes after Israel was proclaimed, it was recognized by the United States, whose example was quickly followed by the Soviet Union, and most Western powers.

Above all else, now, the people of Israel wanted peace with their neighbors—peace and friendship. They would have neither.

7

THE JIHAD
THAT FAILED

Bread of deceit is sweet to a man, but afterwards his mouth shall be filled with gravel.

—Proverbs XX, 17

ON MAY 15, 1948, AT 5:25 A.M., BEN-GURION WAS BROADCASTING from the Tel Aviv radio station Israel's thanks to the United States for prompt recognition. A loud explosion interrupted his speech. After a pause, his American listeners heard him say, "A bomb has just fallen on this city from enemy aircraft flying overhead." The Arab war to "drive the Jews into the sea" had begun in earnest.

The armies of Egypt, Transjordan, Syria, Lebanon, and Iraq —and contingents from Saudi Arabia and Yemen—fell upon Israel from the north, east, and south with twenty-five thousand regular troops supported by modern bombers and fighter planes, artillery, tanks, and armored cars. Officially, the commander-in-chief was King Abdullah of Transjordan, whose right hand as military man was General John Bagot Glubb, honorary pasha, a latterday Lawrence who had created Transjordan's five-thousand-man Arab Legion, the best of the attackers' fighting units. The first Arab communiqué predicted victory within a week.

Had any doubts existed abroad as to the Arabs' intentions, they were quickly dispelled by Azzam Pasha, then secretary-general of the Arab League. At a press conference in Cairo on the day that the invasion of Israel began, he said, "This will be a war of extermination and a momentous massacre which will be spoken of like the Mongolian massacres and the Crusades." [1] His apocalyptic prognosis was confirmed by Ahmed Shukairy, then spokesman for Mufti Husseini's Palestine Arab High Committee. Shukairy said the Arabs' war aims were, simply, "the elimination of the Jewish state." [2] It would be difficult to imagine a clearer statement of Arab war aims in the Middle East. Arab policy as enunciated by Azzam and Shukairy added up to *Judenrein*—a Middle East "free of Jews"—precisely what Hitler had hoped to achieve, and very nearly succeeded in achieving, in Europe.

The Arabs had not disclaimed, indeed, they had flaunted, their responsibility for the outbreak of hostilities in 1947 "for the forcible prevention of the establishment of a Jewish state" [3] envisaged in the United Nations partition plan. They were equally blatant in identifying themselves as the aggressors in 1948: on May 15, the Egyptian foreign minister cabled the United Nations Security Council that with termination of the British Mandate, "the Egyptian armed forces have started to enter Palestine."

The Arabs unleashed full-scale war to destroy Israel less than six hours after it was born, but what was jihad for the Arabs proved to be a War of Independence for the Jews.

The Egyptian army, with Saudi Arabian, Sudanese, and

[1] B.B.C. News broadcast, May 15, 1948.
[2] First Committee, General Assembly, Official Records, p. 650.
[3] *The New York Times*, November 30, 1947.

Yemenite contingents, concentrated on the Palestine frontier with Sinai. It consisted of modern tank units, an artillery regiment, and about ten thousand infantry supported by fighter, bomber, and reconnaissance aircraft. One brigade group advanced along the coast headed for Tel Aviv, while another pushed through Beersheba and Hebron to link up with Glubb Pasha's Arab Legion south of Jerusalem, and to storm the city. The Syrians launched their main attack at Samakh, on the south shore of the Sea of Galilee, with a second thrust directed at Mishmar Hayarden, south of Lake Hula. The Lebanese forces attacked Malkiya, and an Arab pincer movement threatened all of Upper Galilee.

The Iraqi army comprised an armored brigade and eight infantry battalions, a total force of ten thousand men supported by three squadrons of aircraft. They established headquarters at Nablus, in Samaria, and occupied the whole Arab triangle of Nablus-Jenin-Tulkarem, posing a grave hazard to Israel's seacoast, only ten miles away. By the end of the first two weeks of fighting, the Egyptians had advanced as far as Ashdod, some twenty miles south of Tel Aviv, and Bethlehem, near Jerusalem. They ultimately succeeded in cutting off the whole of the northern Negev by establishing themselves along the line from Migdal to Faluja. The Arab Legion had overrun the Jewish quarter of the Old City of Jerusalem, severed communications between Mount Scopus and the New City by capturing Sheikh Jarrah, and cut Jerusalem from Tel Aviv by occupying Latrun. South of Jerusalem the Arab Legion destroyed the Jewish *kibbutzim* of the Etzion bloc—Revadim, Ein Tzurim, Masuot Yitzhak, and Kfar Etzion. On the western shore of the Dead Sea, the kibbutz of Beit Arava, whose inhabitants had made agricultural history by ingeniously desalinating their brackish soil and making it productive, was destroyed. Further north, Atarot and Neve Yaakov were captured, and the Lebanese took Malkiya.

The twenty-five thousand well-armed Arab invaders had behind them the physical and human resources of some forty million people. Opposing them were at most fifteen thousand inadequately armed Israeli defenders of nearly seven hundred thousand Jews. Although by the end of May their jihad was one full week behind schedule, the Arabs still had good reason to anticipate victory, rich booty, and a place in the Moslem heaven for having slain many Jews.

With weapons available for only one in every four of a possible sixty thousand fighters, the Haganah could not as yet mount a counteroffensive. The Jews concentrated on holding a number of settlements in the enemy's rear while "mobile units" —jeeploads of daring young men who charged into action with Bren and Sten guns blazing—harassed the Arabs' flanks.

Israeli ingenuity partly overcame the "weapons gap"; the secret workshops were turning out improvised mortars called Davidkas —"Little Davids"—which did small damage, but made a big noise; the Piper Cubs of the Israeli "air force" dropped home-made grenades from open cockpits; the pilots of two-seater trainers flew low over Arab positions while the copilots strafed with machine guns held over the side.

Very soon other factors came into play that caused jihad to grind to a sudden halt and Arab dreams of plunder to fade. The Israelis compensated for their deficiency in numbers with excellent intelligence, expert use of such weapons as they possessed, careful planning, and high morale. The knowledge that they were engaged in a life-or-death struggle, fighting for repossession of a land that their forefathers had defended against Assyrians, Babylonians, Egyptians, Greeks, and Romans, imbued them with a will to win which their poorly led, ill-motivated, uncoordinated opponents could not approach.

The Israelis stopped the Syrian advance in the north at the Sea of Galilee, and in the south contained the Egyptian advance at Ashdod. In the center the Iraqis were prevented from reaching the coast and cutting the Tel Aviv–Haifa road.

Jerusalem, however, remained besieged by the strong, British-officered Arab Legion. One of a number of desperate, costly, but futile Haganah efforts to break the Legion's hold on Jerusalem was led by an American volunteer, a West Point graduate colonel named David ("Mickey") Marcus, who was killed soon after.

On June 11 the Arabs, realizing victory would be neither swift nor rewarding, gratefully accepted a United Nations cease-fire which previously they had been stubbornly resisting. The truce, negotiated by United Nations mediator Count Folke Bernadotte,[4] prescribed cessation of movement of military materials and distinctly forbade reinforcements of the armies already in the field. Both sides covertly violated the truce, the Arabs in hopes of swift victory, the Israelis to make up a potentially tragic deficit in arms and men. Under its cover, Egypt enlarged its army to 18,000, including volunteers from Sudan, Saudi Arabi, and North Africa; called up Spitfires; and added mortars and field guns to its artillery. The Iraqi force grew to 15,000. During the cease-fire period, the strength of the Arab forces was doubled—from 25,000 to 50,000.[5] The Israelis meanwhile brought in more and heavier weapons from Czechoslovakia and other European sources, and were able to field a fighting force of approximately 30,000.

Count Bernadotte produced terms for an armistice which were unacceptable to both sides. The Israelis agreed to a prolongation of the truce, but the Arabs decided to resume hostilities again in the hope of achieving a swift devastating triumph.

The Egyptians reopened their offensive with an attack in the direction of the Jewish settlement of Beer Tuvia on July 8, a day before the truce was due to expire. They were held and driven back.

The Israelis then launched a counteroffensive that succeeded in containing the Egyptians in the south. On the central front,

[4] Former head of the Swedish Red Cross, appointed May 14, 1948, by a resolution of the United Nations General Assembly.
[5] Edgar O'Ballance, *The Arab-Israeli War 1948*, New York: Praeger, 1957, p. 137.

they wrested Ramleh and Lydda from the Arab Legion, which held on to Latrun, but to do so was forced to withdraw troops from the siege of Jerusalem. In Galilee, Israeli forces defeated Kaukji and took Nazareth. The only Arab gains were by the Syrians at Mishmar Hayarden.

Now truly apprehensive of an impending military debacle, the Arabs welcomed a second truce on July 18. Count Bernadotte proposed the new terms of a final settlement on September 16. Israel proposed, instead, direct negotiations, in a letter addressed to the mediator by Foreign Minister Moshe Sharett. The Arab states rejected both the terms offered by Count Bernadotte and the Israelis' direct-negotiations proposal.

On September 17, Count Bernadotte was assassinated by members of a dissident military organization which had refused to accept the command or discipline of the Haganah. Despite an intensive search for the killers, whose act was universally condemned by the Jewish authorities and populations, they were not discovered.

The second truce ostensibly allowed free access for food supplies to Jewish settlements behind Egyptian lines, but Egyptian forces unremittingly attacked the convoys, and the Israelis took military action to restore communications. The action which began on October 15 soon turned into a major push. The Egyptian forces in the northern Negev were compelled to withdraw. Beersheba was occupied and only two Egyptian strongholds remained—at Gaza on the coast and at Faluja in the east, where the troops were completely surrounded. A young Egyptian intelligence officer named Major Abdel Nasser was among the surrounded forces.

The final stages of the war were now at hand. On January 7, 1949, the last major operation was launched. The Israelis took El Auja, on the border of the Sinai Peninsula, and enveloped the whole Egyptian army by reaching Abut Ageilah, inside the peninsula, and almost cutting off the Gaza Strip by attacking

Rafiah on the coast. The whole of the Sinai Peninsula was now open to the Israeli advance. Britain, which still had a military treaty with Egypt, threatened to intervene, however, and under additional strong pressure from Washington, the Israelis fell back across the old Palestine border. Israel had already agreed to over-all armistice talks, pursuant to a United Nations Security Council resolution of November 16, 1948. Still hopeful of victory, however, the Egyptians stalled for a time, but the reverses in the Negev obliged them to seek an armistice.

This left the Gaza Strip in Egyptian hands. At the same time the forces besieged in the Faluja pocket were allowed to withdraw to Egypt. Meanwhile, Israel had succeeded in breaking the siege of Jerusalem by liberating Galilee and, in fact, in containing the invaders on all fronts. The west bank of the River Jordan remained in Jordanian hands and was eventually annexed. The virtual annexation by Egypt of the Gaza Strip and the formal annexation by Jordan of the west bank, both earmarked as part of the designated Palestine Arab state, was a violation of the United Nations partition decision of November 29, 1947. The annexations prevented creation of an Arab state, its economic union with the projected Jewish nation, and the economic union of both with an international enclave around Jerusalem. Such a union obviously could not be effected because Jordan refused to hand over the Old City of Jerusalem and the territory on the west bank, while Egypt insisted on continued occupation of the Gaza Strip. Instead of economic union of Jewish and Arab states within Palestine, what resulted were the Armistice Agreements, with an economic boycott and a maritime blockade against Israel, and the continuation of not-so-holy war by other means.

Designed as *temporary* measures rapidly to be replaced by *permanent* peace treaties, a series of general armistice agreements with Israel were concluded under United Nations auspices between January and July 1949 and signed by Egypt, Lebanon, Jordan, and Syria. Iraq, whose armies had played so large a part in the invasion, declined to sign on the grounds that it had no common frontier with Israel.

The Armistice Agreements—of which the one between Egypt and Israel, negotiated by Bernadotte's successor, Dr. Ralph Bunche,[6] and signed on the Island of Rhodes on February 24, 1949, was the prototype—laid special emphasis on a number of governing principles. Article I guaranteed the right of each party to security and freedom from fear of attack by the armed forces of the other, and explicitly declared that the Armistice was "accepted as an indispensable step towards the liquidation of armed conflict and the restoration of peace in Palestine"; Article II stipulated that "no element of the land, sea, or air military or para-military forces of either party, including non-regular forces, shall commit any warlike or hostile act against the military or para-military forces of the other party, or against civilians in territory under the control of that party"; Article VII reiterated the parties' intention "to eliminate the threat to peace in Palestine and facilitate the transition from the present truce to permanent peace"; Article XII authorized either party to call upon the United Nations secretary-general to convoke a conference of representatives of the two parties for the purpose of reviewing, revising, or suspending any of the provisions of the Agreement, with participation obligatory.

The Armistice Agreements were one part of a twofold United Nations effort to end the Arab-Israeli conflict once and for all. The second, more ambitious, effort sought to establish lasting peace between Israel and her neighbors. It was assigned by the United Nations to a three-man Palestine Conciliation Commission representing the United States, France, and Turkey.

The Commission first attempted to bring Arabs and Israelis together with the aim of finding common ground upon which a peace settlement could rest. The Arab states refused to sit with Israel's representatives. Israel, on its part, suggested direct

[6] Dr. Bunche was director of the United Nations Trusteeship Division from 1946 to 1955, and was awarded the Nobel Peace Prize in 1950.

negotiations. The Commission chose to convene two separate meetings, one with the Israelis and the other with the Arab states collectively. These were held in Lausanne, Switzerland, in spring 1949, and each meeting ended with the signing of identical protocols dealing with the major problem resulting from the war.

In 1967, eighteen years had elapsed since the protocols, and the Armistice Agreements which superseded them, were signed. But no peace treaties have yet been drawn up, owing to the refusal of the Arab states to negotiate directly with Israel, and the Security Council has been powerless to enforce compliance with the terms of an international contract to which it had solemnly subscribed.[7] Israel has repeatedly drawn attention to the fact that the Armistice Agreements were meant as "transitional steps towards permanent peace," and has since volunteered time and again to enter into negotiations for that purpose. The Arab states have consistently declined.

In successive attempts to bridge the gap between Armistice Agreements and permanent peace, Israel in the last eighteen years has made a series of unilateral peace offers to the Arab states. To mention but a few of these, the Israel delegation at the Paris conference of the Palestine Conciliation Commission, on September 21, 1951, proposed a nonaggression pact; on November 4, 1951, Israel offered to negotiate compensation to Arabs who abandoned their land and dwelling places in Israel; on April 10, 1953, Israel released accounts held by Arab refugees in Israeli banks; on September 17, 1954, Israel offered Jordan

[7] On November 23, 1953, on the request of Israel, Dag Hammarskjöld, then secretary-general of the United Nations, sent a telegram to the minister of foreign affairs of Jordan, invoking Article XII (S/3911). On November 24, 1953, a Security Council resolution assumed a peace conference would take place. On February 18, 1954, the secretary-general again attempted, on Israel's initiative, to invoke Article XII. The Jordanian government persistently refused to honor the article, and on March 24, 1954, Mr. Hammarskjöld wrote to Abba Eban, Israel's Permanent Representative at the United Nations: "I consider that for the present my pursuance of this matter any further is not warranted." (S/3180/add.1).

free port facilities at Haifa as part of a peace settlement with that country; on September 25, 1954, in an Arabic broadcast over Israel's official broadcasting station, Kol Israel, Israel expressed willingness to serve as a "land bridge" between her neighboring Arab states, offering passage across her territory.

Israel has gone so far as to offer the Arabs "complete disarmament in the Middle East with mutual inspection, and if they were not yet ready for peace and complete cooperation, Israel would offer them political, economic and cultural relations, and a non-aggression pact." [8] Ben-Gurion's words were eloquently echoed the same day by Michael Comay, then Israel's Ambassador to the United Nations, in a speech before the United Nations Special Political Committee, in which he said, "Israel seeks nothing from its neighbors but the chance to live in peace with them for the common good of our troubled region." "Despite every discouragement," Comay said, "we cling to this vision of peace and progress for their people and ours, based on respect for each other's political independence and territorial integrity."

These and innumerable other offers to negotiate peace and cooperation in every conceivable form have been scorned or ignored. The experience of the negotiations over the Armistice Agreements as compared with those of the Conciliation Commission clearly indicates that when the Israelis are able to talk directly with Arab governments concrete results ensue. However, nothing has ever yet resulted from negotiations through third parties; there Arab procrastination has been the rule. The only Arab responses have been those of the press and the professional Arab propagandists, and they are invariably along the lines that "Israel is attempting to trap us [the Arab states] into making peace with her."

Indeed, after the "first round" of hostilities in 1947–1949, the Arab states regarded the Armistice Agreements merely as "a

[8] In an interview in the London *Times*, November 13, 1959.

means of bringing about the second round," and derided Israel's "hope that these agreements will act as a bridge toward healing Arab wounds and a possible peace." [9] Cairo's influential *Al Akhbar* put it this way: "In the last analysis the difference between peace and unrest in our region depends upon Israel's annihilation. Any agreement based on this thesis will not be final, but merely equivalent to a 'second truce.' The problem is not one of merely reshaping the borders in this or that place, but is basically, and stands before us, the elimination of Israel." [10]

Unworkable and inefficient though they turned out to be, the Armistice Agreements, which resulted from the military fact of an Arab defeat, endured for eighteen years. They were clearly not meant to last that long, and gradual disintegration was predictable, but the anticipated peace treaties did not materialize. This was due to a number of reasons, among them the Arabs' reluctance to relinquish what obviously, from their point of view, was a most favorable state of affairs; they were having their cake and eating it too.

Backward Hashemite Transjordan, for instance, became Jordan, appropriated territory on the west bank of the Jordan River, and grabbed Jerusalem, acquiring thereby a Palestinian population of better farmers, richer merchants, and politically more sophisticated people than its own preponderantly nomadic Bedouin inhabitants. Jordan, incidentally, annexed the conquered territories and the Old City of Jerusalem totally and politically on April 24, 1950, one year after the Armistice Agreements were signed.[11] It became one of the world's few states completely *Judenrein*; it made itself not only "free of Jews," but eliminated the Jewish presence completely. Not even Jewish cemeteries were allowed to remain; their headstones were used

---

[9] *Al Jihad*, Jordanian newspaper, September 11, 1955.
[10] March 22, 1956.
[11] The United States did not recognize the Jordanian armed conquest in law, but merely accorded *de facto* acceptance of the *fait accompli*.

for retaining walls for goat corrals, footpaths for a Jordanian army camp, and other less dignified purposes.

Egypt also found armistice preferable to peace. It could say, with some justification, that it had not suffered a military defeat. After all, it had sent an expeditionary force into another country and returned with land—the Gaza Strip—it did not have before. Its troops were roundly beaten, but not so decisively as they would be in 1956 and 1967, and Farouk, then still king, could say with small but acceptable plausibility that the army had returned with a fine prize—a strip of new territory.

Syria, despite defeat, also came out ahead as a result of the 1947–1949 war. It lost no territory, and its troops were able to establish themselves on the heights above Galilee, from which they could shell and harass the Jewish settlements below. Lebanon was the only territorial loser in the fighting, but only temporarily. The Israelis occupied the southern part of the country, but withdrew when they signed the armistice.

A major consequence of the Armistice Agreements, aside from the aggrandizement of the aggressors, was the development over the years of a veritable "Chinese Wall" separating the Arab states from their Jewish neighbors. The wall's components, cemented with the mortar of purposeful animus, are the Arabs' illegal economic blockade, incessant harassment of Israeli border settlements, disregard of the elementary rules of international conduct, and an unrelenting propaganda campaign whose only purpose is to keep alive hopes of eventually successful jihad.

The cacophony of hate that pours from the closely controlled Arab press and radio has two main themes—genocide and "politicide." No other people in the world has been obliged to contend, day in and day out, with so real a threat to its existence —as a people and as a state—as the Israelis faced until the summer of 1967.

A recurrent subtheme of Arab propaganda concerns the Arabs who fled Palestine during the 1947–1949 fighting. A few, perhaps, evacuated the country by preference, others out of fear.

But the overwhelming majority went at the instigation of leaders who promised them mass return in a jihad that would enrich them with Jewish booty—land, homes, goods, and money. A large percentage are not refugees at all, but immigrants who entered Palestine while the Jews were making the country into an excellent approximation of a land of milk and honey.

The Arab refugees, genuine or not, represent a large and very human problem in which, as we shall see, Israel is prepared to cooperate wholeheartedly. The Arabs, however, have repeatedly and consistently sought to divest themselves of the problem they created, and to lay its full burden on Israel, on the United Nations—on everybody, in fact, except themselves. In demanding that Israel take into its territory all the refugees, unconditionally, President Nasser clearly disclosed his objective. "If the refugees return to Israel," he said in September 1960, "Israel will cease to exist."

The problem is hardly unique. The division of the subcontinent of India into Hindu and Moslem states that resulted in the creation of Pakistan in 1947 was not entirely peaceful or free of bloodshed. There are still many unsettled territorial and other questions between the two peoples. But the two states exist, trade with each other, diplomatically and politically recognize each other's sovereignty.

Earlier, in 1922, Greece invaded Asia Minor in an attempt to assert sovereignty over disputed Eastern Thrace, territory then heavily inhabited by Greeks. Kemal Ataturk defeated the Greeks, and the Turks subsequently went to the peace table. At the Conference of Lausanne the Turks were awarded sovereignty over the disputed territory. The problem of sorting out and exchanging the populations involved was far more complex than the one now at hand. Two million Greeks returned to Greece from Asia Minor, and the large Turkish minorities residing in Greece were restored to Turkey under an exchange of populations arranged and supervised by the League of Nations. True, Greco-Turkish relations are disturbed from time to time over respective minority problems. But, here again, the two nations recognize each other's existence, exchange ambassadors as well as goods and services. In fact, they are military allies.

In both cases—India versus Pakistan, Greece versus Turkey—the issues involved were settled at the conference table. But in bilateral, not multilateral, face-to-face confrontation such as was skillfully, and wisely, arranged by Dr. Bunche between Egypt and Israel in 1949 on the Island of Rhodes to negotiate the first of the Armistice Agreements.

There seems to be no valid reason to believe that the problems constituting that Chinese Wall now separating Arabs and Israelis could not be solved, one by one, by employing the techniques used at Rhodes. Ideally, each Arab state could individually negotiate actual peace with Israel. Alternatively, given even only minimal good will on the Arabs' side, the divisive problems could be resolved, singly, and not necessarily in order of importance. It is possible, perhaps even probable, that in the changed strategic and political circumstances created by the war of 1967, bilateral negotiations could be initiated to tackle such overpublicized but nevertheless grave questions as the refugee problem.

The situation has changed considerably from what it was prior to June 5, 1967. The Egyptians are no longer in the Gaza Strip, and the Israelis are on the east bank of Suez. Israel is no longer a distant military entity to be crushed by jihad, but an active, dynamic military presence along Egypt's economic jugular—the Suez Canal, whose closure by the Egyptians is costing them approximately $600,000 daily in uncollected transit fees, a sum they cannot long afford to do without. The Egyptians claim that they will not open the canal until they have rid themselves of the Israeli military presence. To attempt to do this by force of arms, however, would be far too risky, as 1949, 1956, and 1967 have proved. The alternative seems to be negotiation.

One of the problems begging for negotiation is the fate of the Arab refugees, a problem far more susceptible of solution than is generally supposed, even without a peace pact. If the Greeks and the Turks, the Pakistanis and the Indians could resolve the population problems generated in the twentieth-century nation-making process, then the Arabs and Israelis can resolve theirs.

But if they have seen that jihad is not the answer to political and economic growth and development, the Arabs may also recognize the realities of the refugee question. Those realities include the fact that the past two decades have produced approximately as many Jewish as Arab refugees. There has been, in fact, an exchange of populations, though entirely one-sided.

Iraq, for example, sent out 110,000 Jews, confiscating their considerable property in the process—and some of the Iraqi Jews were quite wealthy. Israel absorbed the Jews from Iraq, as it absorbed several hundred thousand more from Morocco, Egypt, Syria, Yemen, and other Moslem countries. However, not one of the Arab nations has taken in any of its own people, but has left them in refugee camps as wards of the United Nations and has used them for propaganda purposes as a horrible example of Israeli "aggression"—an aggression they utterly failed to prove before the United Nations in June and July 1967, despite the prestige and help of Alexsei Kosygin, the premier of the Soviet Union.

The Arab delegates who preceded and followed Premier Kosygin to the rostrum to insist that the wars of 1947–1949, 1956, and 1967 were "deliberate acts of Israeli aggression" undoubtedly believed what they said. But the archives of the United Nations Security Council and General Assembly literally bulge with proof irrefutably establishing the Arabs as guilty in law and in fact of having been the aggressors in 1947 and 1948, and of having continued the war ever since in a variety of ways, including using their unfortunate brothers in the refugee camps to generate hatred for Israel—a hatred that is the only unifying force among the rival tribes and sects that constitute the constellation of the Arab states.

8

REFUGEES:
MYTHS AND REALITIES

> And they shall come that were lost in the land of
> Assyria, and they that were dispersed in the land of
> Egypt.
>
> —Isaiah XXVII, 13

ARAB AGGRESSION HAS CREATED NOT ONE BUT TWO GROUPS OF refugees in the Middle East. The world has not been allowed to forget the first but has remained largely unaware of the second. The first group comprises those Arabs who abandoned their homes in Palestine during the 1947–1949 fighting. They numbered 587,000 and are now the charges of the United Nations, which houses, feeds, cares for, and educates them. Because nothing has been done to resettle or rehabilitate them, they constitute a "problem." The second group encompasses the Jews who, between 1947 and 1963, were uprooted from African and Middle Eastern countries where their ancestors had lived for generations and where they were full-fledged citizens until they suddenly became anathema. They numbered about 650,000, and are now productive citizens of Israel. The overwhelming majority were poor people, but they collectively left behind property valued in the hundreds of millions of dollars. All arrived in Israel penniless, many with only the rags on their backs, but they are no longer a "problem"—they are home, secure under their own flag, protected by their own laws, Wandering Jews no longer.

The world has not overly concerned itself about the Jews who were constrained by forces beyond their control—discriminatory laws, persecutions, physical violence, and purposeful exclusion from Arab societies—to flee "to a place of safety," thus meeting Webster's definition of "refugees." Attention has been concentrated instead on the plight of the Arabs who left Palestine voluntarily—persuaded by their own military commanders and politicians that the war against the Jews would be short and their victorious return would be sweet with booty—hence might be categorized more properly as "fugitives" than as "refugees."

The Arab exodus began before the State of Israel was proclaimed, and the Jewish population, the Haganah, and most particular the Jewish authorities did their utmost to prevent the mass flight. According to the Research Group for European Migration Problems, "as early as the first months of 1948 the Arab League issued orders exhorting the people to seek temporary refuge in neighboring countries, later to return to their abodes in the wake of the victorious Arab armies and obtain their share of the abandoned Jewish property." [1] Then, in April, when the Jews repulsed the first serious Arab onslaught, the Arab population panicked and started to flee in large numbers.

At that time, the British superintendent of police in Haifa reported that "every effort is being made by the Jews to persuade the Arab population to stay and carry on with their normal lives, to get their shops and businesses open and to be assured that their lives and interests would be safe." [2] In a later report, he

---

[1] *REMP Bulletin,* The Hague, January–March 1957, p. 10.
[2] British District Police Haifa, "Report to Police Headquarters, Jerusalem, April 26, 1949. Document captured by Haganah.

added: "The Arab National Committee of Haifa admitted that the removal was voluntary and carried out at Arab request. The Jewish representatives expressed their deep regret, and the Jewish mayor adjourned the meeting with a passionate appeal to the Arabs to reconsider their decision. It seems that the Jews intended to prove that the Haifa Arabs could live safely and securely. . . ."

Israel's Proclamation of Independence subsequently appealed specifically to its Arab inhabitants "to return to the ways of peace," and to play their part in the development of the state "with full and equal citizenship and due representation in all its bodies and institutions, provisional and permanent." The fugitive Arabs did not listen. Nimr Al Hawari, former commander of the Arab Youth Organization in Palestine, said later that "The Palestinian Arabs' eyes were blinded and their brains clogged" by the gaudy promises of their leaders whose "ganster-like leadership . . . herded them like docile sheep." [3]

But by any name—fugitives or refugees —the Arabs now living in United Nations camps constitute a problem, although not nearly as huge and unsolvable a one as some well-meaning but misinformed observers would have one believe. Over the years, what should have been a simple exercise in population exchange has become an emotion-charged issue, the *casus belli* of spurious Arab irredentism. Every aspect of the problem has been distorted beyond recognition by the prisms of the Arabs' propaganda, which have magnified the numbers involved, exaggerated the miseries of refugee-camp life, and otherwise used the victims of their own aggression to mobilize public opinion against Israel.

The Arab states have rejected every proposal by Israel—and by various international bodies—for absorption and rehabilitation of the former residents of Palestine, thereby ensuring continuance of conditions which can be exploited to advance the central objective of Arab policy—namely, destruction of Israel.

[3] *The Secret Behind the Disaster*, Nazareth, 1955.

Their refugees do not represent for the Arab states a human problem to be resolved at the earliest possible moment but a propaganda weapon to be preserved at all costs, regardless of the consequences to the people involved.

The only "solution" advanced so far by the Arab states is total "repatriation" of the refugees in a *patria* that no longer exists. This would mean, in effect, their absorption by Israel. Arab leaders make no secret of their motives in making such a patently impossible request. "It is obvious," as Cairo radio put it, "that the return of one million Arabs to Palestine will make them the majority of Israel's inhabitants. Then they will be able to impose their will on the Jews and expel them from Palestine." [4]

From the outset, the Arab League states insisted that the United Nations provide for the wants and needs of the refugees. In 1949 the United Nations assigned the task to the specially created United Nations Relief and Works Agency for Palestine Refugees in the Near East, commonly known as UNRWA. The agency has since spent more than five hundred thirty million dollars, most of it contributed by the United States, in providing housing, food, medical care, and education for the occupants of the fifty-eight refugee camps scattered about in Egypt, Jordan, Syria, and Lebanon. Many continue to receive assistance even though they have found gainful employment in the host countries. None of the Arab states which stripped their Jewish citizens of their possessions before they left has allocated any portion of the confiscated wealth to the care of the Palestine Arab refugees. Israel, on the other hand, has released all bank accounts of the Arab refugees who left Israeli territory, paying out the money abroad in hard currencies despite the fact that this meant adding to the foreign-exchange balances of the very governments waging economic warfare against Israel. Meanwhile, not a penny of the funds left by the Jewish emigrants in Arab banks has ever been returned to them.

[4] Official Egyptian Propaganda Ministry broadcast of September 1, 1960.

A thorough, scientific survey of the whole problem with a view to resolving it humanely, within the shortest possible time, and in the best interests of the men, women, and children involved, is long overdue. At present it is not even certain just how many bona fide refugees are involved. Thanks to a naturally high birth rate and improved health conditions, the 587,000 who fled Palestine in 1947–1949 probably do number 1,330,000, as recently reported.[5] The estimate was based on the number of ration cards that UNRWA had issued to date, but, as the agency itself has repeatedly reported, the refugees make a practice of hiding their dead in order to hold onto old ration cards and have often passed newborn babies around from family to family to acquire new cards.[6]

The Arab governments have played the refugee "numbers game" to great effect in their efforts to maximize the issue politically, but the facts clearly indicate the problem is not nearly as numerically enormous, or unmanageable, as is generally believed. In a report drafted in November 1964, UNRWA estimated the total registered refugees at the time at 1,262,649, with 876,297 actually drawing rations. Of that number, the agency said, many were in fact ineligible because they were "eco-

[5] Frank McGee program, National Broadcasting Company, August 6, 1967.

[6] UNRWA Report, 7th Session, No. 13, United Nations Document A/2171, 1952, p. 3: "To increase or to prevent decreases in their ration issue they [the refugees] eagerly report births, sometimes by passing a newborn baby from family to family, and reluctantly report deaths, resorting often to surreptitious burial to avoid giving up a ration card."

From the *Congressional Record*, Senate, April 2, 1960, p. 7778:

"In 1959, after an enquiry on behalf of the U.S. Senate Committee on Foreign Relations into the administration of the refugee problem, Senators Gore (Tennessee) and McGee (Wyoming) cabled President Eisenhower:

" 'UNRWA officials say fraudulent possession and use of ration cards for Jordanians widespread but Government of Jordan will not permit validation cards now 11 years old. . . .'

"In confidential report on spot investigation October 6 (1959) George Vinson (Field Registration and Eligibility Office in Old Jerusalem) wrote: 'It will be observed out of 145 ration recipients, 61 were found to be ineligible, that is 42 percent.' "

nomically self-supporting, dead, or fraudulently registered." [7] In a later report, UNRWA estimated that the proportions of "ineligibles" drawing rations may be as high as one-third or one-half in some of the four host countries. More recently, *The New York Times* quoted an American State Department spokesman as saying "it is estimated that as many as 200,000 of 450,000 refugee cards issued for Jordanian camps have fallen into the hands of merchants and other unauthorized users." [8]

When victorious Israeli troops arrived at Gaza and at the west bank of the Jordan in June 1967 they found, to their immense surprise, far fewer refugees than they had expected— 315,000 in Gaza, and 400,000 on the Jordanian west bank. Moreover, many of the so-called refugees could not with any degree of accuracy be thus described. The Palestinian Arabs the Israelis found living on the west bank had lived there all their lives. They were refugees not because they had moved, but because the boundary had been moved. They had automatically become "Palestine refugees" when the state of Jordan was established.

It is commonly believed that the Palestinian Arabs were all resettled in the refugee camps in Jordan, Egypt, Syria, and Lebanon. But the camps in these countries have been found to hold only 37 per cent of the total refugee population. It seems a reasonable assumption that those refugees not residing in the UNRWA camps have been absorbed into the economy of the lands of their exile.

The myth of the wretchedness of refugee camps in the Gaza Strip still holds great currency too. A leading magazine recently paraded the statistics of UNRWA relief in a manner meant to make any American shudder: "The UN Relief and Works

[7] As quoted by Assistant Secretary of State for Near Eastern and Asian Affairs Phillips Talbot, before the House Committee on Foreign Affairs, during hearings on H.R. 7750, Foreign Assistance Act of 1965, February 4–March 10, 1965, *Congressional Record.*
[8] June 14, 1966.

Agency provides those who live in refugee camps with a depressingly basic diet of 1,500 calories a day plus one piece of soap a month, a new blanket every three years in cases of 'special needs.'" [9] It left out the fact that free milk is distributed daily to children and neglected to make any comparison between the nutritional level of the refugees to that of their fellows in the Nile Valley or in the slums of Cairo, Beirut, Damascus, and Amman. The differences were noted by an Egyptian officer who, writing in At-Tahrir, the official Egyptian military journal, described the camps in the Gaza area as follows:

> I spent three days in that uncomfortable country where I came to recognize as such all the lies that we read in the newspapers about refugees, disease, cold, hunger, misery and injustice. Hunger, misery and distress are not to be found. In the refugee camps there is security and plenty. I visited seven of them: Al Bureiga, Al Nusseirat, Deir el Balah, Khan Yunis, Gabalia, Gaza and Rafah. In all of them I saw people eating their full, drinking milk and living in comfort . . . happy. The men lay on their backs in the sunshine or played dice, women carried their pink-cheeked babies, not the pale sickly babies which you see in our villages, where there are no refugees . . . Do our weak children drink milk? Have you ever heard of an Egyptian fellah wearing shoes? [10]

I visited the same camps in 1956, in the wake of Israeli forces which struck at Egypt in retaliation for years of border violations by *fedayeen* guerrillas. I can vouch for the accuracy of the Egyptian officer's report, and add that the Arab "refugees" I saw in those camps were far better housed, dressed, fed, and cared for than their Arab brothers in the average Egyptian or Syrian village.

What is more, the refugees are becoming an intellectual elite

[9] *Newsweek*, June 12, 1967, p. 41.
[10] Cairo, March 25, 1953.

among the Arabs. Nearly all male children and almost 25 per
cent of the females attend school. Hundreds of refugees are now
studying in various universities on UNRWA scholarships.

For nineteen years the Arabs have insisted on 100 per cent
repatriation, not to Israel, but to the political entity which
would ensue only from Israel's destruction. The official Arab
position was expounded in 1949 by Mohammed Salah el Din
Bin Bey, then foreign minister of Egypt. "In demanding the
restoration of the refugees to Palestine, the Arabs intend that
they return as masters . . . more explicitly: they intend to
annihilate the state of Israel." [11] This and similar iterations have
had their effect on the refugee mentality. "We will stay here,"
a Gaza refugee recently told an American reporter, "until we
can fight again and take back our land." [12]

In July 1949, Israel offered to incorporate the Gaza refugees it
had at that time. The offer was refused by the Arabs. Israel then
offered to make the refugee problem the first item of business on
the agenda of peace negotiations, but this offer too was rejected.
Israel then offered to take back one hundred thousand refugees,
no questions asked. The Arabs ignored the offer, and it was with-
drawn in July 1950. In 1963, Israel again announced in the
United Nations her readiness to negotiate directly on the refugee solution. The Arab governments never even acknowledged
the offer.

For nearly two decades Israel has been offering compensation
for the landed property left behind by Arab refugees and taken
over by Israel and, to this end, has had a United Nations body
appraise the properties. The Arab governments would have no
part of any such compensatory schemes because, as far as they
are concerned, that would imply that their claims had been disposed of. Their obstructionism elicited sharp criticism from one
of their own number, King Hussein of Jordan. "Since 1948," he
said, "Arab leaders have approached the Palestinian problem in

[11] *Al Misri*, October 11, 1949.
[12] Curtis G. Pepper, *Newsweek*, June 26, 1967, p. 23.

an irresponsible manner . . . They have used the Palestine people for selfish purposes." [13]

The refugees' only hope of a useful and productive future seems to lie in resettlement in the Arab countries. In most respects, the task involved is not as onerous as skeptics have pictured it. To begin with, resettling an Arab from a mud-walled hovel in Rafa to a farm in Syria is not nearly as difficult as taking a Jewish tailor from Berlin and turning him into a tractor driver on a kibbutz. There are few linguistic, social, or climatic complications. Nor is space a problem. There is plenty of room for the Palestine Arabs in the underpopulated but as yet under-developed areas of the Middle East. Perhaps not in Egypt, which is unable to feed its present population, or in tiny Lebanon, which is already somewhat overcrowded.

The Arabs cannot claim, as can the Israelis, that they have limited absorptive capacity. Syria—as large as the states of New York and West Virginia combined, with only four million inhabitants—is definitely underpopulated. An American agronomist once estimated that Syria could support forty million people. Syria herself agrees about her capacity, but not who should fill it. On December 6, 1957, L'Orient, a Beirut paper, quoted Akham Hourani, speaker of the Syrian Parliament, as saying: "The Egyptians are mistaken when they think of the Sudan in considering emigration. The natural emigration should be north. Syria has millions of acres of fertile land. These immense areas are today abandoned and need labor. Millions of Egyptians could be easily absorbed there."

Iraq is even more underpopulated, with only five million inhabitants in a country nearly as large as California. It needs farmers and shepherds, and laborers for its oil fields. Speaking to a group of American correspondents on April 8, 1957, the foreign minister of Iraq said: "The refugee problem is being used by Egypt as a political football. Iraq alone is capable of absorbing all the Arab refugees, amounting to more than a million

[13] Associated Press interview, 1960.

souls. In Iraq, there are wide expanses of uncultivated agricultural lands waiting to be tilled. It is within Iraq's capacity to absorb more than five million people." [14] The coup which took the life of King Faisal radically altered the possibility of implementing this idea, but the space and the need are still there.

In 1951, UNRWA recommended that a two-hundred-million-dollar fund be established for a program to reintegrate and rehabilitate the refugees in Middle Eastern countries. It was adopted on January 26, 1952, endorsed in the General Assembly by even the Arab states. Various plans were laid out. The Sinai Peninsula would be irrigated; a program of agricultural exploitation would be utilized to provide power and irrigation; the Jordan's waters would be diverted and used to develop the Jordan Valley in a parallel to the Tennessee Valley Authority.[15] None of these plans was ever implemented.

The Arab motivation for refusing to solve the refugee problem is well expressed by a member of the Jordan parliament: "The existence of the refugee problem is an important harassing factor vis-à-vis the Jews and the West. As long as it remains unsolved, Israel's political and economic existences are actually endangered.[16] As Robert Galloway, a former UNRWA representative to Jordan, has said, "It is perfectly clear that the Arab nations do not want to solve the refugee problem. They want to keep it as an open sore, as an affront against the United Nations,

---

[14] *Rose el Yussef* (Cairo magazine), April 8, 1957.

[15] In 1955, after nearly three years' study, the late Eric Johnston drafted a unified plan integrating all positive features of previous schemes. The United States promised financial support. Johnston's plan, negotiated with the Arab states and Israel, assured a fair share of the Jordan River water system to each state concerned, and brought together the essential elements of two separate schemes—an Israeli one and an Arab one. It satisfied the needs of each of the Arab states for enough water to meet all agricultural and other requirements. Israel was ready to ratify the plan, and the Arab governments accepted it at the technical level, but the Arab League, meeting in Cairo in October 1955, withheld political approval on the ground that the plan would mean cooperating with and benefiting Israel.

[16] Mizra Khan, "The Arab Refugees—A Study in Frustration," *Midstream*, 1956, p. 14.

and as a weapon against Israel. Arab leaders don't give a damn whether the refugees live or die."

It is not generally known that the number of Arabs who fled the newly formed state of Israel has been surpassed by the number of Jews who have been forced to emigrate from Arab countries. During the 1947 United Nations debates, the head of the Egyptian delegation warned that "the lives of a million Jews in Moslem countries will be jeopardized by the establishment of the Jewish State." Haj Amin el-Husseini, chairman of the Palestine Arab Higher Executive, told that body, "If a Jewish State were established in Palestine, the position of the Jews in the Arab countries would become very precarious." "Governments," he added ominously, "have always been unable to prevent mob excitement and violence." When the state was established, the Jews in the Arab countries became, to all intents, outcasts in their own lands.

A review of the behavior of the various Arab countries toward their Jewish minorities reveals a sharp difference between Arab treatment of the Jews and Israeli treatment of the Arabs. Less than a year after Israeli independence was declared in 1948, repressive measures were taken by Iraq. Thousands of Jews were imprisoned or taken into "protective custody" on charges of "Zionism." Jews applied in large numbers for exit permits to Israel, but legislation was quickly passed freezing Jewish bank accounts and forbidding Jews to dispose of their property without special permission; Jewish emigrants who succeeded in obtaining exit visas were allowed to take only fifty kilograms (about one hundred and ten pounds) of luggage per person. Soon after, a decree was issued blocking the property of all Iraqi Jews who, by leaving the country, "had relinquished their nationality." Jewish property was sold at public auction. A year later laws were passed restricting the movements of Jews, barring them from schools, hospitals, and other public institutions, and refusing them import and export licenses to carry on their businesses. The program was effective: by the middle of July 1950 more than 110,000 Iraqi Jews had registered for emigration, and by June 1951 they had departed for Israel, leaving all their possessions behind.

Jews had begun to leave Yemen in the 1880s, when some 2500 had made their way to Jerusalem and Jaffa. But it was after World War I, when Yemen became independent, that anti-Jewish feeling in that country made emigration imperative. Laws which had lain dormant for years were revived. Jews were not permitted to walk on pavements—or to ride horses. In court, a Jew's evidence was not accepted against that of a Moslem. Jewish orphans had to be converted to Islam, and anyone who helped such children to escape did so on pain of death. When a Jew emigrated, he had to leave all his property. In spite of this, between 1923 and 1945 a total of 17,000 Yemenite Jews entered Palestine.

After the war, thousands more Yemenite Jews wanted to come to Palestine, but the White Paper was still in force and those who left Yemen ended up in crowded slums in Aden, where serious riots broke out in 1947, after the United Nations decided on partition. Many Jews were killed, and the Jewish quarter was burned to the ground. It was not until September 1948 that the British authorities in Aden allowed the refugees to proceed to Israel. The Egyptians had closed the Suez Canal and the Strait of Tiran to Israeli vessels, so the immigrants had to be airlifted to the new nation. By March 1949, all the Yemenite refugees in Aden had been brought to Israel.

In Syria, the now-familiar restrictions were placed on Jews: they were forbidden to buy and sell property; their bank accounts were frozen; exit permits became exorbitantly expensive. In 1943 there were 29,000 Jews in Syria; by 1960 the number was 6000. Most have since made their way to Israel.

Libya's 35,000 Jews had greatly suffered during the war years, for the country had been under Axis control and many Jews died in the concentration camps at Giado. In November 1945, when anti-Jewish riots broke out in neighboring Egypt, a pogrom took place in Tripoli in which 130 Jews were murdered. In the wake of this violence, more than 31,000 Jews departed for Israel. Now Libya too is very nearly *Judenrein*.

The 1947 Egyptian census reported 65,639 Jewish residents of that country. Unofficial estimates ran as high as 90,000. Today there are fewer than 14,000 Jewish residents. When Egypt joined in the 1948 invasion of Israel, it also promulgated anti-Jewish decrees, taking severe measures against those suspected of "Zionist" activities. Jewish property was confiscated, and hundreds of Jewish families were dispossessed. Jewish homes were bombed, and many Jews were killed or wounded. A mob attacked the Jewish quarter of Cairo, killing a number of Jews and looting their houses and shops. By November 1950, about 27,000 Jews had left the country: 21,000 of them made new lives in Israel.

In 1956, the Egyptians undertook a ruthless "Islamization" of the economic and political life with measures aimed specifically at the Jews in their midst. Many leaders of the large Egyptian-Jewish community were arrested, led through the streets of Cairo and Alexandria, and stoned. Foreign Jews, including families who had resided in Egypt for generations but had not been granted citizenship, were evicted. A government order was read in every mosque that Jews were to be regarded as "enemies."

Bank accounts were blocked, private and commercial property was confiscated, business firms were liquidated, and Jewish employees were discharged. Jewish department stores, banks, and other businesses were taken over, as were the Jewish hospitals. Synagogues were closed. Jewish lawyers were expelled from the bar, and Jewish engineers were denied the right to practice. The Egyptian Medical Association instructed the population not to consult Jewish physicians and surgeons. Approximately 36,000 Egyptian Jews managed to emigrate to Israel.

The nationalist extremism that accompanied the independence movements in the Maghrib—Algeria, Tunisia, and Morocco—also endangered the lives and property of some four hundred thousand Jews residing in those countries. About one hundred fifty thousand made their way to Israel between 1948 and 1957 from those nations. Many more would leave if they could.

The refugees from the Arab lands arrived in Israel while the country was straining its resources to absorb another half million newcomers from Central and Eastern Europe. Nevertheless, their integration in the economic and social life of the country was smoothly accomplished. The new arrivals were provided with housing, job training, and a multitude of social services, and frightened, destitute people soon became proud, productive human beings, free men in a free society. Generous financial help was provided by world Jewry, and some economic aid came from friendly nations, but Israel itself bore the brunt of the burden.

But while the Jewish refugees from the Arab lands have been absorbed and continue to be absorbed in Israel at Israeli expense, the Palestine refugees remain in their camps, a thirty-five-million-dollar annual charge on the United Nations. Obviously, a solution is long overdue. To leave matters as they are is to perpetuate a colossal racket whose victims are human beings condemned to unproductive lives as wards of UNRWA. While it is true, as Secretary of State Dean Rusk said before a Senate Subcommittee recently that "almost half a million refugees . . . have jobs and some of them at some distance from the camps, living reasonably normal lives," [17] several hundred thousand remain in unhappy statelessness, easy prey to the hate-Israel propa-

[17] On July 14, 1966, Mr. Rusk reported to the Senate Subcommittee on Refugees and Escapees: "There are almost half-a-million refugees who have registered refugee status but who, in fact, have jobs and some of them at some distance from the camps, living reasonably normal lives. They want to retain their registered status, yet we would like to see continuation of the rolls, so that the funds that are available will be used as wisely as possible."

ganda and recruiting officers of the so-called Palestine Liberation Organization.

The Organization was established in 1964, at Egypt's instigation. Its declared aim was to wipe out Israel, and in September of that year the Arab League approved its plan to recruit a "Palestine Liberation Army" from among the refugees. This army, conceived as an integral part of the Egyptian-led Unified Arab Military Command, was actually voted fifteen million dollars by Arab states, which have never appropriated a penny for refugee relief or rehabilitation. Training facilities were provided by Egypt in the Gaza Strip and Sinai, and by Syria and Iraq in their own territories. The Organization introduced conscription in the Gaza Strip of all residents born between 1937 and 1944, and in March 1965 began training about 6000 refugee students. Subsequent reliable estimates placed the number of card-holding refugees serving in the "Liberation Army" at between 8000 and 12,000, which meant that a United Nations agency was being exploited to support a movement for the destruction of a United Nations member-state. On June 20, 1966, following complaints by member delegations, the United Nations secretary-general called for a full investigation.

The military events of June 1967 inevitably produced its own quota of refugees. When, after years of having a cocked pistol held at her head, Israel's forces moved to eliminate the threat to her national existence, they occupied the west bank of the Jordan, which had a population of 900,000, and the Gaza Strip, with 300,000 inhabitants. As Israel's army approached, a flow of refugees began moving eastward across the Jordan. In the first days of the occupation, under Israel's policy of minimal interference in the internal civilian affairs of the area, approximately 100,000 residents of the West Bank moved into Jordan. But when Arab propagandists began abusing this freedom by claiming that Israel was expelling west bank inhabitants, the government announced passage eastward would be permitted "only to those who request it freely in writing, and upon the approval of their local mayor, the head of the village or another local authority." Shortly afterward, on July 2, 1967, Israel announced it would allow west bank residents to return if they so desired and could prove previous residence.

Most of those who crossed into Jordan, it was discovered, were refugees from the camps, but some were Jordanian troops who had changed into civilian clothes, and others were Jordanian government officials and their families. Mayors and other local west bank authorities testified that comparatively few indigenous residents of the area joined the eastward flow. There were strong economic reasons for the refugees to leave their camps and cross over into Jordan. Thousands receive monthly remittances from relatives living and working in Kuwait, and in other Arab and non-Arab countries. The remittances amount to more than fifty million dollars a year, and they are now transferred to banks with branches east of the Jordan. Other refugees vacated the camps because they feared, unjustifiably, that they would lose the UNRWA rations; still others left to be reunited with their families.

Israel's policy for administering the west bank, as stated by Abba Eban, was designed to bring to an end the "injury and suffering of war." "Our policy," he said, "is to maintain a just, a humane attitude towards all the populations to whom we now have this responsibility. The communications, the food supply, the power supply to the villages, all these are working well, and it is not our policy . . . to bring about or to encourage any expulsion or migrations." [18]

How Israel's policy was being translated into action was subsequently documented amply by the American and British press. The London *Times* correspondent observed on June 23, 1967, that UNRWA stores had been reopened in the camps, and that the (Israeli) army was distributing bread and milk. "The inhabitants of the West Bank who fled but did not cross the Jordan are now returning home," the *Times* reporter wrote, adding,

[18] Television interview, New York, June 14, 1967.

"Relations between the Army and the civil population seem excellent." Following the occupation, steps were taken to restore normal conditions of living and repair the dislocation of war. Free movement of population and vehicles was authorized; vehicles were handed back to their owners; commerce between cities and countryside became again active; all municipalities resumed functioning as normal; the telephone network was restored; and electricity and water supplies were repaired and put into operation.

In the Gaza Strip, where conditions were more difficult, a similar situation soon prevailed. On entering the area the Israel authorities found it to be a virtual concentration camp, its three hundred thousand inhabitants almost totally banned by the Egyptian military administration from traveling outside the area, even to Egypt. Israel rescinded the travel restrictions, and, for the first time in almost two decades, residents of the Gaza Strip were able to travel to the west bank of the Jordan and renew contacts with relatives and friends.

While attention focused on the welfare of Arab populations in Israel-administered areas, little notice was taken of the fate of the one hundred twenty thousand Jews in Arab lands in the wake of the June 1967 hostilities. Everywhere, Jews in these countries were treated as hostages and many fled in the face of officially inspired mob terror, rampant destruction and confiscation of their properties, pillage, murder, and arbitrary arrest. In Egypt alone some six hundred Jews were imprisoned, beaten, and held for long periods of time without food or water. Pogroms took place in Syria, Libya, and Aden, where scores of Jews were beaten to death. In Libya Jewish shops were destroyed, and the main synagogue was burned in Tunis alongside other Jewish property.

Israel believes that the conditions created in the Middle East as a consequence of the events of June 1967 offer a new opportunity to resolve the refugee question. In statements at the

United Nations and elsewhere, Israel has emphasized its readiness to meet with Arab representatives face to face to negotiate a final settlement of the problem, and to seek a solution to all outstanding questions with a view to lasting peace.

Meanwhile, Israel is taking steps to improve the lot of the Arab refugees in the territory under its control. A high-level commission is carrying out a study of refugee conditions in the areas of the west bank of the Jordan and the Gaza Strip. This represents the first tangible, constructive effort to devise a program which could extend to the refugees actual facilities for creative rehabilitation. Israel brings to the refugee problem its total experience in absorbing its own refugees—1,250,000 of them in nineteen years. The Israelis have become experts in the art of integrating and rehabilitating human beings of diverse cultural and racial backgrounds. They have developed modern techniques for creating productive jobs and for providing housing, schools, medical care, and a multitude of social services for the displaced and the unwanted which are clearly applicable to the case of the Palestinians. The Israelis have offered to place their "know-how" at the disposal of their Arab neighbors for a new, massive, cooperative assault on the problem. A positive response would mean a first important step toward a negotiated settlement of Arab-Jewish differences in the Middle East and the dawn of a new era of peace and prosperity for the whole region.

The plight of the Arab refugees weighs heavily on Israeli minds, for they are a compassionate people, knowing better than most what it means to be unwanted and stateless. More important, they see the Palestine Arabs less as a "problem" than as more hands with which to build a nation. The prospect of absorbing the refugees of the Gaza Strip in Israel's economy—should it come to that—does not frighten them. They faced it once before, in 1956.

I recall an interview on the subject with big, burly David Tuvyahu, then mayor of Beersheba, the booming capital of the Negev. Israel had occupied the Gaza Strip at the time, and seriously considered holding onto it until persuaded by President Eisenhower to evacuate it. There were only about two hundred thousand refugees in the strip then, and Tuvyahu was among those who were not in the least frightened at the prospect of adding that many Arabs to the country's population. He said this:

> We are building houses, garages, machine shops. We need hands here to mix and pour the concrete and to load and unload the trucks and the railway cars. We need them to make new farms in the desert. Yes, we need more hands, for there is so much to do. If we must arrange the matter of the refugees, then we will arrange it. In a Beersheba of 60,000 people, we can have 20,000 Arabs. Why not? There is room in the Negev for ten villages or towns of Arabs and plenty of work for them to do.
>
> One hundred thousand refugees, two hundred thousand, what does it matter? They hate us? Maybe so. They will come closer to us with time and education and patience. And through them we shall come closer to the East. This we must never forget. We are a Western society, yes. But we are becoming more and more orientalized. The time will come when we shall not know whether we are an orientalized Western country or a westernized Oriental nation. Our future is in the Orient. Asia can become our economic hinterland, the Arab countries consumers of our products and we of theirs. But we must have peace, and if taking in the refugees is a way to peace, why not?

But the refugee problem is a *result*, not a *cause*, of war. Refugees do not make war. Wars are made by Arab governments and by Arab armies which, except for a few "volunteers," are not refugee armies. It is war itself that must be eliminated in the Middle East if the region is to realize its immense potential for economic development and well-being.

9

WAR BY HARASSMENT

If you want a war, nourish a doctrine. Doctrines are the most fearful tyrants to which men are ever subject, because doctrines get inside of a man's own reason and betray him against himself.

—W. G. Sumner, War, 1903

IN NOURISHING THEIR DOCTRINE OF *Judenrein* IN THE MIDDLE EAST, the Arab states have used—and continue to use—every known means of covert aggression, as well as overt warfare, in blatant violation not only of the Armistice Agreements, but of the letter and spirit of the Charter of the United Nations. Eighteen years of Arab war by harassment have aggravated and perpetuated tensions in the Middle East, retarded the economic, social, and political development of the area, corroded the foundations of United Nations authority in international affairs, and twice endangered world peace—in 1956 and 1967. It is beyond the scope of this book to analyze Arab behavior, a task which this writer gladly leaves to other hands. But Arab actions between the signature of the Armistice Agreements in August 1949 and the massing of Arab armies for another futile jihad in May 1967 compels one to the conclusion that under present leaders the Arabs constitute as great a threat to world peace and stability and to international morality as did the Germans and the Italians under the Nazis and the Fascists.

One of the great challenges faced by contemporary statesmen is how to redeem from mindless leaders bent on pursuing an impossible dream of Pan-Arabism a once-great people which gave the world invaluable new knowledge in higher mathematics, chemistry, medicine, and agriculture but which has contributed almost nothing to mankind's progress or enlightenment since its conquest by the Ottoman Turks in 1517. Its only contribution during most of the last fifty years—and particularly since its long exposure to the Nazi and Fascist propaganda of the 1930s—has been in devising ways and means of destroying Jews.

The dust of the battle had not yet settled in Sinai, Galilee, and the Judean hills in 1949—nor the ink dried on the Armistice Agreements—when the Arab states launched a new offensive against Israel. Its weapons were economic boycott, border and guerrilla attacks, maritime blockade, and a relentless propaganda campaign as luridly anti-Jewish as if Goebbels himself had been directing it. At the same time, the Arab countries, having lost the "first round" against Israel, embarked on an armaments buildup which they openly proclaimed was in preparation for a "second round" to destroy the Jewish state.

All this despite the fact that at one of the final sessions of the armistice negotiations successfully conducted at Rhodes by Dr. Bunche, two eminent Arab delegates gave the United Nations mediator their personal assurances of their full awareness of the obligations and responsibilities which their countries had undertaken in signing the Agreements.[1] The Egyptian delegate, Mahmoud Fawzi, later foreign minister of Egypt, said he understood that the agreements were "tantamount to a non-

[1] Security Council Official Records, Fourth Year, 434th meeting, August 4, 1949.

aggression pact," that they constituted "a provisional settlement which could only be supplemented by a peace settlement," and that they "bound [Egypt] to unequivocal assurances and commitments not to resort to force, and even plan or threaten to resort to force" in settlement of the Palestine question. Syrian delegate Rafiq Asha was no less explicit. "My government," he said, "did not authorize the signing of the Armistice Agreement until it had examined every provision most carefully. The Government of Syria honors its words and fully respects agreements into which it enters."

Whereupon the Arab states, led specifically by Egypt and Syria, proceeded singly and collectively to demonstrate that their professions of good faith were intended only to delude Dr. Bunche, Israel, and the world in general while they continued the war by other than conventional means. The financial, physical, and psychological methods which they employed would lead to two more wars—in 1956 and 1967—and two more disastrous defeats, the last perhaps far more decisive than was generally realized by August 1967.

An all-inclusive economic boycott of Israel and her products and services began on an organized world-wide scale in 1955, when thirteen Arab League members and four Persian Gulf sheikdoms created an apparatus known as the Arab Boycott of Israel. A Central Boycott Office was established in Damascus, with branches in each member nation, for the purpose of "preventing Israel's goods from reaching the Arab countries and Arab goods from reaching Israel, sabotaging the industrialization of Israel, and obstructing export of Israel's commodities." [2]

To that end, the Arab countries passed legislation forbidding their nationals to maintain any contacts or commercial relations with Israel. Penalties of up to ten years' imprisonment at hard labor and fines ranging up to fourteen thousand dollars were decreed for violators. Postal, telephone, and telegraph facilities,

[2] *Le Commerce du Levant* (Beirut), August 1954.

and all communications by sea, air, road, or rail between the Arab states and Israel were severed and never restored. During the last twelve years, the Boycott Office has resorted to blackmail and coercion in its efforts to accomplish by economic warfare what its member-states failed to achieve by force of arms. Hundreds of businesses operating in both the Arab countries and Israel have been subjected to unrelenting and frequently successful pressures to force them to abandon operations in Israel or give up their markets in the Arab countries.

Although foreign business firms first became aware of the Arabs' campaign in 1955–1956, when they began receiving strange questionnaires from Cairo and other Arab capitals pressing them for information on whether they were "guilty" of having Jewish ownership or participation, the boycott was not a new technique in Arab aggression. Hitler's henchman Husseini first used it back in Mandate days, when he succeeded in having the authorities deny Palestine's Jewish community free use of the port facilities at Haifa, whereupon the Jews built their own harbor at Tel Aviv. But as the neighboring Arab governments fell increasingly under Nazi and Fascist influence in the late 1930s, and as the Jews increasingly identified themselves with the democracies, the boycott crystallized into established Arab policy.

The policy was developed into a total boycott by Awni Abdul Hadi, then one of the most influential members of Husseini's Arab Higher Committee, which controlled the Arab Bank of Palestine and the Arab press. Hadi influenced the first formal boycott declaration by the Council of the Arab League in December 1945. It stated that "Jewish products and manufactured goods shall be considered undesirable to the Arab countries" and called upon all Arab "institutions, organizations, merchants, commission agents, and individuals . . . to refuse to deal in, distribute, or consume Zionist products and manufactured goods." Six months later the Arab League adopted regulations aimed at achieving the economic strangulation of the Jewish community in Palestine. They provided, among other things, for the "allocation of 50 per cent of the value of confiscated goods to guides and officials, in order to encourage the communication of secret information about the smuggling of Zionist goods and products. . . ."

Up to that time, it will be noted, the boycott was aimed only against Arab purchases of "Zionist goods." It was not directed at third parties or at preventing the sale of "Zionist goods" to markets other than those of the Arab states. The Arab League took no further formal decisions regarding the conduct of the boycott until the spring of 1950, when the drive was expanded to include shipping services in an attempt to obstruct the flow of refugees from Arab countries to Israel. The Arab League decreed, "It shall be forbidden to provision or carry cargo on ships on which are impounded contraband goods or which carry Jewish immigrants to Palestine; it shall also be forbidden to provision or carry cargo on ships which are known to carry immigrants or contraband goods to Israel."

It is evident from the foregoing that the Arab states, though members of the United Nations by grace of the victors of World War II, are contemptuous of international law governing commercial and maritime traffic and consider themselves in such matters a law unto themselves. In its present highly developed form the boycott hampers the work of international bodies and stultifies the purposes for which they were founded. Arab League members, for instance, will not attend meetings if Israel is represented; and behavior wrecked the United States–sponsored Johnston Plan for multilateral development of Middle East water resources.

Stemming as it does from the mufti's solidarity with the Axis before and during World War II, the boycott can be regarded as a postwar projection of Hitlerian anti-Semitism and an integral part of the Arab doctrine of a *Judenrein* Middle East. It remains an appalling fact that no concerted international effort has been made by the appropriate disciplinary bodies of the

United Nations to condemn outrageous contravention of its Charter, bought with Allied (not Arab) blood and treasure in World War II.

Arab refusal to join a unified flight-information center for the Middle East jeopardizes the safety of air travelers in the Mediterranean. Planes making use of Israeli facilities are forbidden to fly over Arab territories, seek flight information, or obtain rescue services. Saudi Arabia went so far as to vow to shoot down any aircraft bound to or from Israel. The restrictions and threats clearly violate the International Convention Governing Civil Aviation and the International Air Service Transit Agreement.[3] In refusing to participate in international meetings or commissions with Israeli representatives, the Arabs also impede the operations of the United Nations Locust Control Commission and render ineffective the work of the Regional Council of the World Health Organization as well as other specialized agencies of the United Nations in the Middle East.

The boycott, however, is not limited to Israel and its citizens, but for some years has reached to Jews and Jewish firms, private or commercial, though they may have no connection with the country. The leader in this aspect of the Boycott Office's activities is oil-rich Saudi Arabia, which discriminates against Jews and against any concern employing them in any capacity. Since 1945, this darling of American oil companies—and recipient of considerable United States economic and military assistance—has refused to allow American Jews to be stationed on its territory as members of the United States armed forces at Dhahran Air Base. The agreement, signed in 1951 and renewed in 1957, requires the United States Mission to submit a "detailed list of the names and identities" of its members and employees so that it will not include "individuals objectionable to the Saudi Arabian Government."[4]

Under boycott rules, American citizens and nationals of other

[3] United Nations Treaty Series, Vol. 15, 1948.
[4] *United States Treaties and other International Acts Series*, No. 2290.

countries visiting Israel are not allowed to enter Arab territory directly, and are refused visas if they have visited or intend to visit Israel. Saudi Arabia, Jordan, Iraq, Syria, and Yemen refuse entry or transit visas to Jews regardless of nationality, although Egypt—until recently at least—would permit Jews to visit provided they swore they were not Zionists, or their names did not appear on the Egyptian Zionist Blacklist.

Shipping lines are seriously hampered by the boycott's regulations. Vessels may not call at ports in Israel and at Arab ports on the same run. American Export Lines, for example, must run a second expensive and time-consuming Middle East service to accommodate traffic to Haifa and Tel Aviv. More than one hundred and twenty ships of foreign registry, including a number of American vessels, have been blacklisted for sailing to Israel.

Not surprisingly, in view of their two-and-one-half-billion-dollar stake in the Middle East, oil companies anxious to please their Arab landlords have strictly observed the boycott. But only a few American businesses have shut down operations in Israel in preference to dropping their Arab markets. The American reaction has typically been to fight back, and such companies as Hilton Hotel Corporation, Sheraton Hotel Corporation, Music Corporation of America, General Tire and Rubber Company, General Motors, Twentieth-Century Fox, International Telephone and Telegraph, and Chrysler have all defied the regulations.

The Arab states themselves have been reluctant to ban lucrative trade with foreign companies simply to meet the ideological objectives of the boycott. When West Germany was threatened with loss of Arab business if it signed a reparations agreement with Israel, Bonn went ahead and signed, and the Arab countries, needing the German market more than the Germans needed the Arab markets, looked the other way.

Viewed from the purely economic point of view, the Arab boycott has been a thunderous failure. Since 1950, Israel has enjoyed an economic growth rate of 10 per cent annually, one of the world's highest; annual per capita income is $1000, compared with approximately $75 in the Arab states, and Israel's gross national product has outstripped population growth by 2.38 to 1, an unusually good performance in comparison with other developing nations. Israel's imports have increased from $423,106,000 in 1958 to $826,233,000 in 1964, and exports have risen during the same period from $139,102,000 to $351,821,000.

Far from "strangling" Israel, the boycott actually may have stimulated the country's economic development by "promoting greater self-reliance." Nevertheless, few Israelis would regret exchanging the boycott for a more sensible economic stimulus: the free exchange of goods with all Arab neighbors, the bare beginnings of which already are discernible in reunited Jerusalem —where Israeli soda pop and ice cream are being widely sold by Arabs in the Old City!

Before the boycott, Jewish Palestine absorbed approximately 90 per cent of Jordan's exports and was also a profitable market for agricultural products from Syria, Lebanon, and Iraq. In turn, Jewish industry in Palestine found a natural outlet in all neighboring countries. Resumption of trade between Israel and the Arab bloc would provide a much-needed impetus to the economic development of the entire region. Viewed politically, the boycott is another matter. It sins against the Armistice Agreements of 1949 and thwarts the main purpose of those agreements—peace negotiations. But if the boycott did not hurt Israel, the naval blockade did, for it isolated the country from its African and Asian hinterland.

Egypt announced imposition of a maritime blockade against Israel in the spring of 1948 as part of its over-all invasion plan to destroy the new Jewish state. But with the signing of the Israeli-Egyptian armistice, which categorically enjoined both parties against "any warlike or hostile act," it was taken for granted the blockade would be terminated. After the armistice had been signed, Dr. Bunche told the United Nations Security Council that it was his understanding that "There should be free movement for legitimate shipping and no vestiges of the wartime blockade should be allowed to remain, as they are inconsistent with both the letter and spirit of the Armistice Agreements." [5] The Mixed Armistice Commission of Egyptian, Israeli, and United Nations representatives, charged with implementing the armistice, supported Dr. Bunche's view and went on record as claiming "the right to demand that the Egyptian Government shall not interfere with the passage of goods to Israel through the Suez Canal." [6]

Egypt was also subject to the wider obligations of Article IV of the Constantinople Convention of 1888, stating that "The Suez Maritime Canal shall always be free and open in time of war as in time of peace, to every vessel of commerce or war, without distinction of flag." The Convention further stipulated that the signatories were obligated "not to interfere in any way with the free use of the Canal, in time of war as in time of peace." "The Canal," the Convention specified, "shall never be subjected to the exercise of the right of blockade."

The Egyptians claimed that the wording of the Convention's Articles IX and X permitted them to secure with their own forces "the defense of Egypt and the maintenance of public order." True to form, they did not read as far as Article XI, which specified, "The measures taken in cases provided for by Articles IX and X of the present treaty shall not interfere with the free use of the Canal." Even if Egypt had belligerent rights, as she claimed, she still lacked authority under the convention to obstruct Israel's freedom of passage through Suez.

Toward the end of 1949, Egypt, in addition to denying Israel the use of the Suez Canal, fortified Tiran and Sanafir, the islands at the mouth of the Gulf of Aqaba, and planted guns on Ras Nasrani, facing the Strait of Tiran, Israel's back door to

[5] United Nations Security Council Meeting, July 26, 1949.
[6] United Nations Document S/2047, August 29, 1949.

Asia and Africa. This was followed by new regulations designed by Egypt to strengthen the blockade and to prevent trans-shipments of goods to Israel via a third country. The regulations required ships' captains to present declarations countersigned by Egyptian consuls in the country of destination, showing that their cargoes had actually been discharged and were for local consumption. Subsequently, Egyptian port authorities announced that they would deny drinking water and food to vessels "blacklisted" for trading with Israel.

By the middle of 1950, this "blacklist" already included eighty-eight ships, of which seventy were oil tankers, and in September the Egyptian government introduced increasingly burdensome restrictions, such as the requirement of a guarantee by ships' captains and, in particular, by captains of oil tankers that their ships would not ultimately discharge at an Israeli port. Another regulation called for the submission of log books by tankers intending to proceed southward through the Suez Canal. Vessels found to have called at any Israeli port were placed on the blacklist and denied stores, fuel, and repair facilities in Egyptian ports. Egypt then formulated a long list of "strategic goods" which might not be shipped to Israel under penalty of confiscation, including such items as petroleum, pharmaceuticals, chemicals, ships, motor cars, money, and gold. The obvious aim was to deny Israel use of the canal for her most important import—oil. The list subsequently was enlarged to include foodstuffs and consumer goods.

Israel protested these measures to the United Nations Security Council in July 1951, and the representatives of the great maritime powers strongly censured the Egyptian action. The United States' Warren Austin condemned Egypt for maintaining the blockade "for so long a period after the signing of the Armistice Agreement," and said it was having a "damaging effect . . . on the legitimate interests of various maritime nations, including the United States." The British delegate, Sir Gladwyn Jebb, saw "no justification for the attempt by Egypt to maintain restrictions against Israel," adding that Egypt had been given "the most ample time and opportunity for lifting these restrictions."

The Security Council subsequently ordered Egypt "to terminate the restrictions on the passage of international commercial shipping and goods through the Suez Canal wherever bound, and to cease all interference with such shipping." The United Nations dismissed Egyptian claims that a state of war with Israel justified such action, stating that "neither party can reasonably assert that it is actively a belligerent or requires to exercise the right of visit, search or seizure for self-defense," and denounced such practice as "an abuse" of the privilege.[7]

Egypt continued the blockade in direct defiance of the Security Council, and enlarged the list of so-called contraband goods to include all "commodities likely to strengthen the war potential of the Zionists."

The more flagrant Egyptian blockade practices after the censure by the Security Council included confiscation of a cargo of Israel-bound meat on the Norwegian vessel *Rimfrost;* seizure of building materials and Israel-manufactured automobiles from the Greek vessel *Parnon* at Port Said; confiscation of a cargo of meat and hides from the Italian vessel *Franca Maria;* of clothing and bicycles from the Norwegian ship *Laritan;* and detention and seizure of the Israel vessel *Bat Galim,* carrying meat, plywood, and hides from Massawa to Haifa, at the entrance of the Suez Canal. The crew of the vessel was imprisoned and maltreated for three months, and was released only at the intervention of the United Nations Truce Supervisory Organization. The *Bat Galim* remains in Egyptian hands to this day.

Faced with this Egyptian defiance, Israel again took its case to the Security Council on February 5, 1954, and again the great maritime powers censured Egypt's illegal blockade. The Council's President, Sir Leslie Munro of New Zealand, said, "any impartial survey of events since . . . 1951 must record that the Egyptian Government has with every appearance of delib-

[7] United Nations Document No. S/2322 (1951).

eration ignored the injunctions of this Council." [8] A draft resolution of the Security Council called upon Egypt "to terminate the restriction on the passage of international commercial shipping and goods through the Suez Canal wherever bound and to cease all interference with such shipping. . . ." [9] Eight members, including the United States, Britain, France, Brazil, Denmark, Colombia, New Zealand, and Turkey voted for the resolution—but the Soviet Union vetoed it. Egypt had found friends in Moscow.

The Egyptian government, bolstered in its adamancy by the Soviet Union, continued its illegal blockade against Israel. The Greek vessel *Panagia* was detained at Port Said in the spring of 1956, and its captain and crew were subjected to inhuman treatment for three months. The vessel's water supply was curtailed, and, despite sickness among the sailors, its crew was forbidden to share privileges. In July, the Swedish freighter *Birkaland* was stopped and searched. A member of its crew was found to hold an Israeli passport and was arrested. In the meantime, the blacklist of foreign ships had swelled to one hundred twenty names, including vessels of British, Scandinavian, and American registry, and Israel was being subjected to another, more direct, more violent form of harassment—guerrilla attacks.

The tightening of the anti-Israel boycott, the broadening of the maritime blockade, and the unremitting guerrilla and propaganda warfare that followed resulted from major political changes and realignments in Middle Eastern politics. One was the emergence of Gamal Abdel Nasser as master of the destinies of twenty-three million Egyptians, following the 1952 revolution which ousted King Farouk. Another was the decline of Western power and influence in the area, and the ascendancy of the

[8] Security Council Official Records, 662nd meeting, 23 March, 1954, S/PV 662.
[9] *Ibid.*

Soviet Union as chief banker of economic reforms and supplier of armaments.

The revolution that overthrew Farouk's corrupt, xenophobic, anti-Western regime brought to power a Revolutionary Command Council, or junta, composed of eleven young officers ostensibly headed by the fatherly, benevolent Major General Mohammed Naguib. It announced sweeping reforms to emancipate the country from "imperialism and feudalism," and to ensure social justice, economic progress, and dignity to the hapless hordes of fellaheen. Hopes rose that Egypt might pursue a less intransigent policy toward the West, perhaps even negotiate peace with Israel, as Egyptian policy turned inward with ambitious new programs for providing land for the landless, and flotation of a one-billion-dollar national loan to finance irrigation, reclamation, and development schemes, including construction of a high dam at Aswan and transformation of the huge estates of the rich into farms for the poor. These hopes faded, however, as the junta abrogated the constitution and outlawed all political parties except its own National Union. Egypt became a full-fledged dictatorship within a nominally republican form of government. Heading it with a coterie of militarists and supernationalists of the "Free Officers' Society," who had helped him engineer the 1952 revolution was Lieutenant-Colonel Gamal Abdel Nasser.

Early in his regime, Nasser indicated that Egypt leaned toward the West, and that Russia and Communism represented "the only conceivable danger to Egypt's security." This was in reply to Western efforts, spearheaded by the United States, to draw Egypt into regional-security schemes against Russian penetration, such as the Baghdad Pact. "Left alone," Nasser added, "the Arabs will naturally turn toward the West to ask it for arms and assistance." He further justified Egypt's refusal to participate in any formal alliances by declaring that "Cooperation based on trust and friendship, even though it is not specified in any written agreement, is better than a treaty that is regarded suspiciously by the average Egyptian." [10]

One of the two real objectives of Nasser's foreign policy—a *Judenrein* Middle East with the destruction of Israel—became apparent in 1953–1954 as Arab infiltrations and raids increased in frequency and violence along the country's six-hundred-mile frontier. Nasser's second major goal—Pan-Arabism—was clearly revealed by his vigorous objection to Iraq's participation in the Central Treaty Organization, the defensive alliance formed in 1955 with Iran, Iraq, Turkey, Pakistan, and Great Britain. He then accused Iraq of betraying the Arab cause,[11] and was the leading spokesman for neutralism at the Bandung Afro-Asian Conference in April 1955.

Nasser's policy of ever-increasing opposition to Western security pacts made him a natural ally of the Soviet bloc. In the summer of 1955 he tried to buy armaments from Britain and the United States, but met with refusal unless he undertook to live up to the Armistice Agreements with Israel by negotiating a peace settlement. He turned to other, more willing, and less squeamish suppliers—Communist Czechoslovakia and the Soviet Union—for undisclosed quantities of jet bombers, tanks, and submarines in exchange for cotton.

What was spoken of openly in Arab capitals as the "second round" to obliterate Israel started—with the infiltrations and guerrilla attacks indicated earlier—soon after the 1952 revolution brought Nasser to power in Cairo. It was plain that the raids were planned and executed at the direction of the Egyptian general staff, now composed of those intimates of Nasser who had formed part of his Free Officers' Society, an organization patterned on Hitler's early *Schutzstaffel*—an elite group sworn to loyalty to the death. It was composed of disgruntled,

---

[10] *The New York Times*, September 3, 1954.
[11] Iraq withdrew from the alliance in 1958 as a result of pressure from Nasser.

intensely nationalistic young men drawn from the lower middle class, with some education and military training. All had read *Mein Kampf*, which became required reading for Egyptian officers from the rank of lieutenant up; all subscribed whole-heartedly to the idea of a *Judenrein* Middle East. (When I revisited Egypt in 1957, the country was startlingly reminiscent in "feeling" of Mussolini's Italy and Hitler's Germany. What I saw lacked the theatrical finesse of Fascism or the efficiency of Nazism, but had all the attributes of a police state: a rigidly controlled press, tapped telephones, hotel rooms wired for sound, and an elaborate network of police spies. Visitors were even subject to nightly "bed-checks." These conditions were even more noticeable in 1958 and 1959.)

Israel at first adhered to a policy of self-restraint in dealing with the provocations. But by 1953 there had been 7896 cases of Arab infiltration, sabotage, and murder, with 639 Jewish casualties. Israel began to retaliate, taking care, however, to strike directly at the Arab terrorists' bases. This was borne out by the fact that while up to this time nearly 70 per cent of Arab casualties were sustained by military or paramilitary personnel, about 80 per cent of the Jewish casualties involved civilians— usually peaceful farmers killed or wounded while plowing their fields, driving along a country road, or asleep in their homes.

On January 9, 1954, King Saud of Saudi Arabia declared in an interview that, if necessary, the Arabs would "sacrifice up to ten million men in order to eradicate Israel," which he described as a "cancer" on the Arab body. One result of such statesmanship was an Arab raid on a bus at the Scorpion Pass, near Beersheba, in which eleven Israelis were killed. Israel promptly accused Jordan of the deed, but the Mixed Armistice Commission, pleading lack of evidence, refused to condemn the Jordanian government. Israel retaliated by boycotting the Commission, and eleven days after the Scorpion Pass killings, Israeli troops attacked the village of Nahhalin, in Jordanian territory, killed nine Jordanians, and wounded nineteen.

By early 1955, a well-defined pattern of Arab aggression had emerged. The military pacts between the Arab states included arrangement for alternating attacks on Israel from one frontier to the other. The next major attack came from the refugee-populated Gaza Strip, and on February 28 an Israeli force of approximately battalion strength attacked and destroyed the Gaza garrison headquarters of the Egyptian army, killing thirty-eight and wounding thirty-one Egyptians. The United Nations Security Council censured Israel for the retaliatory action, although in his report to the Council, General Burns, chief of staff of the Truce Supervision Organization, admitted that "Infiltration from Egyptian controlled territory has not been the only cause of present tension, but has undoubtedly been one of its main causes." [12]

The Gaza incident culminated a long series of Egyptian provocations and aggressions. Between September 1, 1954, and February 1, 1955, Egypt was condemned no fewer than twenty-seven times for violations of the Armistice Agreement. On January 21, 1955, an Egyptian army unit crossed the lines and attacked an Israel military post, killing or wounding all its occupants. This attack was condemned by the Israel-Egyptian Armistice Commission three days later, but that failed to restrain the Egyptians. The condemnation, in the form of a resolution adopted on January 24, 1955, was one of the strongest ever made by the Mixed Armistice Commission. It said, in part, that "an Egyptian military patrol, commanded by an officer, attacked an Israeli post in Israel, manned by three Israeli soldiers, killing one and wounding the other two," noted that the "Armistice demarcation line was clearly marked near the place of the attack," and decided that this aggressive action by a unit of the Egyptian army, commanded by an officer, was "a flagrant violation by Egypt of the General Armistice Agreement."

The Commission called upon the Egyptians "to terminate

[12] United Nations Document S/3373, March 17, 1955.

these aggressive acts against Israel," [13] but three days later, an Egyptian armed band attacked the settlement of Ein Hashlosha and ambushed its farmers.

During the last week of February, Egyptian units penetrated about thirty miles into Israeli territory on an espionage and murder mission. They broke into government offices at Rishon Le-Zion and stole documents, and on February 25 they killed a cyclist near Rehovot. The Armistice Commission found Egypt guilty on all counts. Three days later an Egyptian military unit attacked an Israeli post across the border. Israeli troops chased the Egyptians back across the frontier into the Gaza Strip.

The raids, it was ascertained, were being conducted by commando groups known as *fedayeen*, roughly equivalent to the wartime Japanese kamikaze, literally "self-sacrificers," or "suicide troops." The *fedayeen* were paid twice the Egyptian soldier's regular wages, and were highly trained in murder and sabotage. Often operating at night, they ambushed road traffic, killed men, women, and children, blew up wells and water installations, mined roads, demolished houses in which farmers and their families were asleep, and stole anything that could be carried off—irrigation pipe, farm animals, produce, implements.

The *fedayeen* guerrillas' activities reached a peak of intensity between August 25 and 29, 1955. During that period, they carried out thirteen armed raids on Israeli villages, twelve attacks against Israeli patrols. Eight Israelis were killed and twenty wounded. Egypt, which previously had denied knowledge of the existence of the *fedayeen* and disclaimed any responsibility for their attacks, now not only admitted the commandos existed but gloried in the commandos' achievements.

In April of the following year, the late Dag Hammarskjöld, then United Nations secretary-general, managed to negotiate a cease-fire along the Israeli-Egyptian border, but to the Egyp-

[13] Decision of Emergency Session of Israeli-Egyptian Mixed Armistice Commission, January 24, 1955.

tians the agreement was merely another scrap of United Nations paper. Nasser himself defied it in a Cairo radio broadcast on May 28. "The *fedayeen*, which started as a small force of one thousand men last year," he boasted, "is today greater in number and better in training and equipment. I believe in the strength, the ability, the loyalty, and the courage of this Palestine army. Its soldiers will be responsible for taking revenge for their homeland and people."

During the next six months, *fedayeen* raiders carried out twenty-nine attacks from Egyptian and Jordanian bases, killing twenty-eight Israelis and wounding one hundred twenty-seven, and causing heavy damage to installations and crops.

Appearing before the Security Council on October 31, 1956, Abba Eban, Israel's foreign minister, detailed incident after mournful incident, and underscored the fact that from the time the armistice was negotiated in 1949 his country had been subjected to armed robbery and theft 1943 times, had endured 1339 armed clashes with Egyptian armed forces, suffered 435 incursions from Egyptian-controlled territory, and documented 172 cases of sabotage perpetrated by Egyptian military units and *fedayeen* raiders. The toll in Israeli dead was 101, in wounded, 364. Clearly, the situation had become intolerable.

10

ISRAEL STRIKES BACK

They have sown the wind, and they shall reap the whirlwind.

—Hosea VIII, 7

ISRAEL'S FIRST MAJOR MILITARY REACTION TO YEARS OF ARAB threats and harassment was the Sinai campaign of 1956. Ostensibly, it was triggered by the increasing frequency and intensity of the Arabs' *fedayeen* raids—Israel was the only country in the world whose inhabitants were at the mercy of assassins organized and dispatched by neighboring governments. Actually, Operation Kaddish,[1] as the Sinai strike of 1956 was called, was the product of many factors, which added up to such clear and evident danger to Israel's existence that it was fight—or die.

The alternative to the use of force—settlement of outstanding differences with the Arabs by negotiation—was denied to Israel. The Arabs simply refused to negotiate, a refusal that sprang from their declared desire to exterminate the Jewish state, and it is axiomatic that annihilation cannot be negotiated over a conference table with the party to be annihilated!

[1] Kaddish is a Hebrew word for services memorializing the dead, in this case those Jews who died at the hands of *fedayeen* marauders.

Nor could Israel hope for help from the United Nations in resolving her many problems. The United Nations apparatus had proved incapable of reopening the Suez Canal or the Strait of Tiran to Israeli shipping, nor could it guarantee Israel's territorial integrity and prevent the continued systematic murder of Israeli citizens.

However, the most compelling factor in Israel's decision to resort to force in 1956 was the flow of Russian and Soviet-bloc armaments into Egypt. The flow had begun as a trickle in 1953–1954 with Russian T-34 tanks infinitely superior to the Israelis' old Sherman Mark IIIs, and MIG and Illyushin warplanes years ahead in design and performance of Israel's Meteors and Ouragans. But after Nasser's 1955 arms deal with Czechoslovakia, the trickle became a flood. Until then, a rough if unfavorable weapons balance had existed between Israel and Egypt: each had about two hundred tanks, and Egypt possessed about eighty jet fighters to Israel's fifty. But as green summer ripened into golden autumn in 1956 the balance tipped perilously in favor of Egypt.

By summer's end, Egypt had received from Czechoslovakia five hundred thirty armored vehicles—two hundred thirty tanks, two hundred armored troop carriers, and a hundred self-propelled guns—plus about five hundred pieces of artillery; some two hundred fighter aircraft, bombers, and transport planes; and many warships, including submarines, destroyers, and motor torpedo boats.

Obviously, Egypt nourished large-scale aggressive intentions. These had already become apparent the year before, on October 19, 1955, when Cairo and Damascus temporarily suppressed their rivalries and animosities, and established a Joint Egyptian-Syrian Military Command. Syria, too, had begun receiving Russian weapons and, like Egypt, platoons of Soviet technicians to teach Arab soldiers how to use their lethal hardware.

Contracts signed in Moscow by Syria's then defense minister, Khaled Azm, called for delivery of from a hundred twenty to a hundred forty T-34 tanks, two hundred BTR-152 armored personnel carriers, at least forty 85mm. antiaircraft guns, sixty 122mm. gun-howitzers, twenty 152mm. gun-howitzers, fifty 111mm. self-propelled guns, one hundred 37mm. antiaircraft guns, fifteen thousand late-model Czech rifles, and enormous quantities of automatic small rams and ammunition. In addition, Syria received forty MIG-15s, but like the other weapons in Syrian hands they presented no immediate threat to Israel, whose excellent intelligence services estimated it would take years for the Syrians to train the troops and pilots needed to man the new armaments.

Egypt was another matter. The Egyptians had been training under Russian supervision for many months, and had fielded in Sinai an army of some sixty thousand troops, with a partly trained reserve of upwards of one hundred thousand. Given their quantitative and qualitative preponderance of land, sea, and air weapons, the Egyptians represented—at least on paper—a most formidable array, and Israel could have no doubt against whom it would be used.

To correct the potentially lethal imbalance created by the Russian supplies to her self-declared enemies, Israel turned to France, which agreed to supply tanks and airplanes. "At least," said Ben-Gurion, after having appealed in vain to the United States for weapons, "Israel has found a true ally."

The Israeli General Staff was busy planning how best to neutralize the mounting threat from Egypt and how to speed up training to absorb the new weapons which Israel was receiving from France, when a new, although not wholly unexpected, element entered their calculations. From the Israeli military attaché in Paris came an urgent signal disclosing that the British and French planned a joint military action to seize the Suez Canal, which Nasser had swiftly, ruthlessly, and successfully nationalized in July.

The news was almost too good to be true, for if the Anglo-French attempt succeeded, the international status of the Suez

Canal would be restored, and one of Israel's major problems would disappear. Clearly, it behooved Israel to be ready to exploit whatever military advantages might accrue from the proposed Anglo-French operation, which was to be called Musketeer, but, as it developed, might better have been dubbed Snafu.

General Moshe Dayan, then chief of the Israeli General Staff, spent a month assessing the capabilities of his country's defense forces and testing alternative plans of action with his officers, and on October 1 flew to Paris to talk with the French Chief of Staff, General Ely. Ely was reluctant to talk of French plans for Suez but indicated he was disposed to be "helpful" to Israel, particularly with air support.

Musketeer was one of the worst-kept secrets in the history of modern military operations, and Dayan had little difficulty assembling from various sources a fairly accurate evaluation of the probable strength of the Anglo-French effort, its strategy and tactics, and the approximate date of the intended strike. From their studies, Dayan and his staff concluded that their principal objective should be the conquest of the Sinai peninsula.

Some members of the Israeli government doubted the wisdom of a major Sinai campaign, but political developments in Jordan quickly dissolved their opposition. As a result of national elections, a strongly pro-Nasser, anti-Western government came to power in Amman on October 23. The same day, General Amer, the Egyptian commander-in-chief, arrived in the Jordanian capital to exploit the success of the country's pro-Egyptian politicians. Within twenty-four hours a military pact was signed linking Jordan to Egypt and Syria under a unified command with Amer as generalissimo.

For Israel, this was the last straw. It would be only a matter of time before Egypt would strike. If any advantage was to be derived from the planned Anglo-French seizure of the Suez Canal, Israel needed to act promptly. To fail to do so could be fatal. In Ben-Gurion's words, Israel wanted peace, "but not suicide."

He obtained Cabinet approval for an action "for our very survival, in sheer self-defense."

Accordingly, on October 25, Dayan informed his Operations Branch that the government had approved plans for a Sinai campaign. Stress would be placed on creation of a "threat" to the Suez Canal, although Israel had no intention of penetrating that far into Egypt; her real objectives would be to capture Sharm el-Sheikh, the Egyptian positions commanding the Strait of Tiran, confound the organization of the Egyptian forces, and bring about their collapse. According to Dayan's information, D-Day for Musketeer had been set for October 31. Kaddish would be launched on October 29 and complete the capture of the Sinai peninsula, Dayan estimated, within seven to ten days.

The next day, October 26, Israel quietly mobilized her reserves. Already in the field was her regular army of upwards of thirty thousand men. Behind it, within forty-eight hours, approximately two hundred thousand Israeli men and women answered telegrams, telephone calls, and other prearranged signals calling them to the colors.

On the eve of the war, where once nearly all of Egypt's army of sixty thousand had ranged the Sinai, now little more than thirty thousand remained: Nasser had pulled the rest back to defend the Suez Canal and his capital. But though ground forces were more or less equal in number, if not in skill and morale, Egypt held the balance in armor and air power. The Egyptian air force was composed exclusively of jets. The Egyptians had about two hundred MIG-15 fighters deployed in four squadrons, and some fifty Russian Illyushin-28 bombers, plus four squadrons of British Meteors and Vampires—an additional one hundred thirty planes. Against these were eight jet squadrons, totaling seventy-nine planes—thirty-seven Mystères and forty-two Meteors and Ouragans. Against Egypt's fifty bombers, Israel had exactly two: piston-engine B-17s, relics of World War II! A ragtag collection of sixty-four piston-engine fighters completed the Israeli force. Outnumbered something like two or three to one, the Israelis would have to rely on the fact that they knew their equipment better and were better trained.

The Israeli attack was launched at 1700 hours October 29 with paratroopers dropped at the Mitla Pass, the connecting link between the Sinai and the Canal Zone. Israeli's three invading columns fanned into a seventy-mile-wide arc and ground westward into the Sinai's barren dunes, plateaus, and lifeless mountains. The northernmost column pushed easily past Quseima and fishhooked to the northwest to cut off the Gaza Strip. The southernmost column drove past Eilat without resistance and raced toward the heart of the peninsula. Its objective was Nakhl, there to reinforce the paratroopers who had been dropped at Mitla. The center column, moving past Kuntilla, drew blood only a few miles inside Sinai, where it encountered Egyptian armor, mostly Soviet T-34 tanks. After sixteen hours, it scattered the Egyptians.

By dawn on October 30, the Israeli southern column had, in effect, cut off all southern Sinai and was even turning some of Egypt's own T-34s against the defenders. Egypt fought back mostly with windy communiqués—"We have annihilated the invasion forces"—a few ineffectual air sorties at Tel Aviv (the pilots dropped their bombs in empty fields and turned tail), and a tragicomic attempt by an Egyptian frigate to shell Haifa. The ship was crippled by Israeli aircraft rockets and ran up a white flag. Egyptian Navy headquarters in Alexandria ordered the captain to scuttle the ship, but he could not find the keys to the sea cocks. The ship was towed into port while Israelis cheered from Haifa's rooftops.

It was on the third day, October 31, that the Egyptians threw their one fierce punch in a stretch of dune coutnry in north-central Sinai, at a vital road junction called Abu Aweigila. Israeli Shermans and AMX tanks ran into a strong battalion of Egyptian armor and veered away from it while Israeli infantry moved to the attack. Overhead, Israeli Mystères spotted a major reinforcing column—apparently a full corps of up to fifty thousand men—lumbering eastward along the black-topped road from Ismailia. Egyptian Vampires and MIGs came in to cover the reinforcements and fell into battle with Israeli fighters. By late in the day, it was still a battle; the Egyptians were fighting with more skill and courage than they had in 1948.

The day before an astounding ultimatum had come from the French and British. It required: stoppage of all warlike action on land, sea, and in the air forthwith; withdrawal of all armed forces to a distance of ten miles from the Suez Canal; and the Egyptian government's agreement "in order to guarantee freedom of transit through the Suez Canal by the ships of all nations and in order to separate the belligerents, to accept the temporary occupation by Anglo-French forces of key positions at Port Said, Ismailia and Suez."

Compliance was requested within twelve hours, but the Anglo-French forces chose not to act until twenty-five hours later, at dusk October 31. Now the first Anglo-French bombers hit Egypt's airfields. It was all the help the Israelis at Abu Aweigila needed. With Egypt's air harassment all but eliminated, Israel's thin-skinned but speedy French tanks engaged the heavier T-34s. Soon the hillsides were smoky with burning tanks, both Egyptian and Israeli, but by nightfall the Israelis' speed proved decisive.

West of Suez, British twin Canberra jets whistled in from Cyprus to strike at Egyptian airfields. The political hope in London and Paris was that their air strikes alone, combined with the Israeli sweep across the Sinai, would persuade Egypt to surrender —or blast Nasser from power. But the basic military intent was to clear the skies for Anglo-French invasion.

As dawn broke over the tank battlefield of Abu Aweigila on November 1, the Israelis discovered that in the darkness the Egyptians had pulled out what was left of their armor to scurry to safety west of the Suez. A considerable remnant had got away, but the Egyptians' one big effort had failed.

Over Cairo, the Anglo-French bombing spread from airports to military barracks and munitions depots. The British command warned the Egyptians of what Anglo-French airmen were going to do before they did it, with the double purpose of preventing casualties and of spreading despair.

In Tel Aviv, an Israeli army spokesman proudly announced: "We have conquered the bulk of Sinai."

On the fifth day, Anglo-French forces finished the destruction of the Egyptian air force on the ground, then turned to strafing and bombing Egyptian motor convoys and strategic points which might hinder the landing in the Canal Zone. In frustration, the Egyptians sank seven blockships at various points in the Suez Canal. That morning Israeli forces marched into El Arish on the way along the Mediterranean coast to a point ten miles from the Canal. The city had been evacuated by the Egyptians, and it was apparent that, when the withdrawal order was given, everyone had simply left his post and rushed to join the convoys leaving the city.

The hospital offered a gruesome sight. On the operating table lay the body of an Egyptian soldier whose leg had just been amputated. He had been abandoned in the middle of the operation. No doctor or nurse had stopped to bandage him, and he died from loss of blood. Hundreds of wounded had been similarly left to their fate. The Israelis did what they could to help them.

On the sixth day, November 3, Israeli forces marched triumphantly into the ancient and grubby city of Gaza, where a blinded Samson once had pulled down the pillars and destroyed the Temple. They found only a handful of dull-eyed, curious Arabs, the remnants of an Egyptian division whose members had shucked their uniforms and were walking around in shorts or pajamas to blend with the population. The Egyptian governor-general of the Gaza Strip put his name to surrender papers and handed the Strip, with all its problems, over to Israel. Meanwhile, the British-French invasion of the Canal Zone finally got under way.

By Monday, November 5, the eighth day of the war, Israel defense-force units occupied Sharm el-Sheikh, commanding the Strait of Tiran. By the time the United Nations cease-fire orders arrived Tuesday at midnight, the Sinai Peninsula was firmly in Israeli hands.

Kaddish had ended victoriously, but Musketeer dragged its feet. The Anglo-French command had had seven days—October 29 to November 4—in which to exploit Israeli-Egyptian hostilities but as yet had landed no troops in the Canal Zone. Now time was running out, politically and militarily. Shouts of "Eden must go!" rose in the British Parliament from Labor members fearful of Russian intervention and escalation of the Suez war into another world war.

Israel had striven to end the Sinai fighting before coming into conflict with the will of the United Nations and, in fact, had succeeded. Although she had rejected the UN's demands for unconditional immediate withdrawal, she had accepted the cease-fire order. Now, Britain asked Israel to reverse herself and *reject* the cease-fire—so that Musketeer troops could occupy the Canal Zone on the pretext that they were acting to separate warring Egyptian and Israeli armies! Israel reluctantly agreed, although this placed her in the role of an aggressor against whom the British and French were taking military action, to ensure cessation of hostilities and Israel's withdrawal from Sinai. It was a bitter pill for Israel to swallow, but swallow it she did out of consideration for the French, who had proved themselves staunch friends when Israel needed weapons.

International tensions increased as the first Anglo-French paratroopers began landing in the Canal Zone at dawn on November 5. War-scare headlines blackened the front pages of newspapers everywhere, and Moscow added to the mounting apprehension. Having crushed the Hungarian uprising which had occupied her attention during the last week in October, the Soviet Union now reacted forcefully on behalf of her Arab friends. Twenty-four Russian-manned MIG-17s, accompanied by Soviet transports bringing technicians and radar equipment, landed in Syria. Bulganin sent stern notes to Britain, France, and Israel threatening Soviet military action, including bombardment by ballistic missiles.

The Russian note to Israel was particularly offensive. Ben-Gurion read it on the night of November 5, furious at its insulting tone but without any trembling at the knees. The note expressed "unqualified condemnation" of what it called "the armed aggressions of Israel," which Russia accused of "acting as an instrument of external imperialistic forces." "The Government of Israel," the note added, "is criminally and irresponsibly playing with the fate of peace and with the fate of its own people. It is sowing hatred of the State of Israel among the Eastern peoples, which cannot but leave its impression on the future of Israel and which puts a question mark against the very existence of Israel as a State. Vitally interested in the maintenance of peace and the preservation of tranquillity in the Middle East, the Soviet Government is at this moment taking steps to put an end to the war and to restrain the aggressors . . . the Soviet Government has decided to ask its Ambassador in Tel Aviv to leave Israel . . . without delay. . . ." All as though the USSR had not sent hundreds of millions of dollars worth of armaments to Egypt to be used against Israel.

Then, a personal message to Ben-Gurion from President Eisenhower. The United States had reached a stern decision: Unless Israel agreed to retreat from the Sinai peninsula, as the United Nations asked, she could not expect any American help in the event of a Soviet attack. The White House had already made it clear to Britain and France that America did not consider her NATO commitments binding in the Middle East. Eisenhower informed the Kremlin, however, that the United States would not allow any "new force" to intervene in the area without a mandate from the United Nations. Ben-Gurion drafted a reply and read it over the air in a hoarse, halting voice: "The Government is prepared to withdraw its forces from the territory of Egypt immediately after the entry of an international emergency force into the Canal Zone."

Israel's Sinai campaign was over, and Musketeer had to be called off within hours of complete success—occupation of the Canal Zone and, very probably, Nasser's downfall.

Militarily, Operation Kaddish was a smashing success. At a cost of only one hundred seventy-two killed, eight hundred seventeen wounded, three missing, and one captured—a Piper Cub pilot who crashed behind the Egyptian lines—the Israelis routed at least fifty thousand Egyptians, and in less than eight days conquered the whole of the Sinai peninsula. The Egyptians lost upwards of three thousand dead, seven thousand prisoners, twelve jets, more than one hundred tanks, nearly two hundred pieces of artillery, and huge stocks of gasoline.

Significantly, none of Egypt's Arab allies rushed to help her in Sinai, not even to the extent of making threatening gestures along Israel's exposed frontiers.

More than four and a half months passed before the United Nations Emergency Force, envisioned in the General Assembly's November 4 resolution, materialized. But on March 16, 1957, Israeli forces withdrew behind the old armistice lines, and UNEF troops took their places in the Gaza Strip and at Sharm el-Sheikh. There they would remain until a certain fateful day in May ten years later.

The withdrawal from the Wilderness, where earlier children of Israel had wandered forty years before entering the Promised Land, was carried out in great solemnity. I witnessed it and can testify to the general sense of disappointment that prevailed in the rank and file of the country's citizens' army. The certainty of having to "do it again someday" was almost unanimous. Many doubted UNEF's ability to prevent *fedayeen* raids from

Gaza or to keep open the Strait of Tiran to Israeli shipping—vital to Israel's growing export trade in potash, phosphates, and manufactured goods to Afro-Asian markets.

As the UNEF elements moved in, the security of the Jewish state's frontier with the Gaza Strip reverted largely to the border settlements. *Kibbutzim* like Nahal Oz and a score of others on the green side of the Strip resumed their round-the-clock vigils as the Israeli army began evacuating the area. The searchlights swept back and forth along the frontier, and the men who manned them knew that in a few years—whenever Egypt, Syria, or their Soviet masters decided—there would be "another round."

"We'll win the next one, of course," said a young major on the way back to Tel Aviv from the Strip, "as we won the first round back in 1948, and the second, now, in Sinai. But that's not the point. Why must there be a third round or, who knows, a fourth or fifth? Why can't we have the peace we so earnestly desire and so desperately need, we *and* the Arabs?"

The Sinai campaign accomplished three important purposes: freedom of shipping for Israeli vessels through the Strait of Tiran and the Gulf of Aqaba was restored; Gaza Strip *fedayeen* bases were destroyed; and the threat of a coordinated Egyptian-Jordanian-Syrian attack on Israel was neutralized. But Operation Kaddish did not end, as Israel had hoped it would, with winner and loser sitting face to face across the negotiating table and achieving mutual agreements. The "peace terms" were negotiated by a third party, United Nations Secretary-General Dag Hammarskjöld—or General E. L. M. Burns, Commander of UNEF. It was a complicated and altogether unsatisfactory arrangement, devised to comply with Nasser's refusal to meet the Israelis face to face as vanquished meeting victor.

In the long run, the results proved no more satisfactory than the methods employed in attaining them. Although Israel obtained freedom of the Tiran Strait, whatever specific commitment Nasser made to that effect was made to Hammarskjöld, not to Israel directly. Similarly, Nasser's agreement to yield the administration of the Gaza Strip to the UNEF was made with the Secretary-General, not as part of a negotiated settlement with Israel. So it was, also, with UNEF occupation of the positions guarding the Tiran Strait at Sharm el-Sheikh. Israel had no solid guarantees of any kind that Egypt would keep "promises" made to a third party. Subsequent events proved that Egypt and the Arab governments regarded the 1957 arrangements merely as a shield behind which to marshal new strength, with Soviet help, for the next attempt at jihad.

Following the Sinai campaign, Israel became a nation more acted upon than acting. She was at the mercy of the whims of Arab policy on the one hand and, on the other, was the indirect victim of the great-power struggle between Washington and Moscow for control of the Mediterranean—a struggle Israel could do little or nothing to influence to her own advantage.

The United Nations' efforts to make Nasser stop shooting at Israel—militarily with his *fedayeen*, economically with his boycott, and politically with his propaganda—were ineffective. The only help Israel received in its lonely struggle for survival came from the United States: In January 1957, President Eisenhower, in one of the major foreign-policy decisions of his administration, committed the United States to using its armed forces to protect Middle Eastern countries requesting help against "overt armed aggression from any nation controlled by international Communism." Congress authorized two hundred million dollars for economic and military aid in support of the Eisenhower Doctrine, and fervent avowals of anti-Communist sentiments were immediately forthcoming from Lebanon, Libya, and Jordan—all three eventually received generous arms shipments. Egypt and Syria, now virtual satellites of Moscow, greeted the Eisenhower Doctrine with vast silence.

In December 1958, the Syrians started systematically shelling Israel's northern border villages from gun emplacements in the hills above Galilee, the first attacks of the kind since the invasion of 1949. This bombardment was followed by a similar attack the next month, and simultaneously the Egyptians renewed their interference with the free passage of shipping through Suez. By the end of the year, despite the presence of the UNEF garrisons along the Egyptian side of the Gaza Strip border, *fedayeen* marauders resumed operations against Israeli settlements.

The disastrous consequences of the Sinai campaign to the Egyptian military establishment should have demonstrated to President Nasser the impossibility of eliminating Israel from the map of the Middle East, for the Jewish state had proved its considerable capacity to defend by force or arms its right to exist. Nasser persisted, however, in his homicidal intentions toward Israel. In this he was aided by two main factors: the Arabs' inability to see the world as it really is, and the Soviet Union's ambitions in the Mediterranean.

First, the psychological factor. Arabs have no monopoly on fantasy, but they carry it to the extreme of utterly confusing fancy with reality, as in pretending that Israel does not occupy a certain minimal number of square miles of Middle Eastern real estate or in assuming that one day they actually will "drive the Jews into the sea." In their unreal world they do not see war as it really is, or themselves as they really are, hence cannot admit any deficiencies as soldiers and must attribute defeat to extraneous causes. They are easily persuaded that "Jews are not fighters," and if Jewish soldiers made a junk heap of the Egyptian army in Sinai in 1956, someone else must have done it.

The loss of hundreds of millions of dollars' worth of Czech and Soviet equipment were never publicly admitted after the Sinai debacle. Nasser, a master of Middle East propaganda, managed to convey to his fanatic followers the idea that the real cause of the defeat was the Anglo-French intervention. The Egyptians ignored the fact that their army was beaten in the field. There can be little doubt that "the cream of Nasser's troops were in Sinai in 1956; the division at Abu Aweigila was the best in the army," [2] and fought well, but when the chips were down, the Egyptians proved to be inferior to the Israelis. To this day, however, few Egyptians know this. They sit enthralled, eyes shining, before performances of a traveling propaganda-ministry road show purporting to demonstrate how Egyptian arms prevailed over their enemies in 1956. Not over the Israelis—who are ignored in the elaborate pantomime—but over the mighty British and French.

As indicated earlier, the Arabs are encouraged to a false view of themselves and the world around them by an Islamic theology which inhibits political development. In the hands of ambitious leaders, Islam becomes a convenient means for generating unity —where none exists—in pursuit of impossible propositions, such as the dream of pan-Arabism or the annihilation of a neighbor state merely because it happens to be Jewish.

The eminent Swiss historian, Jacob Burckhardt,[3] describes Islam as a force exerting "a stranglehold on national feelings," which, with its "miserable constitutional and legal systems grafted onto religion" has been unable to achieve the modern condition known as the "State." Only in non-Arab countries has Mohammedanism changed with the times, Turkey being an outstanding example. Kemal Ataturk brought his country into the twentieth century after World War I by separating church and state, replacing Islamic law with European legal codes in secular matters, encouraging his people to enter commerce and industry instead of the priesthood, and, among other things, changing from Arabic to Latin writing. The Islamic Arab states have had no leaders of Kemal's kidney. So far they have known only Farouks—and Nassers.

[2] A. J. Barker, *Suez: The Seven Day War*, London: Faber and Faber, Ltd., 1964.
[3] *Force and Freedom*, New York: Pantheon, 1964.

Had he not burdened his country's already enfeebled economy with enormous armaments expenditures to fulfill his self-assumed role of Fuehrer of Pan-Arabia, and avenger of the Arab defeat of 1948, Nasser might have been able to finance the much-needed reforms which he proposed on assuming Egypt's leadership, possibly even achieving renown as an Arab Kemal. However, history probably will remember him for brave beginnings rather than solid accomplishments in resolving Egypt's corruption, peasant landlessness, illiteracy, sickness, and unemployment.

It was plain from 1955 onward that Egypt's economy—almost wholly based on cotton exports, tourism, and Suez Canal tolls—could not afford a huge military establishment as well as the Aswan High Dam, the land reform and industrialization programs, and the schools, hospitals, and housing Nasser proposed. The United States refused him loans and credits for his grandiose schemes without guarantees that Egypt would pursue peaceful policies in the Middle East, and Nasser turned to Moscow and the Soviet bloc.

The Kremlin attached no conditions to its economic and military assistance, at least none that prevented Nasser from pursuing a foreign policy predicated on annihilation of Israel. Within two years, he was irrevocably committed to move with the Soviet Union in its political, economic, and military march into the Mediterranean, and the Kremlin became the aider and abettor of Arab designs against Israel.

This marked a 180-degree turn in Soviet policy toward Israel, who had no stauncher supporter than Russia at the United Nations back in 1947–1948. Time and again, Russian representatives rose before the General Assembly or the Security Council during the debates on partition to defend Jewish aspirations to nationhood and to denounce the Arabs as aggressors for invading Israel after she had proclaimed her independence.

Memorable was the May 14, 1947, speech by Andrei Gromyko, then Soviet Ambassador to the United Nations, in which he said, "The fact that no Western European state has been able to ensure the defense of the elementary rights of the Jewish people, and to safeguard it against the violence of Fascist executioners, explains the aspirations of the Jews to establish their own state. It would be unjust not to take this into consideration and to deny the right of the Jewish people to realize this aspiration."

Equally memorable was the May 30, 1948, speech by another Russian delegate, Ambassador Tarassenco, denouncing the Arabs' concerted attack on newborn Israel: "I should like to point out that none of the [Arab] states whose troops have entered Palestine can claim that Palestine forms part of its territory. It is an altogether separate territory without any relationship to the territories of the states which have sent their troops into Palestine." A few days later, Tarassenco was denouncing "the unlawful invasion by a number of states of the territory of Palestine," and declaring that "Jewish immigration cannot constitute a threat to the security of the Arab states; it is insignificant in comparison with the population of the Arab countries."

A decade later, the same Soviet Union would attempt to have Israel branded by the General Assembly as the aggressor in the June 1967 six-day war. It would fail, for the world knew by then the extent of the Soviet Union's responsibility for the tensions and bloodshed that continued to characterize Israeli-Arab relations after the Sinai campaign of 1956.

Emboldened by Soviet economic, political, and military support, Nasser began mounting another jihad, making certain, however, that this time he would be joined by all the Arab states. By the summer of 1959, less than three years after the Sinai debacle, the propaganda preparation for the "third round" was in full cry. Mere one-line excerpts from the hate-Israel editorials, statements, and declarations of Arab leaders during the years leading up to the events of June 1967 would fill several fat volumes. But a few samples will suffice.

"We want a decisive battle to annihilate Israel," said Nasser in a speech in Alexandria on July 29, 1959." All the Arabs want a decisive battle." Later, to make certain he was being understood, he declared, "In secret documents we say the same things as in our speeches and discussions. Our movement is along a broad battlefront, starting with words and ending with the firing of guns." Subsequently, he was even more explicit: "We will launch a full-scale war when the right moment comes." Then, over Radio Cairo on February 22, 1964, he said, "The prospects are for war with Israel. But this time it is we who will dictate the time; we who will dictate the place."

The theme recurred over and over again in the Egyptian press, and in the broadcasts of Cairo's "Voice of the Arabs" radio station. Hardly a day passed without similar threats from other Arab leaders. On November 2, 1964, President Abdul Salem Aref of Iraq declared, "We must put an end to Israel's existence, and with the help of Allah, and the support of all nations that believe in justice, we shall." At about the same time, Syrian Chief of Staff Salah Jedid was saying over Radio Damascus, "Our army will accept nothing short of the disappearance of Israel."

Syria, always on the lookout for opportunities to wrest the initiative in anti-Israeli belligerence from other Arab countries, especially Egypt, now intensified its own attacks against Israel. The most unstable of the Arab states, Syria has experienced more changes in government than any of its Middle East neighbors. At times the changes have reflected alterations in domestic policies or ideologies, at others they have indicated a shift in inter-Arab orientations or in Syria's posture toward West or East. But animosity toward Israel has remained a constant of Syrian policy, most markedly since the rise to power of the pro-Communist, Moscow-oriented Socialist Nationalist Ba'ath party in March 1963.

One of the concepts introduced by the Ba'athists was that of "popular" or "people's war" against Israel. This involved the mobilization of volunteer commandos and their organization into paramilitary units whose task was to infiltrate Israel and plant explosives where they would kill or maim Israelis and damage crops and installations. The raiders, Syrian counterparts of the Egyptian *fedayeen,* were known as *El-Fatah* (The Conquest). Radio Damascus, far from concealing the Syrian government's responsibility in *El-Fatah* activities, boasted of the marauders' achievements and urged extension of the "popular war against Israel." Between January 1965 and May 1967, *El-Fatah* guerrillas carried out one hundred and thirteen acts of sabotage in Israel, killing eleven Israelis and wounding sixty-two.[4]

In most cases, the *El-Fatah* raiders did not strike directly across Israel's border with Syria but were sent by way of Jordan to avoid retaliatory action by Israel against Syria. Sometimes they struck from Lebanon, but wherever they originated the source of their inspiration was always the same—the Syrian end of the Cairo-Damascus axis. President Atassi himself admitted this in a broadcast April 17, 1967, in which he said, "Our method for thwarting Zionism is the method of the popular war of liberation. Our training centers are open to all Arab citizens."

Meanwhile, thousands of Palestinian refugees were being trained by the ubiquitous Ahmed Shukairy, now head of the so-called Palestine Liberation Organization, to fight in regular mili-

[4] Secretary-General of the United Nations U Thant took note of the *El-Fatah* activities, and the menace to peace they represented, at a press conference sponsored by the Correspondents' Association on May 11, 1967. He declared, "In the last few days, the *El-Fatah* type of incidents has increased, unfortunately. Those incidents have occurred in the vicinity of the Lebanese and Syrian lines and are very deplorable especially because, by their nature, they seem to indicate that the individuals who committed them have had more specialized training than has usually been evidenced in *El-Fatah* incidents in the past. That type of activity is insidious, is contrary to the letter and spirit of the Armistice Agreements, and menaces the peace of the area. All governments concerned have an obligation under the General Armistice Agreements, as well as under the Charter of the United Nations and in the interest of peace, to take every measure within their means to put an end to such activities."

tary formations to be attached to the invading Arab armies when the "third round" began against Israel. Shukairy's pronouncements over PLO radio facilities in Cairo and elsewhere provided the Israelis with confirmation of what they had known all along —that a massive, concerted Egyptian-Jordanian-Syrian assault was in the making.

On June 1, four days before the outbreak of hostilities, Shukairy made a speech in Amman that damaged the Arab cause almost as much as a lost battle. He forecast the imminence of another jihad, and declared, "We will allow them [the conquered Israelis] to return to their countries of origin. As for those born in Palestine, they can remain—whatever is left of them. But I doubt that even a single one will survive." [5] The next day, while inciting thousands crowding the Mosque of Omar in the Old City of Jerusalem, he cried, "God will be exalted when we embark upon the holy war for the liberation of Palestine and the cleansing of our holy land from the atheists and infidels." [6]

The extent of Soviet military and political support of the aggressive intentions of the Arab states, particularly Egypt and Syria, was every whit as "sad and shocking" a story as Abba Eban said it was on June 19, 1967. Between 1955 and the spring of 1967, Russia supplied the Arab countries with two thousand modern tanks, of which about thirteen hundred went to Egypt. In addition, the Arab states received from the U.S.S.R. seven hundred modern fighter aircraft and bombers, again most of them going to Egypt. That country alone also received five hundred forty field guns, a hundred thirty medium guns, two hundred 120mm. mortars, large quantities of antiaircraft guns, a hundred seventy-five rocket launchers, six hundred fifty antitank weapons, and a number of Luna M and SPKA-2 ground-to-ground missiles. Egypt's naval forces were augmented by Russia to the tune of seven destroyers and forty-six torpedo boats of

[5] Augusto Guerriero, in *Corriere della Sera*, of Milan, August 31, 1967.
[6] Associated Press dispatch, June 2, 1967.

various types, including vessels equipped to carry and launch missiles. Topping the pile of deadly hardware were several highly sophisticated ground-to-air missile systems. In fact, many of the weapons supplied to Egypt were far in advance of those which Russia had been furnishing its allies in Eastern Europe.

To acquire that arsenal, Egypt went into debt to the extent of an estimated two billion dollars. Half that amount spent on developmental programs would have rescued the country from its deepening economic and social difficulties.

The Soviet Union backed up its military support of the Arab states with massive political assistance at the United Nations. Five times it exercised its veto rights in the Security Council to frustrate Western efforts to improve Arab-Israeli relations.

On January 22, 1954, Russia nullified a Franco-British-American resolution to facilitate construction of the Bnot Yaakov Canal Project on the west bank of the Jordan, and thus held up regional water development for several years. Two months later, the U.S.S.R. killed a New Zealand resolution reiterating United Nations opposition to Egypt's denial of freedom of passage through the Suez Canal for Israeli ships. On August 19, 1963, Moscow vetoed a British-American resolution denouncing the murder by Arab marauders of two Israelis at Almagor. On December 21, 1964, the U.S.S.R. vetoed an Anglo-American resolution deploring the shelling by the Syrians of Israeli settlements at Tel Dan, Dan, Dafne, and Shaar Yashuv. Then, on November 2, 1966, Argentina, Japan, the Netherlands, New Zealand, and Nigeria jointly expressed regret at "infiltration from Syria and loss of human life caused by the incidents in October and November 1966." Although the resolution was sponsored by five member-states, representing as many continents, the Russians again exercised their veto.

The Russian *nyets* had a dual effect: they prevented the adoption of any resolution to which an Arab state was opposed and inhibited the Security Council from taking any constructive action in disputes between Arab states and Israel—because of the certain knowledge that any measure unfavorable to the Arab countries would automatically evoke a Soviet veto. Israel was thus denied equitable treatment within the Security Council, while the Council's authority, and its function as a constructive force in Middle East affairs, was proportionately eroded.

Now began a significant parallelism between the propaganda output of Arab press and radio and the corresponding Soviet media. Arab speeches, statements, and editorials iterated and reiterated the objective of their governments as "total destruction of Israel." Soviet propaganda sidestepped this well-worn Arab theme and sought to justify support of the Arab cause by accusing Israel of serving the interests of "imperialism," "neocolonialism," and "reaction."

In the Soviet press Egypt and Syria soon could do no wrong, and Israel—or more precisely "reactionary circles" in Israel— "supported" by the West, could do nothing but evil. Characteristically, the wildest rumors from Cairo and/or Damascus were prominently displayed in *Pravda* and *Izvestia*, while official Israeli communiqués or impartial reports about Israel from other sources were ignored or distorted. For instance, Syrian artillery never shelled Israeli settlements, Israeli civilians were only "allegedly" murdered by *El-Fatah* gangs, Arab terrorists who mined Israeli roads were "mythical," and saboteurs who blew up the "kibbutzniks'" water pumps were only "so-called" saboteurs. The Soviet propaganda apparatus had no difficulty in justifying the huge arms supplies to Egypt and Syria as indispensable to the prevention of Israel's "imperialist-backed aggression."

Again, an entire volume would be required to document fully the Moscow-Cairo and Moscow-Damascus propaganda parallelisms, but an example or two might serve.

Al-Ba'ath, the Syrian daily, wrote on March 13, 1966:

The revolutionary forces in the Arab homeland and the Ba'ath at their head preach a genuine Arab Palestine Libera-

tion, on the soil of Palestine, and they have had enough of the traditional methods. . . . It has become evident that our problem will only be solved by an armed struggle to repel the rapacious enemy and put an end to the Zionist presence. The Arab people demand armed struggle, and day-by-day incessant confrontation, through a total war of liberation in which all the Arabs will take part. . . .

K. Ivanov said, in *Izvestia*, May 2, 1966:

The Western press now . . . clamors about the movement of ships of the American Sixth Fleet in the eastern Mediterranean and about the confidential talks between the American diplomats and military officials and the Israeli General Staff. No secret is made of the fact that this is connected with the policies of Syria and of other independent Arab countries that do not wish to be servants of neocolonialism. However, this is just an additional exposure of neocolonialism and its agents in Tel Aviv. They shouldn't forget the lessons of Suez and the fiasco of their adventure in that region. . . .

Izvestia produced another masterpiece on May 19, 1966, to justify Russian-Egyptian collaboration. The newspaper printed a joint U.S.S.R.–Egypt communiqué, which stated: "The Soviet side fully supports the lawful and inalienable rights of the Palestine Arabs. It supports the struggle and the efforts undertaken by the Arab states against the aggressive intrigues of the imperialist forces striving to exploit the Palestine problem for an intensification of tension in the Near East. . . ." A clearer example of the technique of the Big Lie had not appeared in print since Goebbels' time.

The Big Lie strategy soon gave way to the tactic of open provocation. The Arabs clearly stated their homicidal intentions, and in Moscow the Soviet press egged the Arabs on. Said Cairo Radio on May 15, 1967: "The Arab people are determined to wipe Israel off the map and to return Arab honor to Palestine."

In *Izvestia,* next day, came this counterpoint: "In one word, the atmosphere is becoming more and more charged. It is difficult to call Israel's actions anything but provoking. This is the evaluation that is given them by the Arab press and by newspapers of many countries throughout the world."

The Soviet Union did not content itself with supplying the weapons and creating the climate for war, but actually lighted the fuse that exploded the lethal mixture. This was disclosed by Nasser himself in the course of his spurious resignation of June 9, 1967, when he had reaped the whirlwind. He said:

> "We all know how the crisis began in the first half of last May. There was an enemy plan to invade Syria, and the statements by his [Israel's] politicians and all his military commanders declared that frankly. The evidence was ample. The sources of our Syrian brothers and our own reliable information were categorical on this. Even our friends in the Soviet Union told the [Egyptian] parliamentary delegation which was visiting Moscow early last month that there was a calculated intention. It was our duty not to accept this in silence."

The fiction of a planned Israeli attack on Syria was readily believed by a Nasser preparing for war. On May 15 he began moving troops into Sinai, and on May 18 he demanded withdrawal of the UNEF "shield" from Gaza and Sharm el-Sheikh. The UNEF troops were gone by May 22, whereupon he closed the Strait of Tiran by reoccupying Sharm el-Sheikh, and poured seven divisions and nine hundred tanks into Sinai. On May 30 Nasser completed military encirclement of Israel by signing a new military alliance with Jordan, and on June 4 Cairo Radio announced that Egypt was "burning with a desire for the battle to start." Shortly before 0800 hours on the morning of June 5, the Israeli radar screen picked up Egyptian warplanes headed for Israeli targets. What followed is history too recent to warrant detailing here.

It is highly relevant, however, that since the Israeli defeat of the Arab armies' third attempt at jihad, Soviet replenishment of the approximately one-and-a-half-billion-dollars' worth of Egyptian military hardware destroyed in Sinai has begun. Israeli intelligence estimates three months after the fighting ended were that approximately 80 per cent of Egypt's fighter planes had been replaced.

11

IN SEARCH OF PEACE

The aim of war is to be able to live unhurt in peace.
—Cicero, *De Officiis*, I, 78 B.C.

PEACE HAS BEEN THE PARAMOUNT DESIRE OF ISRAEL EVER SINCE its return to the land of its origin. So keen was the Israelis' desire for peace with their Arab neighbors that they made it a fundamental precept of their Declaration of Independence: "We extend the hand of peace and good-neighborliness to all the states around us, and to their peoples, and we call upon them to cooperate in mutual helpfulness with the independent Jewish nation. The State of Israel is prepared to make its contribution in a concerted effort for the advancement of the entire Middle East."

Thereafter, the record abounds with expressions of the Israelis' readiness to submit their differences with the Arabs to negotiation, and with affirmations of their hopes for the establishment of normal relationships which would promote the social, economic, and political development of their common area. That record is remarkable for the frequency of Israeli overtures, and

the totality of Arab rejection. Besides reiterated offers to negotiate peaceful settlements of outstanding issues, Israel made
many specific proposals favorable to Arab interests. It offered
Jordan use of the port of Haifa; compensation to refugees for the
lands they abandoned in 1947–1948; release of blocked refugee
bank accounts; [1] overland communications between Egypt and
landlocked Jordan. A comprehensive Arab-Israeli peace settlement was outlined to the General Assembly by Abba Eban in
1954. The Arab response was always the same: rejection, belligerency, threats, arms build-ups, and their inevitable consequence—war.

I visited Israel soon after its third decisive victory over its self-
proclaimed enemies. I found the Israelis' desire for peace
stronger than ever, as was their willingness to be helpful in solving their neighbors' many social and economic problems. But
equally firm, in fact to the point of immobility, was their determination to deal with their neighbors directly in any eventual
peacemaking process, and not through intermediaries, no matter
how prestigious or well-intentioned.

On this point, as on all others related to foreign policy, there
was complete unanimity among the country's leaders and its
people, and among the people themselves. There were sharp differences among Israelis concerning the propriety of separating
men from women worshipers at their regained Wailing Wall in
Jerusalem, divergences over internal politics, and—as always—
resentments between Oriental Sephardim and European Ash-
kenazim, but there was a ringing national consensus about dealing face to face with the Arabs in pursuit of a final, definitive,
realistic peace.

The Israelis want the security of their frontiers and their freedom of navigation guaranteed not by third-party middlemen but
by the Arab states with whom they have been in mortal conflict
and whom they have soundly beaten on the battlefield. While
there was none of the strut and swagger of the victors about

[1] Actually effected April 10, 1952.

them, they plainly coveted the victors' right to make peace with the vanquished and, uniquely, a peace not imposed but on terms to be mutually agreed upon across the conference table. Their adamancy is born of sad experience with the impermanence of cease-fires, armistices, and conciliations arranged by organs of the United Nations, or by the secretary-general himself. Such arrangements invariably have served the Arabs' interests by enabling them to prepare for armed warfare against Israel while waging warfare by other means. Besides, the conflict in the Middle East is not between Israel and the United Nations but between Israel and the Arab states, hence logically can be resolved only in frank confrontations between the parties intimately concerned. Anything short of a peace negotiated by Israel with her Arab enemies will merely recreate and perpetuate the intolerable state of affairs prevalent prior to 1948, 1956, and 1967.

As this was written—in a room in Jerusalem's King David Hotel overlooking the moon-lacquered, crenelated walls of an Old City no longer alien to the New—the one certainty of Israeli public opinion, however healthy divided on domestic issues, was its single-mindedness about rejecting any stopgap solutions to Arab-Israeli differences. Such solutions would only enable the Arabs to avoid the necessity of coming face to face with the geographic and strategic realities of the Middle East. As long as the Arabs believe that they can avoid peace negotiations, they will continue to pursue those policies which have given the Middle East three wars in twenty years and are certain to breed another war, and another, and another, each with all-too-obvious potentialities for escalation into atomic holocaust.

It was my impression, however, that the Israelis did not delude themselves that the Arabs would quickly abandon their cherished posture of belligerency and face the new realities created by the six-day war. Those realities are geographic, military, and strategic. Israel is nearly four times bigger than when the war started, is easily the strongest power in the Middle East, and is no longer vulnerable to surprise air-land attack from any direction. But the Israelis are all too familiar with Arab reluctance, or inability, to see things as they are. They have no illusions, therefore, that the suggestion of one of the Arabs' own leaders, Tunisian President Habib Bourguiba—to recognize Israel's existence and stop talking about wiping it off the map— would be heeded by his colleagues in Cairo, Amman, and Damascus. But the Israelis are accustomed to living with cease-fires and are prepared to live with this one for as long as necessary to bring their Arab antagonists to the peace table.

If the Arabs are as concerned about the loss of territories as their demand for Israel's unconditional withdrawal to the old armistice lines indicated, then it would behoove them to move quickly from belligerency to peace. It was plain some months after the cease-fire went into effect on June 11, 1967—that the longer the Arabs delayed a decision to recognize Israel and enter into peace negotiations, the less negotiable the territory held by the victors was likely to be. Some areas already seemed beyond negotiation.

Although as this book went to press Israel had not formally annexed any of the territories which its army had conquered, administrative fusion of the Old City of Jerusalem was an accomplished fact. Its power grid and water mains had been connected to those of New Jerusalem, and the economies and social services of the ancient and modern halves of the city of David and Solomon had been merged. It is difficult to imagine any Israeli government long surviving a decision to give up Jerusalem, object of millennial Jewish longings, or making any concessions beyond those designed to respect the religious rights of others.

Nor is it conceivable that the Israelis would relinquish the Golan Heights above Galilee. To do so would be madness from a military point of view. One needs only to stand, as I did, on the rubble of the miniature triple Maginot line which the

Syrians built across the forty-mile stretch between the Lebanese and Jordanian frontiers and look down into the neat parallelograms of tilled Israeli fields to know this. From bunkers, emplacements, and dug-in tank positions, the Syrians overlooked the Jordan Valley and could fire at will into a score of northern settlements—Kfar Szold, Gonen, Notera, Ashmura, Gadot, Tel Qazir. Sparsely inhabited by Druses who hate the Syrians and are friendly to Israel, the region is not likely to return to Syria.

In the minds of many Israelis, the Gaza Strip, long-time *fedayeen* base and thorn in the Israeli flesh, has become another "unnegotiable item." Twenty-five miles long by five miles wide, it was never territorially a part of Egypt proper. Strategic considerations render inadvisable its reversion to Egyptian control, and, like Jerusalem and its environs, may be considered as part of the new map of Israel. The Egyptians took the Gaza Strip by conquest during their armed effort to frustrate partition in 1947; ironically, it was territory destined to be part of the Arab state as conceived by the UN partition resolution.

That is also true of all or most of the west bank of the Jordan. The Jordanians took all of it not from Israel but from what Arab Palestine would have been in accordance with the United Nations partition plan. They have no rightful claim to the fertile, heavily populated area that includes Bethlehem and Nablus south of Jerusalem, and Ramallah, Nablus, and Jenin north of the capital. Since the Jordan River and the Dead Sea are Israel's "natural frontier" with Jordan, King Hussein's chances of regaining any lost portion of his kingdom were not very bright, unless he chose peace over belligerency.

Finally, Sinai. The Israelis held the east bank of the Suez Canal and the western shore of the peninsula from opposite the city of Suez to Sharm el-Sheikh and the entrance to the Gulf of Aqaba. Whether Egypt would regain any substantial portion of Sinai—the Israelis can hardly be expected to relinquish Sharm el-Sheikh, or allow remilitarization of any part of the peninsula —depended on whether Nasser would be willing to recognize

Israel's existence and negotiate with his Israeli conquerors. My impression from talks with political, diplomatic, and military leaders was that the longer Nasser delayed negotiations the tougher Israel's peace terms would become. The Israelis were to be bargaining from strength, and they seemed very aware of this three months after victory. The Sinai peninsula has never been part of Egypt in law. It was part of the Vilayet of Syria and was ceded by the Ottoman Empire to the Allied powers in 1918. Egypt may have great difficulty in establishing its claim to the whole of this territory.

A solution to Arab-Israeli tensions is at once extremely simple and devilishly complex—simple because all that is needed to break the deadlock is a statement by the Arab states that they recognize Israel's right to exist and want peace, and complex because the Arabs will not move toward peace while they are encouraged to believe that some magic formula can be devised by the United Nations, the great powers, or an Arab ally like Yugoslavia's Marshal Tito to enable them to return to the situation which existed prior to June 5, 1967. None of the problems arising from the Israeli-Arab conflict—refugees, development of the area's water resources, navigation rights, inter-Arab overland communications, territorial issues, and a multitude of others— can be solved without peace. And with peace, as Abba Eban has said, "there are no problems."

In a peaceful context, for instance, the refugee problem becomes a mere exercise in resettlement. The moment peace "happens," the refugees cease to be refugees and become people, potential producers and consumers for whom the respective governments involved assume responsibility. With the aid of international agencies, land, homes, and work are found for them, and people who are now a charge on the economies of other nations become an asset to the economies of the countries in which they reside.

So it could be with the water problem. There is a definite

water shortage in the Israel-Jordan area, though it is far more acute in Jordan than in Israel. But if the deficit is studied and resolved on an area basis, as could be done given peaceful relations among the several countries concerned, another problem automatically vanishes. There is more than ample unused water in Syria and Lebanon to supply the needs for agricultural and industrial development of the entire region. Lebanon's Litani River, for instance, flows unimpeded into the sea, providing neither irrigation nor power. Tied into a TVA-on-the-Jordan, such as the late Eric Johnston envisioned back in 1946, the Litani's resources, together with those of Syria's Euphrates and other rivers, could immensely benefit the whole of the Middle East. To date, the Syrians have spent far more money, time, and energy trying to divert the Baniyas headwaters of the Jordan, so that the river's flow through Israel would be reduced, than on utilizing them themselves. Those headwaters, incidentally, are now safely in Israeli hands.

All problems arising from Israeli-Arab tensions remain problems only as long as the Arabs continue to insist that they are at war with Israel. The moment there is peace, the Suez Canal is reopened to Israeli shipping, and still another problem disappears. In peaceful conditions, it is not difficult to imagine railway and highway communications running northward from Haifa to Beirut, Damascus, and Istanbul; eastward to Amman and beyond; and southward to Cairo. Communication could be resumed across the Negev between the Nile Valley and the Fertile Crescent, and what is now a geographic wedge between Arab lands—the land mass of Israel—could become a bridge. Jordan, now cut off from the Mediterranean, could freely import and export its products from the Israeli coast—in exchange for peace, Hussein could have free port facilities at Haifa.

With peace, the Middle East, geographic crossroads of three continents, could become a great air-communications center, at present impossible because the Arab boycott necessitates circuitous routes. Radio, telephone, and postal communications which now end abruptly in mid-air could be restored to help reunite a region too long divided. One immediate result would be the development—to everyone's advantage—of the area's immense touristic possibilities.

There are almost no limits to what peace could mean to the Middle East in social and economic terms. Cooperation in agricultural and industrial development could lead to common-market arrangements similar to those enjoyed by the Europeans. Specialized agencies of the United Nations would be facilitated in supporting health and educational development with greater efficiency than is now possible. To help fill the area's great need for water, joint ventures in the desalination of sea water could materialize.

In a harmonious context, Israel would only too gladly place at its neighbors' disposal the technical facilities and knowledge which in recent years have helped more than fifty underdeveloped nations in the Americas, Africa, and Asia. Perhaps best of all, young Israeli and Arab students could attend each other's schools and universities in a cultural interchange which, within a generation or less, would replace old prejudices with new understanding and mutual respect. Finally, military budgets could be reduced in favor of developmental budgets, and the Middle East would enter a new era of unprecedented prosperity and well-being.

None of the issues dividing Arabs and Israelis is insoluble if both sides approach them in a spirit of good will. No progress can be made, however, if only one side is ready to negotiate. So far, the Arab states have uncompromisingly declined to do so, an attitude that was confirmed at the summit meeting of Arab leaders at Khartoum at the end of August 1967.

Arab nationalism, or more properly Nasserism with its overriding theme of pan-Arabism, remained the principal obstacle to peace between the Arab states and Israel. The kind of Arab oneness which Nasser seeks has little to support it in Arab history. Indeed, Arab unity has been the exception rather than the rule, and nothing has divided the Arab world more than the Egyptian dictator's efforts to unite it.

Egypt has as unifying elements with the Arab world a common religion and language, but these are not sufficiently strong to persuade Jordan, Lebanon, Tunisia, Iraq, and Yemen to accept centralized domination by Cairo. Each has struggled continuously, and at times violently, to preserve its individual sovereignty. Within the inter-Arab conflict, moreover, is the historic rivalry between Egypt and Syria and the clash of interests between the oil-producing have countries and the have-nots.

As directed by Nasser, the Arab union movement emphasizes political structures, such as the Arab League and the Palestine Liberation Organization, and ignores common economic and social development. This is much like building a house in mid-air. Historically, Nasser's efforts are no more justifiable than would be an attempt by Argentina, for instance, to assert its hegemony over the whole of South America merely because, like Argentina, South America is Catholic and, with the exception of Brazil, Spanish-speaking.

Contrary to Nasser's view of the Arab world, the Middle East is not an exclusively Arab domain. There are nearly as many non-Arabs in the Middle East, and Nasser's dream of a united Arab empire reaching from the Atlantic to the Persian Gulf offends what has been called "the region's essential diversity," generating conflicts, resentments, and extremisms and complicating Arab-Israeli relations. Taking language as a criterion, there are some eighty million Arabs in the "world" Nasser would unite, but there are also about seventy-five million non-Arabs. A non-Arab Middle East extends from Turkey and Iran through Israel to Ethiopia. If the area is enlarged to include Pakistan and Afghanistan, the predominantly non-Arab character of the region becomes even more apparent.

The pan-Arabism which Nasser proposes offends international peace and distorts history, geography, and law. Ethnically and linguistically exclusive, it is inspired more by reaction to "ene-mies" (Israeli "colonialist-imperialists," etc.) than by positive impulses of self-realization. In pursuit of pan-Arabism, Nasser has purposefully promoted the idea that the Jewish state should be exterminated. In acquiring the enormous arsenal of modern weapons required for the task, he also acquired the prestige essential to fulfillment of his ambitions.

Unfortunately for all concerned—Israel, the Arab states, and the Western world—the Soviet Union chose to support Nasser in his pan-Arabist efforts with massive economic and military assistance. The extent to which Russia will continue to aid and abet Nasser in his self-chosen role of re-creator of an Arab Empire remained, at this writing, one of the imponderables of the Arab-Israeli peacemaking process. Clearly, continued Soviet assistance can only encourage Nasser and the Arabs in the belief that an-other jihad is possible, hence will hold back the dawn of a new epoch of peace, prosperity, and progress in the Middle East.

Far more constructive was President Johnson's approach to the Middle East crisis. His five principles for peace in the area, enunciated in a major policy address delivered on August 19, 1967, provide the only sound basis for a long-range solution of the Middle East's multitudinous ailments yet made. The Presi-dent said, in part,

> The Middle East is rich in history, rich in its people and its resources. It has no need to live in civil war. It has the power to build its own life, as one of the prosperous regions of the world in which we live. And if the nations of the Middle East will turn toward the works of peace, they can count with confidence upon the friendship and help of all of the people of the United States of America.
>
> In a climate of peace, we here will do our full share to help with a solution for the refugees. We here will do our full share in support of regional cooperation. We here will do our full share and more to see that the peaceful promise of nuclear energy is applied to the critical problems of

desalting water to make the deserts bloom. Our country is committed—and we here reiterate that commitment today —to a peace that is based on five principles:

First, the recognized right of national life. Second, justice for the refugees. Third, innocent maritime passage. Fourth, limits on the wasteful and destructive arms race. And fifth, political independence, and territorial integrity for all.

This is not a time for malice but for magnanimity; not for propaganda but for patience; not for vituperation but for vision. On the basis of peace, we offer our help to the people of the Middle East. That land that's known to us since childhood as the birthplace of the great religions and learning can flourish once again in our time. And we here in the United States shall do all in our power to help make it so.[2]

President Johnson's speech was greeted with satisfaction in Jerusalem, for it held the promise of a genuine effort to persuade Israel's Arab antagonists to move toward the peace table rather than toward another attempt at jihad. It remained to be seen, however, whether President Johnson's five principles would bear fruit.

As I write these final paragraphs, the Egyptians have violated the cease-fire along the Suez Canal, and the Jordanians have been firing on Israeli positions along the Jordan. Peace is still elusive, and distant, but Israel was never more sure of itself, never more secure. For the first time since the state's creation, no Israeli village is within direct range of Arab guns, and Israel's straightened frontiers, previously winding and vulnerable, are only half as long as before but more than twice as safe. Egyptian planes are no longer based in Sinai within seven minutes' striking distance of Tel Aviv; instead, Israel's warplanes are

[2] Before the National Foreign Policy Conference for Educators, *The New York Times*, August 20, 1967.

poised close to Egypt's heart—the Nile Delta. Should the Arabs succeed in mounting another jihad, the fighting would start right where they live, for the Israelis now have what military experts call strategic depth.

Although the Israelis still hope to distill from their victory a peace negotiated directly with their Arab neighbors, they are fully prepared to accept the possible, even probable, alternative: the present *status quo*. But even if the Arabs should ultimately recognize that the earth is really round, that it contains nations peopled by non-Arabs as well as Arabs, and that overwhelming numbers of troops and weapons do not necessarily add up to victorious holy war, and in so recognizing decide to make peace, they will have to be prepared to accept Israel on terms of equality without compromise.

The Israelis are well aware that a bad peace would be even worse than war, hence are not likely to give way to pressures from the great powers, as they did after the Sinai campaign in 1956, to agree to withdraw from conquered territory in return for unreliable guarantees of any kind. The Israelis never made war except for peace, but if they could not have peace they were willing to settle for a peace that was no peace, confident in their ability to solve the innumerable problems victory had brought, confident also in their capacity for containing any future Arab aggression.

"In Israel's national memory," said Abba Eban, "David's victory over Goliath was a result not of his smallness but of his compensating agility and talent for improvisation." The qualities that have enabled Israel to survive nineteen years of Arab hostility seem certain to continue operative for another nineteen years and beyond.

BIBLIOGRAPHY

APPENDICES

INDEX

BIBLIOGRAPHY

Aldington, Richard. *Lawrence of Arabia, A Biographical Enquiry.*
New York: Regnery, 1955.

Arberry, A. J., and Landau, Rom (Eds.). *Islam Today.* London: Faber
and Faber, Ltd., 1943.

Bein, Alexander. *Theodor Herzl: A Biography.* Philadelphia: Jewish
Publication Society of America, 1941.

Ben-Gurion, David. *Rebirth and Destiny of Israel.* Ed. and trans.
from the Hebrew under superv. of Mordekhai Nurock. New
York: Philosophical Library, 1954.

*Bigotry and Blackmail: A Report on the Arab Boycott Against
Americans.* New York: The Presidents of Major American
Jewish Organizations, 1958.

Bilby, Kenneth W. *New Star in the Near East.* New York: Doubleday, 1950.

Bonné, Alfred. *State and Economics in the Middle East, A Society in Transition*, Rev. ed. London: Routledge & Kegan Paul, Ltd., 1955.

Burckhardt, Jacob. *Force and Freedom, Reflections on History.* New York: Pantheon, 1964.

Cahn, Zvi. *The Philosophy of Judaism.* New York: Macmillan, 1962.

Comay, Joan. *Ben-Gurion and the Birth of Israel.* New York: Random House, 1967.

Crum, Bartley C. *Behind the Silken Curtain, A Personal Account of Anglo-American Diplomacy in Palestine and the Middle East.* New York: Simon and Schuster, 1947.

Dayan, Moshe. *Diary of the Sinai Campaign.* New York: Harper and Row, 1965.

Dimont, Max I. *Jews, God and History.* New York: New American Library, 1964.

Eban, Abba Solomon. *Voice of Israel.* New York: Horizon Press, 1957.

Elath, Eliahu. *Israel and Her Neighbors: Lectures Delivered at Brandeis University.* Cleveland: World Publishing Co., 1957.

Esco Foundation for Palestine, Inc. *Palestine: A Study of Jewish, Arab and British Policies.* New Haven: Yale University Press, 1942, 2 v.

Eytan, Walter. *The First Ten Years: A Diplomatic History of Israel.* New York: Simon and Schuster, 1958.

Freud, Sigmund. *Moses and Monotheism.* New York: Knopf, 1939.

García-Granados, Jorge. *The Birth of Israel: The Drama As I Saw It.* New York: Knopf, 1948.

Government of Palestine. *Survey of Palestine 1946.* Jerusalem: Government Printer, 1947.

Henriques, R. *One Hundred Hours to Suez.* New York: Viking, 1957.

Horowitz, David. *State in the Making* (Trans. Julian Meltzer). New York: Knopf, 1953.

Institute of Jewish Affairs. *Jews in Moslem Lands.* New York: World Jewish Congress, 1959.

International Bank for Reconstruction and Development. *The Eco-*

nomic Development of Syria. Baltimore: Johns Hopkins Press, 1956.

Laqueur, Walter Z. *Communism and Nationalism in the Middle East.* New York: Praeger, 1957.

Lenczowski, George. *The Middle East in World Affairs,* 2nd ed. Ithaca, N.Y.: Cornell University Press, 1956.

Lengyel, Emil. *The Changing Middle East.* New York: John Day, 1960.

Litvinoff, Barnet. *Ben-Gurion of Israel.* New York: Praeger, 1954.

Lowdermilk, Walter Clay. *Palestine, Land of Promise.* New York: Harper and Brothers, 1944.

Ludwig, Emil. *The Mediterranean, Saga of a Sea.* New York: McGraw-Hill, 1942.

Marshall, S. L. A. *Sinai Victory.* New York: William Morrow, 1957.

Nathan, Robert R.; Gass, Oscar; and Creamer, Daniel. *Palestine: Problem and Promise.* Washington, D.C.: Public Affairs Press of the American Council on Public Affairs, 1946.

Northrop, F. S. C. *The Meeting of East and West: An Inquiry Concerning World Understanding.* New York: Macmillan, 1946.

O'Ballance, Edgar. *The Arab-Israeli War 1948.* New York: Praeger, 1957.

Owen, George Frederick. *Abraham to the Middle East Crisis,* 4th ed. Grand Rapids, Mich.: Eerdmans, 1957.

Patai, Raphael. *Israel Between East and West: A Study in Human Relations.* Philadelphia: Jewish Publication Society of America, 1953.

Pearlman, Moshe. *The Army of Israel.* New York: Philosophical Library, 1950.

Royal Institute of International Affairs. *Great Britain and Palestine.* New York: Oxford University Press, 1939.

Siegfried, André. *The Mediterranean* (Trans. Doris Hemming), New York: Duell, Sloan and Pearce, 1947.

Simmel, Ernst (Ed.). *Anti-Semitism, A Social Disease.* New York: International Universities Press, 1946.

Speiser, E. A. *The United States and the Near East.* Cambridge: Harvard University Press, 1950.

Tritton, A. S. *Islam: Belief and Practice*. London: Hutchinson's University Library, 1954.

Twain, Mark. *The Innocents Abroad*.

Uris, Leon. *Exodus*. New York: Doubleday, 1959.

Voss, Carl Hermann. *The Palestine Problem Today: Israel and Its Neighbors*. Boston: Beacon Press, 1953.

Wavell, A. P. *The Palestine Campaigns*, 3d ed. London: Constable and Co. Ltd., 1938.

Weizmann, Chaim. *Trial and Error: The Autobiography of Chaim Weizmann*. Philadelphia: Jewish Publication Society of America, 1949.

Ziff, William B. *The Rape of Palestine*. New York: Longmans, Green and Co., 1938.

APPENDICES

Appendix 1

ENDORSEMENT AND ADOPTION OF THE BALFOUR DECLARATION BY THE ALLIED AND ASSOCIATED POWERS OF WORLD WAR I

[The Palestine Royal Commission of 1937 found and stated as a fact that]

The text of the Declaration had been submitted to President Wilson [of the United States of America] and had been approved by him before its publication. On the 14th February and the 9th May, 1918, the French and Italian Governments publicly endorsed it.

[The other Allies of the First World War likewise endorsed the Declaration shortly thereafter (Hanna, British Policy in Palestine, p. 36).]

Appendix 2

TREATY OF PEACE BETWEEN THE PRINCIPAL ALLIED POWERS AND TURKEY

Sèvres, August 10, 1920

Article 95

The High Contracting Parties agree to entrust, by application of the provisions of Article 22, the administration of Palestine, within such boundaries as may be determined by the Principal Allied Powers, to a Mandatory to be selected by the said Powers. The Mandatory will be responsible for putting into effect the declaration originally made on November 2, 1917, by the British Government, and adopted by the other Allied Powers, in favor of the establishment in Palestine of a national home for the Jewish people, it being clearly understood that nothing shall be done which may prejudice the civil and religious rights of existing non-Jewish communities in Palestine or the rights and political status enjoyed by Jews in any other country.

Appendix 3

ACCORD AND DECISION OF THE CONFERENCE OF THE PRINCIPAL ALLIED POWERS AT SAN REMO, 1920

[At the San Remo Conference held in April 1920, the principal Allied powers decided that the Mandate for the government of Palestine should be entrusted to Great Britian and that] The Mandatory Power will be responsible for putting into effect the Declaration originally made on November 2nd, 1917, by the British Government in favour of the establishment of a National Home for the Jewish people, subject to the conditions included in the Declaration itself (Duke of Devonshire, House of Lords, June 27, 1923).

Appendix 4

AGREEMENT BETWEEN EMIR FEISAL
AND DR. WEIZMANN

January 3, 1919 [1]

His Royal Highness the Emir Feisal, representing and acting on behalf of the Arab Kingdom of Hedjaz, and Dr. Chaim Weizmann, representing and acting on behalf of the Zionist Organization, mindful of the racial kinship and ancient bonds existing between the Arabs and the Jewish people, and realizing that the surest means of working out the consummation of their national aspirations is through the closest possible collaboration in the development of the Arab State and Palestine, and being desirous further of confirming the good understanding which exists between them, have agreed upon the following Articles:

Article I

The Arab State and Palestine in all their relations and undertakings shall be controlled by the most cordial goodwill and understanding, and to this end Arab and Jewish duly accredited agents shall be established and maintained in the respective territories.

Article II

Immediately following the completion of the deliberations of the Peace Conference, the definite boundaries between the Arab State and Palestine shall be determined by a Commission to be agreed upon by the parties hereto.

Article III

In the estabishment of the Constitution and Administration of Palestine all such measures shall be adopted as will afford the fullest guarantees for carrying into effect the British Government's Declaration of the 2nd of November, 1917.

[1] *Book of Documents* submitted to the General Assembly of the United Nations (Jewish Agency for Palestine, New York, May 1947). Spelling as in the original.

Article IV

All necessary measures shall be taken to encourage and stimulate immigration of Jews into Palestine on a large scale, and as quickly as possible to settle Jewish immigrants upon the land through closer settlement and intensive cultivation of the soil. In taking such measures the Arab peasant and tenant farmers shall be protected in their rights, and shall be assisted in forwarding their economic development.

Article V

No regulation nor law shall be made prohibiting or interfering in any way with the free exercise of religion; and further the free exercise and enjoyment of religious profession and worship without discrimination or preference shall forever be allowed. No religious test shall ever be required for the exercise of civil or political rights.

Article VI

The Mohammedan Holy Places shall be under Mohammedan control.

Article VII

The Zionist Organization proposes to send to Palestine a Commission of experts to make a survey of the economic possibilities of the country, and to report upon the best means for its development. The Zionist Organization will place the aforementioned Commission at the disposal of the Arab State for the purpose of a survey of the economic possibilities of the Arab State and to report upon the best means for its development. The Zionist Organization will use its best efforts to assist the Arab State in providing the means for developing the natural resources and economic possibilities thereof.

Article VIII

The parties hereto agree to act in complete accord and harmony on all matters embraced herein before the Peace Conference.

Article IX

Any matters of dispute which may arise between the contracting parties shall be referred to the British Government for arbitration.

Given under our hand at London, England, the third day of January, one thousand nine hundred and nineteen.

CHAIM WEIZMANN
FEISAL IBN-HUSSEIN

Reservation by the Emir Feisal

If the Arabs are established as I have asked in my manifesto of January 4th addressed to the British Secretary of State for Foreign Affairs, I will carry out what is written in this agreement. If changes are made, I cannot be answerable for failing to carry out this agreement.

FEISAL IBN-HUSSEIN

Appendix 5

JOINT RESOLUTION OF THE CONGRESS OF THE UNITED STATES ADOPTED JUNE 30, 1922, AND SIGNED BY PRESIDENT HARDING ON SEPTEMBER 20, 1922 [2]

Whereas the Jewish people have for many centuries believed in and yearned for the rebuilding of their ancient homeland; and

Whereas owing to the outcome of the World War and their part therein, the Jewish people are to be enabled to re-create and reorganize a national home in the land of their fathers, which will give to the House of Israel its long-denied opportunity to re-establish a fruitful Jewish life and culture in the ancient Jewish land: therefore be it

Resolved by the Senate and House of Representatives of the

[2] *Congressional Record*, 67th Cong., 2nd Session (June 30, 1922), p. 9800.

United States of America in Congress assembled, that the United States of America favors the establishment in Palestine of a national home for the Jewish people, it being clearly understood that nothing shall be done which may prejudice the civil and religious rights of Christian and all other non-Jewish communities in Palestine, and that the holy places and religious buildings and sites in Palestine shall be adquately protected.

Appendix 6

LEAGUE OF NATIONS MANDATE FOR PALESTINE [3]

[The following preamble and articles of the League of Nations Mandate for Palestine are its fundamental clauses.]

The Council of the League of Nations:

Whereas the Principal Allied Powers have agreed, for the purpose of giving effect to the provisions of Article 22 of the Covenant of the League of Nations, to entrust to a Mandatory selected by the said Powers the administration of the territory of Palestine, which formerly belonged to the Turkish Empire, within such boundaries as may be fixed by them; and

Whereas the Principal Allied Powers have also agreed that the Mandatory should be responsible for putting into effect the declaration originally made on November 2nd, 1917, by the Government of His Britannic Majesty, and adopted by the said Powers, in favour of the establishment in Palestine of a national home for the Jewish people, it being clearly understood that nothing should be done which might prejudice the civil and religious rights of existing non-Jewish communities in Palestine, or the rights and political status enjoyed by Jews in any other country; and

Whereas recognition has thereby been given to the historical connection of the Jewish people with Palestine and to the grounds for reconstituting their national home in that country; and

[3] Approved by the Council of the League of Nations on July 24, 1922. Went into effect on September 29, 1923. See Great Britain, *Parliamentary Papers 1922*, Cmd. 1785, pp. 1–11.

Whereas the Principal Allied Powers have selected His Britannic Majesty as the Mandatory for Palestine; and

Whereas the mandate in respect of Palestine has been formulated in the following terms and submitted to the Council of the League for approval; and

Whereas His Britannic Majesty has accepted the mandate in respect of Palestine and undertaken to exercise it on behalf of the League of Nations in conformity with the following provisions; and

Whereas by the afore-mentioned Article 22 (paragraph 8), it is provided that the degree of authority, control or administration to be exercised by the Mandatory, not having been previously agreed upon by the Members of the League, shall be explicity defined by the Council of the League of Nations;

Confirming the said mandate defines its terms as follows:

Article I

The Mandatory shall have full powers of legislation and of administration, save as they may be limited by the terms of this mandate.

Article II

The Mandatory shall be responsible for placing the country under such political, administrative and economic conditions as will secure the establishment of the Jewish national home, as laid down in the preamble, and the development of self-governing institutions, and also for safeguarding the civil and religious rights of all the inhabitants of Palestine, irrespective of race and religion.

Article III

The Mandatory shall, so far as circumstances permit, encourage local autonomy.

Article IV

An appropriate Jewish agency shall be recognized as a public body for the purpose of advising and cooperating with the Administration of Palestine in such economic, social and other matters as may affect the establishment of the Jewish national home and the interests of the Jewish population in Palestine, and, subject always to the control of the Administration, to assist and take part in the development of the country.

The Zionist Organization, so long as its organization and constitution are in the opinion of the Mandatory appropriate, shall be recognized as such agency. It shall take steps in consultation with His Britannic Majesty's Government to secure the cooperation of all Jews who are willing to assist in the establishment of the Jewish national home.

Article V

The Mandatory shall be responsible for seeing that no Palestine territory shall be ceded or leased to, or in any way placed under the control of, the Government of any foreign Power.

Article VI

The Administration of Palestine, while ensuring that the rights and position of other sections of the population are not prejudiced, shall facilitate Jewish immigration under suitable conditions and shall encourage, in cooperation with the Jewish agency referred to in Article IV, close settlement by Jews on the land, including State lands and waste lands not required for public purposes.

Article VII

The consent of the Council of the League of Nations is required for any modification of the terms of this mandate.

From the Certified true copy:

For the Secretary-General
RAPPARD
Director of the Mandates Section

Appendix 7

CONCURRENT RESOLUTION OF THE CONGRESS OF THE UNITED STATES, DECEMBER 19, 1945 [4]

79th Congress
1st Session   **S.Con.Res.44**

Concurrent Resolution

Whereas the Sixty-seventh Congress of the United States on June 30, 1922, unanimously resolved "That the United States of America favors the establishment in Palestine of a national home for the Jewish people, it being clearly understood that nothing shall be done which may prejudice the civil and religious rights of Christians and all other non-Jewish communities in Palestine, and that the holy places and religious buildings and sites in Palestine shall be adequately protected," and

Whereas the ruthless persecution of the Jewish people in Europe has clearly demonstrated the need for a Jewish homeland as a haven for the large numbers who have become homeless as a result of this persecution; and

Whereas these urgent necessities are evidenced by the President's request for the immediate right of entry into Palestine of one hundred thousand additional Jewish refugees; and

Whereas the influx of Jewish immigration into Palestine is resulting in its improvement in agricultural, financial, hygienic, and general economic conditions; and

Whereas the President and the British Prime Minister have agreed upon the appointment of a "Joint Anglo-American Committee of Enquiry" to examine conditions in Palestine as they bear upon the problem of Jewish immigration and the Jewish situation in Europe and have requested a report within one hundred and twenty days:

Therefore Be It

Resolved by the Senate (the House of Representatives concurring),

[4] *United States Statues at Large,* Vol. 59, pp. 848–849.

That the interest shown by the President in the solution of this problem is hereby commended and that the United States shall use its good offices with the mandatory power to the end that Palestine shall be opened for free entry of Jews into that country to the maximum of its agricultural and economic potentialities, and that there shall be full opportunity for colonization and development, so that they may freely proceed with the upbuilding of Palestine as the Jewish national home and, in association with all elements of the population, establish Palestine as a democratic commonwealth in which all men, regardless of race or creed, shall have equal rights.

Passed the Senate December 17 (legislative day, October 29), 1945.

Attest:

LESLIE L. BIFFLE
Secretary

NOTES

(1) The foregoing Resolution likewise passed the House of Representatives on December 19, 1945, as H.Con.Res.113.

(2) Following is the report of the Committee on Foreign Relations of the United States Senate on the foregoing Resolution:

79th Congress } SENATE { Report
1st Session } { No. 855

Restoration of Palestine as a Homeland
for the Jewish People

December 12 (legislative day, October 29), 1945
—Ordered to be printed

Appendix 8

DECLARATIONS BY PRESIDENTS OF THE UNITED STATES ON PALESTINE AND THE JEWISH NATIONAL HOME

President John Adams (October 1818) [5]

I really wish the Jews again in Judaea, an independent Nation, for, as I Believe, the most enlightened men of it have participated in the amelioration of the philosophy of the age; once restored to an independent government, and no longer persecuted, they would soon wear away some of the asperities and pecularities of their character. I wish your nation may be admitted to all the privileges of nations in every part of the world. This country [America] has done much; I wish it may do more, and annul every narrow idea in religion, government and commerce.

President Woodrow Wilson (March 1919)

As for your representations touching Palestine, I have before this expressed my personal approval of the declaration of the British Government regarding the aspirations and historic claims of the Jewish people in regard to Palestine. I am, moreover, persuaded that the Allied Nations, with the fullest concurrence of our own Government and people, are agreed that in Palestine shall be laid the foundations of a Jewish Commonwealth.

President Calvin Coolidge (June 1924)

I have so many times reiterated my interest in this great movement that anything which I might add would be a repetition of former statements, but I am nevertheless glad to have this opportunity to express again my sympathy with the deep and intense longing which finds such fine expression in the Jewish National Homeland in Palestine.

The proposed plan furnishes to the Jewish people an opportunity to devote their great qualities to the upbuilding and preservation of

[5] From discourse on the Restoration of the Jews delivered at the Tabernacle (Congregation) Kabal Kadosh Shearith Israel (The Holy Congregation of the Remnants of Israel), New York City, on October 28 and December 2, 1844, by Mordecai Manuel Noah.

their own homeland and in their own sphere, and I feel sure that the people of the United States will not fail to give that earnest and substantial aid which will be necessary if it is to meet with a full measure of success.

President Herbert Hoover (September 1928)

I have watched with genuine admiration the steady and unmistakable progress made in the rehabilitation of Palestine which, desolate for centuries, is now renewing its youth and vitality through the enthusiasm, hard work, and self-sacrifice of the Jewish pioneers who toil there in a spirit of peace and social justice. It is very gratifying to note that many American Jews, Zionists as well as non-Zionists, have rendered such splendid service to this cause which merits the sympathy and moral encouragement of everyone.

President Franklin D. Roosevelt (July 1936)

The interest which I have had and have frequently manifested in the rebuilding of the ancient Jewish homeland is, I am persuaded, an interest which is shared by all who recognize that every people has the inalienable right to life, liberty and the pursuit of happiness. It is a source of renewed hope and courage, that by international accord and by the moral support of the peoples of the world, men and women of Jewish faith have a right to resettle the land where their faith was born and from which much of our modern civilization has emanated.

President Franklin D. Roosevelt (September 1940)

Efforts will be made to find appropriate ways and means of effectuating this policy as soon as practicable. I know how long and ardently the Jewish people have worked and prayed for the establishment of Palestine as a free and democratic Jewish commonwealth. I am convinced that the American people give their support to this aim and if re-elected I shall help to bring about its realization.

President Harry S. Truman (October 28, 1946)
(Letter to the King of Saudi Arabia)

The Government and the people of the United States have given support to the concept of a Jewish national home in Palestine ever since the termination of the first World War, which resulted in the freeing of a large area of the Near East, including Palestine, and the establishment of a number of independent states which are now members of the United Nations. The United States, which contributed its blood and resources to the winning of that war, could not divest itself of a certain responsibility for the manner in which the freed territories were disposed of, or for the fate of the peoples liberated at that time. It took the position, to which it still adheres, that these peoples should be prepared for self-government and also that a national home for the Jewish people should be established in Palestine. I am happy to note that most of the liberated peoples are now citizens of independent countries. The Jewish national home, however, has not as yet been fully developed.

It is only natural, therefore, that this Government should favor at this time the entry into Palestine of considerable numbers of displaced Jews in Europe, not only that they may find shelter there but also that they may contribute their talents and energies to the upbuilding of the Jewish national home.

Appendix 9

MAJORITY PLAN OF PARTITION WITH ECONOMIC UNION PROPOSED BY THE UNITED NATIONS SPECIAL COMMITTEE ON PALESTINE AND PASSED BY THE UN GENERAL ASSEMBLY ON NOVEMBER 29, 1947, BY OVER TWO-THIRDS' MAJORITY [6,7]

1. The basic premise underlying the partition proposal is that the claims to Palestine of the Arabs and Jews, both possessing va-

[6] UN Doc. A/364, 3 September 1947.
[7] UN Official Records of the Second Session of the General Assembly, Resolutions (16 September–29 November 1947), pp. 131–150.

lidity, are irreconcilable, and that among all of the solutions advanced, partition will provide the most realistic and practicable settlement, and is the most likely to afford a workable basis for meeting in part the claims and national aspirations of both parties.

2. It is a fact that both of these peoples have their historic roots in Palestine, and that both make vital contributions to the economic and cultural life of the country. The partition solution takes these considerations fully into account.

3. The basic conflict in Palestine is a clash of two intense nationalisms. Regardless of the historical origins of the conflict, the rights and wrongs of the promises and counter-promises, and the international intervention incident to the Mandate, there are now in Palestine some 650,000 Jews and some 1,200,000 Arabs who are dissimilar in their ways of living and, for the time being, separated by political interests which render difficult full and effective political cooperation among them, whether voluntary or induced by constitutional arrangements.

4. Only by means of partition can these conflicting national aspirations find substantial expression and qualify both peoples to take their places as independent nations in the international community in the United Nations.

5. The partition solution provides that finality which is a most urgent need in the solution. Every other proposed solution would tend to induce the two parties to seek modification in their favour by means of persistent pressure. The grant of independence to both States, however, would remove the basis for such efforts.

6. Partition is based on a realistic appraisal of the actual Arab-Jewish relations in Palestine. Full political cooperation would be indispensable to the effective functioning of any single-State scheme, such as the federal-State proposal, except in those cases which frankly envisage either an Arab or a Jewish dominated State.

7. Partition is the only means available by which political and economic responsibility can be placed squarely on both Arabs and Jews, with the prospective result that, confronted with the responsibility for bearing fully the consequences of their own actions, a new and important element of political amelioration would be introduced. In the proposed federal-State solution, this factor would be lacking.

8. Jewish immigration is the central issue in Palestine today and is the one factor, above all others, that rules out the necessary co-operation between the Arab and Jewish communities in a single State. The creation of a Jewish State under a partition scheme is the only hope of removing this issue from the arena of conflict.

9. It is recognized that partition has been strongly opposed by Arabs, but it is felt that the opposition would be lessened by a solution which definitively fixes the extent of territory to be allotted to the Jews with its implicit limitation on immigration. The fact that the solution carries the sanction of the United Nations involves a finality which should allay Arab fears of further expansion of the Jewish State.

10. In view of the limited area and resources of Palestine, it is essential that, to the extent feasible, and consistent with the creation of two independent States, the economic unity of the country should be preserved. The partition proposal, therefore, is a qualified partition, subject to such measures and limitations as are considered essential to the future economic and social well-being of both States. Since the economic self-interest of each State would be vitally involved, it is believed that the minimum measure of economic unity is possible, where that of political unity is not.

11. Such economic unity requires the creation of an economic association by means of a treaty between the two States. The essential objectives of this association would be a common customs system, a common currency and the maintenance of a country-wide system of transport and communications.

12. The maintenance of existing standards of social services in all parts of Palestine depends partly upon the preservation of economic unity, and this is a main consideration underlying the provisions for an economic union as part of the partition scheme. Partition, however, necessarily changes to some extent the fiscal situation in such a manner that, at any rate during the early years of its existence, a partitioned Arab State in Palestine would have some difficulty in raising sufficient revenues to keep up its present standards of public services.

One of the aims of the economic union, therefore, is to distribute surplus revenue to support such standards. It is recommended that the division of the surplus revenue, after certain charges and percentage of surplus to be paid to the City of Jerusalem, are met, should be in equal proportions to the two States. This is an arbitrary proportion but it is considered that it would be acceptable, that it has the merit of simplicity and that, being fixed in this manner, it would be less likely to become a matter of controversy. Provisions are suggested whereby this formula is to be reviewed.

13. This division of customs revenue is justified on three grounds: (1) The Jews will have the more economically developed part of the country embracing practically the whole of the citrus-producing area which includes a large number of Arab producers; (2) the Jewish State would, through the customs union, be guaranteed a larger free trade area for the sale of the products of its industry; (3) it would be to the disadvantage of the Jewish State if the Arab State should be in a financially precarious and poor economic condition.

14. As the Arab State will not be in a position to undertake considerable development expenditure, sympathetic consideration should be given to its claims for assistance from international institutions in the way of loans for expansion of education, public health and other vital social services of a non-self-supporting nature.

15. International financial assistance would also be required for any comprehensive irrigation schemes in the interest of both States, and it is to be hoped that constructive work by the Joint Economic Board will be made possible by means of international loans on favourable terms.

Appendix 10

DECLARATION OF THE ESTABLISHMENT OF THE STATE OF ISRAEL [8]

ERETZ ISRAEL [9] was the birthplace of the Jewish people. Here their spiritual, religious and political identity was shaped. Here they first attained to statehood, created cultural values of national

---

[8] Published in the Official Gazette, No. 1 of the 5th Iyar, 5708 (May 14, 1948).

[9] *Eretz-Israel* (Hebrew)—the Land of Israel, Palestine.—F.G.

and universal significance and gave to the world the eternal Book of Books.

After being forcibly exiled from their land. the people kept faith with it throughout their Dispersion and never ceased to pray and hope for their return to it and for the restoration in it of their political freedom.

Impelled by this historic and traditional attachment, Jews strove in every successive generation to re-establish themselves in their ancient homeland. In recent decades they returned in their masses. Pioneers, ma'pilim [10] and defenders, they made deserts bloom, revived the Hebrew language, built villages and towns, and created a thriving community, controlling its own economy and culture, loving peace but knowing how to defend itself, bringing the blessings of progress to all the country's inhabitants, and aspiring towards independent nationhood.

In the year 5657 (1897), at the summons of the spiritual father of the Jewish State, Theodor Herzl, the First Zionist Congress convened and proclaimed the right of the Jewish people to national rebirth in its own country.

This right was recognized in the Balfour Declaration of the 2nd November, 1917, and re-affirmed in the Mandate of the League of Nations which, in particular, gave international sanction to the historic connection between the Jewish people and Eretz-Israel and to the right of the Jewish people to rebuild its National Home.

The catastrophe which recently befell the Jewish people—the massacre of millions of Jews in Europe—was another clear demonstration of the urgency of solving the problem of its homelessness by re-establishing in Eretz-Israel the Jewish State, which would open the gates of the homeland wide to every Jew and confer upon the Jewish people the status of a fully-privileged member of the comity of nations.

Survivors of the Nazi holocaust in Europe, as well as Jews from other parts of the world, continued to migrate to Eretz-Israel, undaunted by difficulties, restrictions and dangers, and never ceased to assert their right to a life of dignity, freedom and honest toil in their national homeland.

[10] *Ma'pilim* (Hebrew)—immigrants coming to Eretz-Israel in defiance of restrictive legislation.—F.G.

In the Second World War, the Jewish community of this country contributed its full share to the struggle of the freedom- and peace-loving nations against the force of Nazi wickedness and, by the blood of its soldiers and its war effort, gained the right to be reckoned among the peoples who founded the United Nations.

On the 29th November, 1947, the United Nations General Assembly passed a resolution calling for the establishment of a Jewish State in Eretz-Israel; the General Assembly required the inhabitants of Eretz-Israel to take such steps as were necessary on their part for the implementation of that resolution. This recognition by the United Nations of the right of the Jewish people to establish their State is irrevocable.

This right is the natural right of the Jewish people to be masters of their own fate, like all other nations, in their own sovereign State.

ACCORDINGLY WE, MEMBERS OF THE PEOPLE'S COUNCIL, REPRE- SENTATIVES OF THE JEWISH COMMUNITY OF ERETZ-ISRAEL AND OF THE ZIONIST MOVEMENT, ARE HERE ASSEMBLED ON THE DAY OF THE TERMINATION OF THE BRITISH MANDATE OVER ERETZ-ISRAEL AND, BY VIRTUE OF OUR NATURAL AND HISTORIC RIGHT AND ON THE STRENGTH OF THE RESOLUTION OF THE UNITED NATIONS GENERAL ASSEMBLY, HEREBY DECLARE THE ESTABLISHMENT OF A JEWISH STATE IN ERETZ-ISRAEL, TO BE KNOWN AS THE STATE OF ISRAEL.

WE DECLARE that, with effect from the moment of the termina- tion of the Mandate, being tonight, the eve of Sabbath, the 6th Iyar, 5708 (15th May, 1948), until the establishment of the elected, regular authorities of the State in accordance with the Constitution which shall be adopted by the Elected Constituent Assembly not later than the 1st October, 1948, the People's Council shall act as a Provisional Council of State, and its executive organ, the People's Administration, shall be the Provisional Government of the Jewish State, to be called "Israel."

THE STATE OF ISRAEL will be open for Jewish immigration and for the ingathering of the exiles, it will foster the development of the country for the benefit of all inhabitants; it will be based on freedom, justice and peace as envisaged by the prophets of Israel; it will ensure complete equality of social and political rights to all its inhabitants irrespective of religion, race or sex; it will guarantee freedom of religion, conscience, language, education and culture; it will safeguard the Holy Places of all religions; and it will be faithful to the principles of the Charter of the United Nations.

THE STATE OF ISRAEL is prepared to cooperate with the agencies and representatives of the United Nations in implementing the resolution of the General Assembly of the 29th November, 1947, and will take steps to bring about the economic union of the whole of Eretz-Israel.

WE APPEAL to the United Nations to assist the Jewish people in the building-up of its State and to receive the State of Israel into the comity of nations.

WE APPEAL—in the very midst of the onslaught launched against us now for months—to the Arab inhabitants of the State of Israel to preserve peace and participate in the upbuilding of the State on the basis of full and equal citizenship and due representation in all its provisional and permanent institutions.

WE EXTEND our hand to all neighboring States and their peoples in an offer of peace and good neighborliness, and appeal to them to establish bonds of cooperation and mutual help with the sovereign Jewish people settled in its own land. The State of Israel is prepared to do its share in common effort for the advancement of the entire Middle East.

WE APPEAL to the Jewish people throughout the Diaspora to rally round the Jews of Eretz-Israel in the tasks of immigrants and upbuilding and to stand by them in the great struggle for the realization of the age-old dream—the redemption of Israel.

PLACING OUR TRUST IN THE ALMIGHTY, WE AFFIX OUR SIGNATURES TO THIS PROCLAMATION AT THIS SESSION OF THE PROVISIONAL COUNCIL OF STATE, ON THE SOIL OF THE HOMELAND IN THE CITY OF TEL AVIV, ON THIS SABBATH EVE, THE 5TH DAY OF IYAR, 5708 (14TH MAY, 1948).

DAVID BEN-GURION

DANIEL AUSTER	RABBI WOLF GOLD
MORDEKHAI BENTOV	MEIR GRABOVSKY
YITZCHAK BEN ZVI	YITZCHAK GRUENBAUM
ELIYAHU BERLIGNE	DR. ABRAHAM GRANOVSKY
FRITZ BERNSTEIN	ELIYAHU DOBKIN

MEIR WILNER-KOVNER

ZERACH WAHRHAFTIG

HERZL VARDI

RACHEL COHEN

RABBI KALMAN KAHANA

SAADIA KOBASHI

RABBI YITZCHAK MEIR LEVIN

MEIR DAVID LOEVENSTEIN

ZVI LURIA

GOLDA MYERSON

NACHUM NIR

ZVI SEGAL

RABBI YEHUDA LEIB HACOHEN
FISHMAN

DAVID ZVI PINKAS

AHARON ZISLING

MOSHE KOLODNY

ELIEZER KAPLAN

ABRAHAM KATZNELSON

FELIX ROSENBLUETH

DAVID REMEZ

BERL REPETUR

MORDEKHAI SHATTNER

BEN ZION STERNBERG

BEKHOR SHITREET

MOSHE SHAPIRA

MOSHE SHERTOK

Appendix 11

ISRAELI-ARAB ARMISTICE AGREEMENTS, 1949

[The following extracts from the Israel-Jordan Armistice Agreement, signed under United Nations auspices at Rhodes, April 13, 1949, are identical in letter and spirit with the Armistice Agreements signed by Israel and Egypt, Israel and Syria, and Israel and Lebanon.]

Security Council Document S/1302/Rev.1

Cablegram dated 3 April 1949 from the United Nations Acting Mediator to the Secretary-General transmitting the text of the General Agreement between the Hashemite Jordan Kingdom and Israel.

[Original text: English]
Rhodes, 3 April 1949

For the President of the Security Council

I have the honour to inform you that an armistice agreement between the Hashemite Jordan Kingdom and Israel has been signed this evening, 3 April 1949, at Rhodes. The text of the agreement follows.

RALPH J. BUNCHE
Acting Mediator

HASHEMITE JORDAN KINGDOM—ISRAEL GENERAL ARMISTICE AGREEMENT RHODES, 3 APRIL 1949

PREAMBLE

The Parties to the present Agreement,

Responding to the Security Council resolution of 16 November 1948, calling upon them, as a further provisional measure under Article 40 of the Charter of the United Nations and in order to facilitate the translation from the present truce to permanent peace in Palestine, to negotiate an armistice;

Having decided to enter into negotiations under United Nations chairmanship concerning the implementation of the Security Council resolution of 16 November 1948; and having appointed representatives empowered to negotiate and conclude an Armistice Agreement,

The undersigned representatives of their respective Governments, having exchanged their full powers found to be in good and proper form, have agreed upon the following provisions:

ARTICLE I

With a view to promoting the return of permanent peace in Palestine and in recognition of the importance in this regard of mutual assurances concerning the future military operations of the Parties, the following principles, which shall be fully observed by both Parties during the armistice, are hereby affirmed:

1. The injunction of the Security Council against resort to military force in the settlement of the Palestine question shall henceforth be scrupulously respected by both Parties;

2. No aggressive action by the armed forces—land, sea or air—of either Party shall be undertaken, planned, or threatened against the people or the armed forces of the other; it being understood

that the use of the term "planned" in this context has no bearing on normal staff planning as generally practiced in military organization;

3. The right of each Party to its security and freedom from fear of attack by the armed forces of the other shall be fully respected;

4. The establishment of an armistice between the armed forces of the two Parties is accepted as an indispensable step toward the liquidation of armed conflict and the restoration of peace in Palestine.

ARTICLE III

1. In pursuance of the foregoing principles and of the resolution of the Security Council of 16 November 1948, a general armistice between the armed forces of the two Parties—land, sea and air—is hereby established.

2. No element of the land, sea or air, military or para-military forces of either Party, including non-regular forces, shall commit any warlike or hostile act against the military or para-military forces of the other Party, or against civilians in territory under the control of that Party; or shall advance beyond or pass over for any purpose whatsoever the Armistice Demarcation Lines set forth in articles V and VI of this Agreement; or enter into or pass through the air space of the other Party.

3. No warlike act or act of hostility shall be conducted from territory controlled by one of the Parties to this Agreement against the other Party.

[*The following article is specific to the Israel-Jordan Armistice Agreement, as it deals with the agreement between the two countries providing for free access to Mount Scopus, holy places and cultural institutions, use of the cemetery on the Mount of Olives, and other matters connected with the Jerusalem area.*]

ARTICLE VIII

1. A Special Committee, composed of two representatives of each Party designated by the respective Governments, shall be established for the purpose of formulating agreed plans and arrangements designed to enlarge the scope of this Agreement and to effect improvements in its application.

2. The Special Committee shall be organized immediately following the coming into effect of this Agreement and shall direct its attention to the formulation of agreed plans and arrangements for such matters as either Party may submit to it, which, in any case, shall include the following on which agreement in principle already exists: free movement of traffic on vital roads, including the Bethlehem and Latrun–Jerusalem roads; resumption of the normal functioning of the cultural and humanitarian institutions on Mount Scopus and free access thereto: free access to the Holy Places and cultural institutions and use of the cemetery on the Mount of Olives; resumption of operation of the Latrun pumping station; provision of electricity for the Old City; and resumption of operation of the railroad to Jerusalem.

3. The Special Committee shall have exclusive competence over such matters as may be referred to it. Agreed plans and arrangements formulated by it may provide for the exercise of supervisory functions by the Mixed Armistice Commission established in article XI.

ARTICLE XI

1. The execution of the provisions of this Agreement, with the exception of such matters as fall within the exclusive competence of the Special Committee established in article VIII, shall be supervised by a Mixed Armistice Commission composed of five members, of whom each Party to this Agreement shall designate two, and whose chairman shall be the United Nations Chief of Staff of the Truce Supervision Organization or a senior officer from the observer personnel of that organization designated by him following consultation with both Parties to this Agreement.

2. The Mixed Armistice Commission shall maintain its headquarters at Jerusalem and shall hold its meetings at such places and at such times as it may deem necessary for the effective conduct of its work

3. The Mixed Armistice Commission shall be convened in its first meeting by the United Nations Chief of Staff of the Truce Supervision Organization and not later than one week following the signing of this Agreement.

4. Decisions of the Mixed Armistice Commission, to the extent possible, shall be based on the principle of unanimity. In the ab-

sence of unanimity, decisions shall be taken by a majority vote of the members of the Commission present and voting.

5. The Mixed Armistice Commission shall formulate its own rules of procedures. Meetings shall be held only after due notice to the members by the Chairman. The quorum for its meetings shall be a majority of its members.

6. The Commission shall be empowered to employ observers, who may be from among the military organizations of the Parties or from the military personnel of the United Nations Truce Supervision Organization, or from both, in such numbers as may be considered essential to the performance of its functions. In the event United Nations observers should be so employed, they shall remain under the command of the United Nations Chief of Staff of the Truce Supervision Organization. Assignments of a general or special nature given to United Nations observers attached to the Mixed Armistice Commission shall be subject to approval by the United Nations Chief of Staff or his designated representative on the Commission, whichever is serving as Chairman.

7. Claims or complaints presented by either Party relating to the application of this Agreement shall be referred immediately to the Mixed Armistice Commission through its Chairman. The Commission shall take such action on all such claims or complaints by means of its observation and investigation machinery as it may deem appropriate, with a view to equitable and mutually satisfactory settlement.

8. Where interpretation of the meaning of a particular provision of this Agreement, other than the preamble and articles I and II, is at issue, the Commission's interpretation shall prevail. The Commission, in its discretion and as the need arises, may from time to time recommend to the Parties modifications in the provisions of this Agreement.

9. The Mixed Armistice Commission shall submit to both Parties reports on its activities as frequently as it may consider necessary. A copy of such report shall be presented to the Secretary-General of the United Nations for transmission to the appropriate organ or agency of the United Nations.

10. Members of the Commission and its observers shall be accorded such freedom of movement and access in the area covered

by this Agreement as the Commission may determine to be necessary, provided that when such decisions of the Commission are reached by a majority vote United Nations observers only shall be employed.

11. The expenses of the Commission, other than those relating to United Nations observers, shall be apportioned in equal shares between the two Parties to this Agreement.

[Article XII of this Agreement stipulates that the Parties may call upon the UN Secretary-General to convoke a conference of the representatives for the purpose of reviewing, revising, or suspending any of its provisions other than articles I and III.]

ARTICLE XII

1. The present Agreement is not subject to ratification and shall come into force immediately upon being signed.

2. This Agreement, having been negotiated and concluded in pursuance of the resolution of the Security Council of 16 November 1948 calling for the establishment of an armistice in order to eliminate the threat to peace in Palestine and to facilitate the transition from the present truce to permanent peace in Palestine, shall remain in force until a peaceful settlement between the Parties is achieved, except as provided in paragraph 3 of this article.

3. The Parties to this Agreement may, by mutual consent, revise this Agreement or any of its provisions, or may suspend its application, other than articles I and III, at any time. In the absence of mutual agreement and after this Agreement has been in effect for one year from the date of its signing, either of the Parties may call upon the Secretary-General of the United Nations to convoke a conference of representatives of the two Parties for the purpose of reviewing, revising, or suspending any of the provisions of this Agreement other than articles I and III. Participation in such conference shall be obligatory upon the Parties.

4. If the conference provided for in paragraph 3 of this article does not result in an agreed solution of a point in dispute, either Party may bring the matter before the Security Council of the United Nations for the relief sought on the grounds that this Agreement has been concluded in pursuance of Security Council actions toward the end of achieving peace in Palestine.

5. This Agreement is signed in quintuplicate, of which one copy shall be retained by each Party, two copies communicated to the Secretary-General of the United Nations for transmission to the Security Council and to the United Nations Conciliation Commission on Palestine, and one copy to the United Nations Acting Mediator on Palestine.

DONE at Rhodes, Island of Rhodes, Greece, on the third of April one thousand nine hundred and forty-nine in the presence of the United Nations Acting Mediator on Palestine and the United Nations Chief of Staff of the Truce Supervision Organization.

For and on behalf of the Government of the Hashemite Jordan Kingdom

(signed)

COLONEL AHMED SUDKI
EL-JUNDI
LIEUTENANT-COLONEL
MOHAMED MAAYTE

For and on behalf of the Government of Israel

(signed)

REUVEN SHILOAH
LIEUTENANT-COLONEL
MOSHE DAYAN

Appendix 12

FREEDOM OF PASSAGE THROUGH SUEZ CANAL

[Relevant operative Paragraphs of Constantinople Convention of 1888, decisions of United Nations Security Council, 1951 and 1956, and Egyptian declaration of acceptance of ruling of United Nations Security Council.]

Constantinople Convention, 1888

[Articles I and IV of the Treaty of Constantinople establish the principle of freedom of passage.]

[Article I provides]

The Suez Maritime Canal shall always be free and open, in time of war as in time of peace, to every vessel of commerce or of war, without distinction of flag.

Consequently, the High Contracting Parties agree not in any way to interfere with the free use of the Canal, in time of war as in time of peace.

The Canal shall never be subjected to the exercise of the rights of blockade.

[*The first paragraph of Article IV declares*]

The Maritime Canal remaining open in time of war as a free passage, even to ships of war of belligerents, according to the terms of Article I of the present Treaty, the High Contracting Parties agree that no right of war, no act of hostility, nor any act having for its object to obstruct the free navigation of the Canal, shall be committed in the Canal and its ports of access, as well as within a radius of three marine miles from those ports, even though the Ottoman Empire should be one of the belligerent Powers.

ARTICLE X

Similarly, the provisions of Articles IV, V, VII and VIII shall not interfere with the measures which His Majesty the Sultan and His Highness the Khedive, in the name of His Imperial Majesty, and within the limits of the Firmans granted, might find it necessary to take for securing by their own forces the defence of Egypt and the maintenance of public order.

In case His Imperial Majesty the Sultan, or His Highness the Khedive, should find it necessary to avail themselves of the exceptions for which this article provides, the Signatory Powers of the Declaration of London shall be notified thereof by the Imperial Ottoman Government.

It is likewise understood that the provisions of the four Articles aforesaid shall in no case occasion any obstacle to the measures which the Imperial Ottoman Government may think it necessary to take in order to insure by its own forces the defence of its other possessions situated on the eastern coast of the Red Sea.

ARTICLE XI

The measures which shall be taken in the cases provided for by Articles IX and X of the present Treaty shall not interfere with the free use of the Canal. In the same cases, the erection of permanent fortifications contrary to the provisions of Article VIII is prohibited.

ARTICLE XIV

The High Contracting Parties agree that the engagements resulting from the present Treaty shall not be limited by the duration of the Acts of Concession of the Universal Suez Canal Company.

UN Security Council Resolutions

[*The Council's Resolution of September 1, 1915 affirms*]

that since the Armistice [Israel-Egypt Armistice Agreement, 1949] regime which has been in existence for nearly two and a half years is of a permanent character, neither party can reasonably assert that it is actively a belligerent or requires to exercise the right of visit, search, and seizure for any legitimate purpose of self-defence. (Paragraph 5)

that practice cannot in the prevailing circumstances be justified on the grounds that it is necessary for self-defence. (Paragraph 8)

The restrictions on the passage of goods through the Suez Canal to Israeli ports are denying to nations at no time connected with conflict in Palestine valuable supplies required for their economic reconstruction, and . . . these restrictions together with sanctions applied by Egypt to certain ships which have visited Israeli ports represent unjustified interference with the rights of nations to navigate the seas and to trade freely with one another, including the Arab States and Israel. (Paragraph 9)

Calls upon Egypt to terminate the restrictions on the passage of international commercial shipping and goods through the Suez Canal wherever bound and to cease all interference with such shipping beyond that essential to the safety of shipping in the Canal itself and to the observance of the international conventions in force.

[*The Council's Resolution of October 13, 1956, unanimously adopted six principles to govern free international navigation. Following are the two principal ones*]

(1) There should be free and open transit through the Canal without discrimination, overt or covert—this covers both political and technical aspects.

(3) The operation of the Canal should be insulated from the politics of any country.

Declaration by the Egyptian Government to the Secretary-General of the United Nations on 24 April 1957 [11]

It remains the unaltered policy and firm purpose of the Government of Egypt to respect the terms and the spirit of the Constantinople Convention of 1888 and the rights and obligations arising therefrom. The Government will continue to respect, observe and implement them.

The Government of Egypt are more particularly determined:

a. To afford and maintain free and uninterrupted navigation for all nations within the limits of and in accordance with the provisions of the Constantinople Convention of 1888.

[The representative of Egypt stated at the Security Council meeting of May 20, 1957] [12]

The Declaration is in keeping with that Resolution [i.e., of October 13, 1956] and hence with the six principles, and even with the most difficult of them, which states that the operation of the Canal shall be insulated from the politics of any country.

Appendix 13

THE HISTADRUT, THE JEWISH FEDERATION OF WORKERS IN PALESTINE

The Executive Committee 21/1/1948

Appeal to the Arab Workers

Fellow workers!

A fortnight ago we issued an appeal to you in the name of peace and cooperation. This appeal was received by many of you— workers, officials, and farm laborers—with satisfaction.

---

[11] Registered as an international treaty under Article 102 of the Charter (S/3818).
[12] (S/PV 778).

نداء من مجلس عمال حيفا

الى سكان حيفا العرب،

الى العمال والموظفين،

لقد مرت على حيفا فترة طويلة من الزمن، عشنا وعشتم فيها تحت
ظلال الطمأنينة والاخوة والتعاون، فازدهر هذا البلد المشترك
وازدهرت حالة سكانه يهوداً وعرباً، حتى اصبح نموذجاً لباقي البلدان،
وعلى حين غرة انقلبت الحال والهدوء بينا وبينكم قتلاً دموياً طالما
حذرناكم من مغبتها والفراراً من عواقبها الوخيمة،

اما اليوم والحمد لله فقد طهرت المدينة من عراصيل الشر، وفر
الشاغبون خوفاً من ان تطاله يد العدالة، وارتفع عنا نير الاستنار،
فبات هذا البلد يسوده الامن وتعمه الطمأنينة، وارتفعت فيه الحالة
ثانية التقارب بين السكان والتعاون بين العمال والحصول على الرزق الحلال
ان الحاوف التي غرسها الشاغبون في صدوركم لا اساس لها من الصحة
اتفاقم نحب السلم ولا نفكر غير الفكر للامنين السالمين الذين يأبون
مثلكم على العمل الشريف والسعي البشر فلا تخافوا، لا تغريركم
يترككم ايدكم، لا تتطردوا الرزاق بانفسكم، ولا تجلبوا على انفسكم
مشقات الرحيل وعذاب الجلاء،

اعلموا انكم ان اثرتم فلا تنتظروا سوى الفقر والذل والاحتقار،
اما هنا في حيفا فالباب المفتوح منتزح للعودة الى اعمالكم والمحافظة على
بيوتكم واموالكم وراحة عيالكم واطفالكم،

فيا ايها السكان المسلمين،

ان مجلس عمال حيفا في فرع المستورت في هذا البلد يصحكم
بالبقاء، ويدعوكم الرجوع الى اعمالكم الاعتيادية، انا مستعدون
لمساعدتكم على اعادة الامور الى مجاريها الحسنة، وتسهيل الحصول على
حاجيات المعيشة، وفتح ابواب العمل برجوعكم، وادخال الطمأنينة
في قلوبكم،

فيا ايها العمال ان بقاءنا لهذا المشترك حيفا يدعم كل التعاون منا على
تعمير ورقية، وازدهار وتقدمه، فلا تغزوا ولا تغرروا انفسكم،
كونوا على بصيرة من امركم وسهروا الى سبيل الخير والسعادة ذلك خير
لكم،

النقابة العامة لعمال اليهود (المستورت)
مجلس عمال حيفا

حيفا ٢٨-٤-٤٨

קול קורא מאת מועצת פועלי חיפה

אל תושבי חיפה הערבים
אל הפועלים והפקידים

שנים על שנים חיינו יחד בעירנו חיפה בבטחון ובתוך יחסי
הבנה ואחוה, הודות לכך פרחה והתפתחה עירנו לטובת התושבים
היהודים והערבים ושימשה מופת ליתר ערי הארץ.

גורמים עיניים לא יכלו שאת את המצב הזה, והם אשר
סכסכו וקלקלו את היחסים בינינו וביניכם, אך יד הצדק השיגה
אותם. עירנו טהרה מגורמים אלה, אשר ברחו על נפשם ועתה
שוב הושלטו סדר ובטחון בעיר ונפתחה דרך לחדוש יחסי שתוף
והתקרבות בין התושבים והפועלים היהודים והערבים לחיים
תקינים.

עתה הננו רואים צורך לאמר לכם גלויות: עם אהוב שלום
אנחנו! אין כל יסוד לפחד אשר מטילים עליכם, אין בלבנו טינה
וכוונות רעות כלפי התושבים שוחרי השלום האמונים כמונו
על עבודה יצירה. אל פחדו אל תחזיקו את בתיכם במו ידיכם
אל תשמעו את מקורות פרנסתכם ואל תמיטו על עצמכם אסונות
בעקב פזני וטלטולים שלא לצורך. בעקבם הטלטולים ישוממו
עוני והשפלה, אך בעירנו-עירכם חיפה פתוחים לפניכם השערים
לעבודה, לחיים ושלום לכם ולמשפחותיכם.

תושבים ישרים ושוחרי שלום!

מועצת פועלי חיפה וההסתדרות מיעצים לכם
ולטובתכם להשאר בעיר ולחזור לעבודתכם הרגילה
אנו מוכנים לבוא לעזרתכם בהחזרת החיים
למסלולם הטוב, להקל עליכם בהשגת מצרכי אכל,
לפתוח בפניכם מקומות עבודה.

פועלים!

עירנו המשותפת חיפה קוראת אתכם להשתתף
בבנינה, קידומה ופיתוחה. אל תבגדו בה ואל
תבגדו בעצמכם. ראו את עניניכם נכוחה ולכו
בדרך הטוב והישר

ההסתדרות הכללית של העובדים העברים בא"י
מועצת פועלי חיפה
חיפה 28.4.48

Appendix 13
Appeal to the Arab Workers

The Palestine Arab Workers Union, however, challenged our appeal with a long statement attempting to throw dust in your eyes and to mislead you into following the adventurous politicians, by stating that the United Nations decision regarding the establishment of a Jewish and an Arab state in this land is a sterile one.

. . . That union wishes you to believe that the decision of the United Nations is valueless. Were the union sincerely striving for peace it would acknowledge that the United Nations is the supreme world organization representing the will of fifty-seven states and that its decisions obligate even those states which voted against it. The decision regarding the establishment of the two states in this land has, moreover, been resolved upon and supported by the United States and the Soviet Union.

. . . The Jewish Federation of Labor reasserts that there can be no withdrawal from the United Nations decision. That decision opens up a new chapter in the history of this country. Within this chapter an Arab and a Jewish state shall arise. The Arab worker, official, and farm laborer, within the Jewish state will be citizens enjoying all the rights and obligations of citizenship. Within this state there shall be no room for discrimination between workers in regard to labor conditions, wages, education, and social services.

The Jewish Federation of Labor calls, therefore, upon the Arab workers, officials, and farm laborers, to oppose bloodshed and to prepare themselves for the tasks of organization and cooperation for the good of all workers.

Fellow workers: do not be misled and do not be herded like sheep after those shepherds who are leading you to catastrophe.

There are two ways open to you: the path of adventurism which will change nothing and which will scare no one; and the path of acknowledging the realities, and preparing the foundations for peace and tranquillity, for good living and prosperity throughout the length of this land.

If it is the former path that you choose—your lot will assuredly be distress and self-harm; and if it be the latter—then we shall work together for our common good, for your welfare and for the good of the country as a whole.

Histadrut, the Federation of Jewish Workers in Palestine

The Executive Committee

January 1948

APPEAL BY THE HAIFA WORKERS' COUNCIL

To the Arab Residents of Haifa
To the Workers and Officials

For years we lived together in our city, Haifa, in security and in mutual understanding and brotherhood. Thanks to this, our city flourished and developed for the good of both Jewish and Arab residents, and thus did Haifa serve as an example to the other cities in Palestine. Hostile elements have been unable to reconcile themselves to this situation and it has been these elements which have induced conflicts and undermined the relations between you and us. But the hand of justice has overcome them. Our city has been cleared of these elements who fled for their lives and once again order and security have been restored in the city and the way has been opened for the restoration of cooperation and fraternity between the Jewish and Arab workers. At this juncture we believe it necessary to speak in the frankest terms: We are a peace-loving people! There is no cause for the fear which others try to instill in you. There is no hatred in our hearts nor evil in our intentions towards peace-loving residents who, like us, are bent upon work and creative effort. Do not fear! Do not destroy your homes with your own hands; do not block off your sources of livelihood; and do not bring upon yourself tragedy by unnecessary evacuation and self-imposed burdens. By moving out you will be overtaken by poverty and humiliation. But in this city, yours and ours, Haifa, the gates are open for work, for life, and for peace for you and for your families.

UPRIGHT AND PEACE-LOVING WORKERS;

The Haifa Workers' Council and the Histadrut advise you for your own good to remain in the city and to return to your normal work. We are ready to come to your help, in restoring normal conditions, to assist you in obtaining food supplies, and to open up job opportunities.

WORKERS! OUR JOINT CITY, HAIFA, CALLS UPON YOU TO JOIN IN ITS UPBUILDING, ITS ADVANCEMENT, ITS DEVELOPMENT. DO NOT BETRAY YOUR CITY AND DO NOT BETRAY YOURSELVES. FOLLOW

YOUR TRUE INTERESTS AND FOLLOW THE GOOD
AND UPRIGHT PATH.

Federation of Jewish Labor in Palestine
THE HAIFA WORKERS' COUNCIL
28. 4. 48

Appendix 14

EGYPTIAN BATTLE ORDERS

[*Translation of accompanying document dated February 15, 1956, captured in Gaza showing Egyptian preparations for offensive against Israel. This document is one of many of a similar nature captured.*]

Top Secret

3rd Infantry Division   Subject: Directive No. 2 of
(Operations)   Commander 3rd Infantry Div.
Registration No. 558/2/56/2/5/E
Date: 15 February 1956
(From) C.O. Egyptian District, Palestine
(To)   C.O. Reinforced 5th Infantry Brigade

The following is the essence of the Directives of the Commander of the 3rd Division to commanders and officers on the days and dates listed below:

El Arish	Day	1 Feb. 56
Rafah	Day	3 Feb. 56
Khan Yunis	Day	4 Feb. 56
Gaza	Day	4 Feb. 56

Please see to the execution of these Directives by all officers and ensure that these Directives shall not be put down in writing for classification lower than battalion or parallel classification in other units.

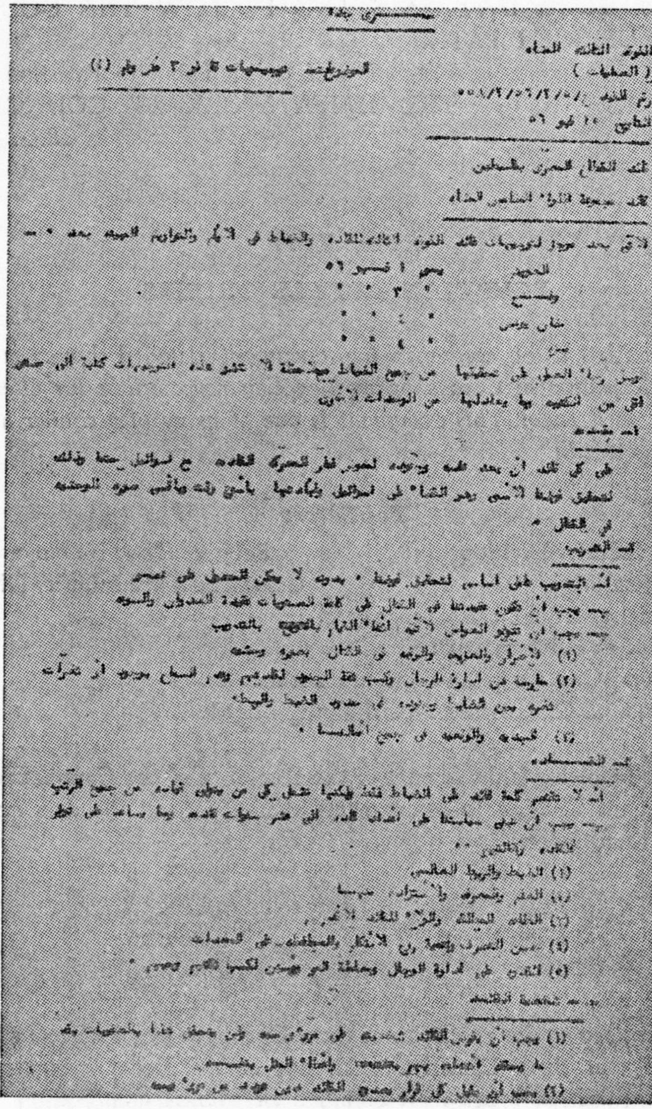

Appendix 14

Egyptian Battle Orders (pp. 221–226)

(1) Introduction

Every commander must prepare himself and his soldiers for the important battle with Israel in which we are fully immersed, with the aim of realizing our lofty tradition, i.e., to overpower and destroy Israel in the shortest possible time and with the greatest brutality and bestiality in battle.

(2) Training

a. Training is the basic factor in the attainment of our goal. Without it, it is impossible to achieve victory.

b. Our faith in battle must be in all ranks, a faith in aggressiveness and speed.

c. The following factors must be part of the training:
1) Perseverance and strong will to fight brutally.
2) Training in leading men and their commanding officers gaining their confidence and affection. Any breach of discipline by soldiers against their officers must be prevented.
3) Earnestness and realism in all our actions.

(3) The Commanders

a. The term Commander is not limited to an officer but applies to anyone of any rank who has to give commands.

b. Our policy must be built up on the preparation of commanders for the next ten years. Aid to prepare commanders and their units . . .
1) High discipline.
2) Knowledge, and the increase of knowledge.
3) Absolute obedience and loyalty to commander.
4) Tact, initiative and care of equipment.
5) Good example in leading men: treating men in order to gain their confidence and affection.

c. Personality of Commander:
1) The commander should control his men more by personal example than by punishment.
2) He must accept every decision of his superior officer without hesitation.
3) When the commander imposes his personality on his unit, hesitations about entering battle are dispelled, regardless of

reasons such as lack of time or equipment. His personality is thus decisive in determining the victorious outcome of the battle.

d. Hence the annual report of officers in general and commanders in particular must include:—

1) The level of ability of the commander.

2) His ability to lead his men.

3) His ability to take care of his equipment.

e. The mistakes made by the commander when he takes fateful decisions or when he executes an order given to him, are not to be condemned, because they teach a lesson that must be put to use. Mistakes emanating from carelessness, however, including those from unifying behavior, should be treated with all severity.

f. Clarity in giving orders, the exposure of errors, the expression of opinions and criticism, are the right and duty of every commander. Forthrightness must be a constructive, and not a destructive factor. It must not be an instrument of degradation. Implied by this is also appreciation of diligence and fitting and constructive guidance of the one who errs.

g. Commanders of all rank must understand that their place is not in offices but rather with their soldiers, either training, directing or educating them, studying their social problems and participating with them in sport and entertainment.

(4) Arms and Equipment

Commanders of all ranks must make certain that:—

a. Every weapon shall be fit for action and efficient use by periodic tests with live ammunition.

b. That vehicles are fit for service. Drivers must be instructed in their proper maintenance. They must be given instructions against overspeeding.

(5) Fortifications

Trenches should be examined to ensure that they are as deep as a man's requirements. Arms must be examined in the light of ability to use them from this position, and with the view of testing the soldier's expertness in aiming and fire.

(6) Inspection

It is expected that a number of commanders of units of the Central District will conduct a tour of inspection in the area of the unit. We must therefore be worthy of appreciation and be able to explain the situation, whether by means of maps or on the ground, each according to his level. Likewise, it is possible that a number of officers and other ranks of the unit will conduct tours of inspection of the battle order of the units of the Central District, within a period of seven hours, beginning and ending in Abu Ageilah.

(7) Hit and Run Policy

Hit and run policy is transformed into aggressive policy as follows:—

a. 5th Brigade—in constant preparedness.

b. 3rd Brigade should arrive by 1st April 1956 for company assault training within the framework of the battalion.

c. 86th Brigade must arrive by 1st April 1956 for company assault training regardless of present shortage of manpower and equipment.

d. The National Guard must complete the training of its volunteers in invasion tactics, without regard to training received preceding their entry into camp. The training of every course must end within seven weeks from arrival at the camp.

(8) Our aim is always "the destruction of Israel."
Remember and act for its attainment.

LIWA (MAJOR-GENERAL) AHMED SALEM, Staff Officer.

Appendix 15

ARAB OPERATIONAL PLANS AND BATTLE ORDERS

On the following pages are reproduced photocopies of portions of the battle orders and operational plans to be used by Arab forces in an attack against Israel. The official Israeli translations of the Arabic text appear on facing pages.

The first document shown is Battle Order Number 6 of the Egyptian Air Force, dated May 26, 1967, and signed by Lieutenant

Colonel Mamdukh Ahmed Taliba, commanding officer of the Egyptian Second Air Brigade. This order, along with similar orders for other units, was captured by advance elements of the Israeli army at El Arish and El-Ser airfields in the Sinai Peninsula. Its special significance is that it establishes a state of readiness for an attack on Israel. This indicates that it is not a contingency plan. Such plans, drawn up for use at an unforeseeable time, and only in case of certain eventualities, necessarily lack an indication of the time when forces are to be mobilized and operations launched. Battle Order Number 6 places the Second Air Brigade in a state of readiness at dawn of May 26, 1967. It may be concluded that an attack was intended to follow shortly thereafter.

Second Air Brigade's mission was to bomb the Israeli airfield at Eilat, together with its aircraft, radar stations, and other ground facilities. Attacking flights were directed to approach designated targets at an altitude of 50 meters. This would have avoided radar detection. Both the assignment and the means of carrying it out indicate a reliance on surprise. From this it may be inferred that Egypt intended not only to attack Israel, but to attack her first.

The next document shown is a Special Operational Order, coded Operation "RA'AD," for the Hashemite Brigade of the Jordanian army. Dated June 7, 1966, and signed by Brigadier General Ahmed Shehada el Huarta, brigade commander, it outlines a plan for a unit of battalion strength to raid the Israeli village of Motzah, in the Jerusalem Hills, to destroy the village and to kill all its inhabitants. Recovered from top-secret safes at brigade headquarters, close to Ramallah, it was found to be identical to operational plans drawn up for each of the six other brigades of the Jordanian army positioned along the west bank of the Jordan River. In all cases, these plans were kept top secret at brigade level, and were to be issued to the battalions only when Jordanian West Front Headquarters gave instructions to commence operations. In all cases, civilian settlements in Israel had been selected as objectives. Code words for various phases of the operation are included in the plans. In the case of Operation "RA'AD," the Brigade Reserve Battalion was instructed to kill all inhabitants of Motzah on receiving the code word "HADHAD" from brigade headquarters. A majority of Motzah's eight hundred inhabitants are women and children.

(سرى للغاية)

قيادة القوات الجوية والدفاع الجوى
قيادة المنطقة الشرقية الجوية
اللواء الجوى الثانى
القيد / ٦٧/١/١/٦٣
التاريخ / ١٩٦٧/٥/٢٦

أمر قتال رقم ٦٧/٦
‏‏‏‏‏‏‏‏‏‏

١ ــ خرائط العاجمة :

مجموعة خرائط مصر وفلسطين ١/ ٥٠٠٠٠٠

٢ ــ مهمة السرب ٢٥ قتال من اللواء الجوى الثانى

ضرب ميناء ايلات ذرية مركزة بقوة سرب

توقيت التنفيذ :

١ ــ تقوم أربعة طائرات بضرب الرادار ومحطة توليد الكهرباء الموجودة بمنتصف الممر وذلك أن تقوم
طائرة القائد ورقم (٢) بضرب منتصف الممر بالصواريخ على رقم (٣) و (٤) ضرب المحطة
بالصواريخ بالدائن شمعض دوران الى جهة اليسار بعد الخروج من الهجوم بالطيران الواطى لمدة
نصف دقيقة (الوقت فوق الهدف من س + ٤ الى س + ٥)

ب ــ تقوم أربعة طائرات بضرب مستودعات الوقود جنوب ايلات ومحطة تحويل المياه بضربة مركزة
بالدائن والصواريخ وعض دوران لجهة اليمين والعودة الى القاعدة بعد الهجوم على أن يقوم القائد
ورقم (٢) بمهاجمة الوقود ويقوم رقم (٣) و (٤) بمهاجمة محطة تحويل المياه (الوقت فوق الهدف
من س + ٥ الى س + ٦)

ج ــ تقوم أربعة الطائرات بضرب محطة الرادار على أن تكون الميناء الجديدة ومخازن البوتاسيوم والفوسفات
التى تباد لنسبى على أن يقوم رقم (١) و (٢) بمهاجمة موتى الرادار ٨ (......)
يقوم رقم (٣) و (٤) (بمهاجمة موتى الرادار (........
ويعطى طابع ثورة لموتى الرادار .

وفى حالة مهاجمة الخزن التبادلى يقوم رقم (١) و (٢) بمهاجمة أونائى الميناء التجارى الجديد
ورقم (٣) و (٤) بمهاجمة مخازن البوتاسيوم على أن يقوم بعمل دوران لليمين بعد الطيران الواطى
لمدة نصف دقيقة تبقى والعودة للقاعدة (الوقت فوق الهدف من س + ٦ الى س + ٧)

د ــ يتم تجنب التشكيلات الثلاث على ارتفاع ٢٠٠ متر والنزول الى ٥٠ متر اثناء الطيران للهدف والعودة
ويعطى طابع خبط الطيران للطائرات الثلاث .

٣ ــ الوحدات المعاونة :

١ ــ سيقوم اللواء الجوى التاسع س ٤٥ بعمل مظلة بقوة ثمانية طائرات من ٢١ لحماية القوة الضاربة من وضع
المظلة الجوية رقم (١) . منطقة المظلة المجرود شمالا وجبل شعيرى جنوبا وحتى ٣٠ كيلو لجهة الغرب
من تل الجبلين . ارتفاع المظلة من ١١ الى ٨ كيلو متر . مدة المظلة من س + ٥٠ الى س + ٩١

ب ــ اللواء الجوى خامس من القاعدة ٢٣٢ س ٤٥ يكون مستعدا فى وضع الاستعداد رقم ١ لتعزيـــز
عملية المظلة الجوية .

٤ ــ تنظيم التعـــاون :

يتم عمل التعاون بين قائد السرب ٢٥ واللواء الجوى ال ٦١ .
ــ بعد ــ

= top secret =

Air Force and Air Defence H Q
Eastern Air Command H Q
2 5 9 Air Base
2 Air Brigade

Reference   63/1/1/67
Date   26/5/1967

BATTLE ORDER NO. 6/67

1.   MAP REFERENCE :   EGYPT and PALESTINE   1: 500,000.

2.   25 Fighter Squadron   2 Air Brigade -- ASSIGNMENTS :

Concentrated bombing of Eilat port by Squadron force

METHOD OF ATTACK:

a. Four aircraft will bomb the airfield and electric power station situated
    halfway along the coastal strip.   The aircraft of the Squadron OC and
    aircraft No. 2 will bomb the strip center with missiles, while Nos. 3 and
    4 will attack the power station with rockets and guns. Within half a
    minute the aircraft will break low altitude formation, turning left.
    Over target: H hour ⊥ 4 to H hour ⊥ 5.

b. Four aircraft will bomb the fuel tanks south of Eilat, and the water
    desalination plant --- concentrated bombing with guns and rockets, turning
    right and returning to air base after attack.   Squadron OC and No. 2
    aircraft attack the fuel dump and Nos. 3 and 4 the desalination plant.
    Over target= H Hour ⊥ 5 to H Hour ⊥ 6.

c. Four aircraft will bomb the radar station with the new port and potash
    and phosphate stores serving as alternate targets.

METHOD

Nos. 1 and 2 will attack 86 Radar Station (FBS - 86); 3 and 4 will attack
Radar Station (FBS 100). Attached is a photo of the radar position.

Alternate mission of Nos. 1 and 2 will be to attack boats anchored in the new
civil port while Nos. 3 and 4 will attack the potash warehouses, turning
right after half a minute, while flying at low altitude and returning to base.
Over target: H Hour ⊥ 6 to H hour ⊥ 7.

d. All three formations will assemble at 200 meters altitude, descending to
    50 meters on course to target and back. Attached is a flight plan for the
    three sorties.

تابــــــــع   (٢)

ه‍ـ الاشـــــــارة

يتم الاتصال بدائرة الاتصال ل ١٤ على الموجة رقم (٤ ٢٢و٣٣٦ الطالب المدنية من الترددالمعي ٢١ وبكترن التردد رقم ١ ٧و١٢٥ ٥ احتياطى ٠

١ ـ مركز قائد اللواء

يتم قيادة التشكيل من الجو وذلك بالطيران قبل د طلعة الا ول‍ـــــــى ١٠ العدد ٣١٠ لاعداء أن أيام جديــدة طارئة عن طريق الدائرة ل ١٤ ٠

٢ ـ وقت الاستعداد

يتم الاستعداد من اول شرؤ يوم ٢٦/٥/١٦٦٧ ٠
تحدد ساعة س بواسطة قائد النوا ت الجوية والدفاع الجوى فى حينــــــــه ٠

مقد م طيار/ صدقى احمد خليبة
قائد اللواء الجوى الثـــــــانى
النوتى/

صورة الى / قائد القاعدة الجوي‍ـــــــ:ة ٢٥٩
صورة الى / قائد الا سراب الخامسة والـ‍.‍ـــــرون
صورة الى / قائد القاعدة الجوي‍ــ ٢٦٠

4. ORGANIZATION OF COORDINATION

    Organized jointly by OC 25 Squadron and 61 Air Brigade.

5. SIGNALS

    Communications will be maintained by an IL-14 aircraft on wavelength 133.3 (4)
    for support request by MIG 21 aircraft.   Frequency 1-7 and 125 will serve as
    reserve.

6. BRIGADE COMMANDERS POSITION

    From the first sortie, command of the formation will be carried out from the
    air while 310 Base will issue emergency orders through the IL- 14 aircraft.

7. DURATION OF STATE OF READINESS

    State of Readiness will commence at dawn of 26.5.1967.
    H. Hour will be determined by OC air forces and Air Defence.

    (signed)

    Lt. Colonel   (PILOT) Mamdukh Ahmed Taliba
                           OC 2 Air Brigade

Copy to=

    OC   259 Air Base
    OCs   25 Squadron
    OC 260 Air Base.

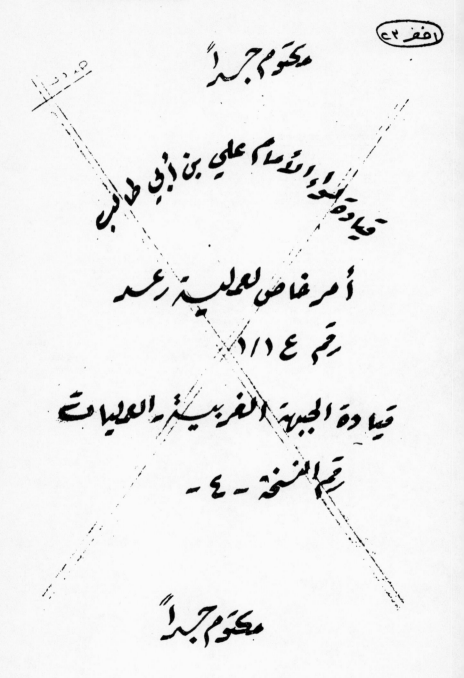

مكتوم جداً

(افقر ٢)

قيادة القوات المسلحة الإسلام علي بن أبي طالب

أمر خاص لعملية رعد

رقم ١٤/١

قيادة الجبهة الغربية - العمليات

قسم الخطة - ٤ -

مكتوم جداً

TOP SECRET

H.Q. Imam Ali ben Abi Taleb Brigade

Special Orders for Operation "RA'AD"

No. A1/1

Headquarters Western Front/Operations

Copy No. 4

TOP SECRET

قائمة التوزيع

الفلقات (ب)	المطبوع (أ)	رقم النسخة	الوحـــــــدة	التسلسل
١	١	١	كلية ليه بن حارثه ٢٢	١
١	١	٢	كلية عبدالرحمن الغافقي ٢٥	٢
١	٢	٣	كلية اسامه بن زيد	٣
١	١	٤	قيادة الجبهة الغربية/المطبعة	٤
١	١	٥	كلية مدفعية الميدان الأولى	٥
١	١	٦	الكاتــــمـــة	٦
١	١	٧	حفظ لدى الركن العسكري	٧

ملاحظة :

لا يوزع هذا الأمر الا في حينه للمعنيين باستثناء قيادة الجبهة الغربية

LIST OF DISTRIBUTION

Serial No.	THE UNIT	Copy No.	Annex "A"	Draught "A'"
1	ZEID BEN HARTHA/33 Battalion	1	1	1
2	ABD EL RAHMAN EL GHAFEQI/35 - Battalion	2	1	1
3	ISSAMU BEN ZEID Battalion	3	1	1
4	H. Q. Western Front /Operations	4	1	1
5	1st Field Arty. Regt.	5	1	1
6	The Brigadier	6	1	1
7	Reserve held by Brigade Major	7	1	1

Remark:

This Order will be distributed only when decided by Order of the H. Q. Western Front.

نسخة جيدا

رقم النسخة (1)

قيادة لواء الاقدم علي بن ابي طالب
(العمليات)
•••••••••••••••••••
الرقم – م / ع / ا /
التاريخ – ٧ حزيران ١٩٦٦

امر عمليات خاص لعملية (وحد)
خرائط المراجعه
التقدير ٥ رقم الله ٥ سلطيت ٥محو
اللمد ٥ مالمائل ايبم ١/ ٠٠٠ر٥٠

الى – قائد كتيبة احتياط اللواء / ٢٧

٠١ الموقف
أ • العدو
(١) لواء العدو في مستعمرة موئسا (١٦٤٧١٣٤٢) يسكن هذه
المستعمره حوالي ٨٠٠ شخصا يحملون السلاح مهيأ لمسم
عظم بحراسة المستعمره •
(٢) تغطي المستعمره خمسة والاف ليله حولها •
(٣) يوجد خنادق محاوره حول المستعمره وتحتل عند الحاجه •
(٤) المستعمره محاطه بلا سلاك الشائكه •
(٥) ميله من الاسلحه وسلوف يحمر ميوتها بالقوميه الاحمر •
(٦) تحتاج لوا المستعمره من ٥ــ٧ دقائق للعبأته واحتلال المراكز
عند الحاجه •
(٧) مراكز العدو الثانيه من المستعمره والتي يمكن ان تتدخل في
المعركه للتجهد •
(ا) معسكر القطلب (١٦٢١٣٢) لوء سريه مشاة مدم
السام مسانده وموقعها الدفاعي في الرطـــــــم
(١٦٣٧١٣٣٧) •
(ب) معسكر نيتني • (١٧٠١٣٢١) به سريه كتف اللوء
السادس •
(ج) معسكر ابولؤز (١٦٠٠١٣٤١) لوته سريه حدود
(٨) السيطره الجويه لصالح العدو •

ب • لواتنا
(١) قصد قيادة الجبهه الغربيه القيام بعمليه للغاره على مستعمره
(موئسا) وتدميرها وقتل من فيها •
(٢) اسند هذا الواجب الى قائد لوء الاقدم علي بن ابـــــي
طالب والذي بدوره اعطى هذه المهمه الى قائد كتيبـــة
احتياط اللوء •

نسخة حدا

Copy No. 4

H.Q. IMAM ALY BEN ABI TALIB Brigade
   (Operations)

Registration No.: A'1/1/1
Date :   7th June 1966

Special Operational Order "Operation (RA'AD)"
Ref. Maps:
Jerusalem, Ramallah, Salfit
Ag'ur, Lud, Yafo—Tel-Aviv
         1:50000

To: Commander Reserve Battalion 27th Brigade.

1. **Situation.**
   A. Enemy.
   1) The enemy forces in MOTZA Colony (16471342). The inhabitants
      number about 800 persons, engage in agriculture and have
      guard details in the colony.

   2) The colony mans five night guard-positions around it.

   3) The colony is surrounded by slit-trenches which are manned
      when necessary.

   4) The colony has barbed-wire fences.

   5) The houses of the colony are built of concrete, and some have
      red-tile roofs.

   6) The forces of the colony need 5-7 minutes to man their positions
      from the moment of surprise.

   7) Enemy camps close to the colony which can take part in the
      campaign and advance reinforcements:--
      a) CASTEL Camp (163133) one Infantry Co. with support detachments.
         The defence position of this unit is on the hill (16371337).
      b) SHNELLER Camp (170132) 6th Brigade Reconaissance Co.
      c) ABU GOSH Camp (16301349) Border Police Co.

   8) Air superiority to enemy.

   B. Own Forces:
   1) The intention of H.Q. Western Front is to carry out a raid on
      MOTZA Colony, to destroy it and to kill all its inhabitants.

   2) This task was allocated to the Brigadier of the IMAM ALY BEN ABI
      TALEB Brigade who will further it to the Brigade Reserve Battalion.

                                                      ../2

- ٢ -

سري للغاية

٠ج - المنفذون والمنتظرون   (عند صدور الامر بالعملية الى الكتيبة الاحتياطيها)
                              خطة الامر   واللواء العسكرية في منطقة الشيخ عبدالعـــزيز
                                              والرداء من الكتيبة الموجوده على يسار والجمعـــة
                                              اللواء ٠

                              بلاسلاك المباشر   بطارية مدفعية الميدان/ ٢ من كتيبة مدفعيـــة
                                              الميدان / ١ ٠
                                              فئة خلد مدفع ميدان
                                              حظيرة حمى مباشر

٠٢ المهمة   كتيبة احتياط اللواء تقوم بحماية النار على مستعمرة موشا وتدميرهـا
                  وتنسل من لهما حال استلام الكتيبة الرئيسه (هدهد) من قيادة اللواء ٠

٠٣ التنفيذ

أ - عام

(١)   تدور العملية ليلا وعلى مرحلة واحده بسرية مشاة ٠ فئة مشاة ٠
        فئة خلد مدفع ميدان اللتحام وتدميره وسريه كالمرتكه ٠ الاسلحة
        المساندة بالكتيبة قوة لاعده وسريه ٠ عناصر تمهيد وخله مــــــ
        لفح التجمعاء ٠

(٢)   جميع الكتيبة تتحرك من منطقة التنزيل بالسيارات عليها على الاقدام
        الى منطقة التجمع وتلملة التوزيع ٠

ب - سرية مشاة   سرية التحام وتدمير ٠

(١)   الواجب ٠   تدمير مستعمرة موشا واقل من لهما ٠

(٢)   التجمع ٠   فايط ملاحظة مدفعية
                        فئة خلد مدفع ميدان

(٣)   اجاده التندابر

(أ)   بعد انتهاء الواجب تنسحب الى نقطة الالتقاء الخاص
        بها ثم تتابع مسيرها الى النقط (١٦٤٤٦٣١٢) جنوب
        غرب قرية بيت صوبها ٠

(ب)   تصلك بطريق انسحابها من شرق الشيخ عبدالعزيز في
        الطريق الترابي المؤدى الى قرية بيت صوبها وحسكل
        منطقة التجمع (١٦٤١٣٧٠) ٠

(ج)   تتحرك مع الكتيبة بالسيارات من طريق مثلث الجبير/بدو
        الى مثلث بيت عور/ بدو ثم الى مزائرها مرتفعات جنابوثا ٠

ج - سرية مشاة ٠ الاسلحة الثانية بالكتيبة ٠   قوة التاخده ٠

(١)   الواجب

(أ)   تنظيم الحماوه الى قوة الالتحام بسلمة الهدف بمايلة
        عند يده عند نفح الدجيم وعند الانتهاء من التدمير ٠

مكتم جدا.

- 2 -

C. **Attached and Detached:** (When giving Reserve Battalion the Order
to proceed)

Under Command
The forces in position at SHEIH' ABD
EL AZIZ Area and the RADAR from the
Battalion responsible for the Left
wing of the Brigade.

Direct Support
2nd Field Battery 1st Field Arty.
Regt. 1 platoon Field Engineers.
1 section casualty collecting.

2. **The Task:** The Brigade Reserve Battalion will raid MOTZA Colony, will
destroy it and will kill all persons in it upon receiving the code-
word "HADHAD" from Brigade H. Q.

3. **Method.**
   A. **General.**
      1) Night raid in one phase by Infantry Co. plus platoon plus
         Engineer platoon for the breaching and destroying, one
         Infantry Co. less one platoon plus battalion support weapons
         as firm base, one infantry Co. plus elements of pioneers and
         field engineers for blocking off reinforcements.

      2) The whole battalion will march from the place of disembarkment
         from the vehicles, to the dispersal area.

   B. **One Company plus one platoon** - for breaching and destroying.

      1) **The task:** The destruction of the colony and killing all
         its inhabitants.

      2) **Attached:** A.A.O. (Advanced Artillery Observer)
         One platoon field engineers.

      3) **Reorganisation:**
         a) On finishing the mission it will retire to the assembly
            point allocated to it and from there will march to point
            16441366, South-West of BEIT SORIK Village.
         b) Axis of retreat, East of SHEIH ABD EL AZIZ and from there
            by track leading to BEIT SORIK and up to the deployment
            area (16401370).
         c) The Company will travel with the Battalion in vehicles
            from ELG'IB BIDU cross-roads to BIR A'WAR-BIDU cross-
            roads and from there to its base in the BETUNYA Hills.

   C. **One Company less a platoon plus Battalion Support Weapons.-** Firm Base.

      1) **The Task:**
         a) Supporting the breaching force and harassing the target
            with heavy fire when the raiding party is discovered and
            after it finishes the destruction.

../3

- ٣ -

تكتم جداً

(ب) ستر الالتحاق - قوة الالتحام لتصميم على مساكة أمنه من نصوان العدو .

(ج) تتحرك من نقطة التزويح الى مكان المقاعده الثلاثه (ج) في التقاطه (١١٤٤١٣٥٢)

(د) تتسحب هذه السريه بعد انسحاب حمى اللواء وعجب ان يكاتم قائد هذه اللواء من ان سريه اللواء قد قادرت من تنفيذ الواجب .

(٢) التحميع   حلب ولطة حداة بند لحمه
             ماسها على مشرك

(٣) قاعدة التسليم

(أ) تتسحب بعد التربة العملية بكله رمزيه من قائد الكتيبه وتسلك الطريق الترابي من أسمين عبدالعزيز الى قيمة بيت سوية. ثم الى نقطة التحمع والركوب بالسيارات .

(ب) تتحرك بالسيارات مع الكتيبه الى مراكز الكتيبه الحمى (بطونها) عن طريق شكلت الجمير / بيث مور فيمانونها .

صرية • لانة التعديد •   لمنع وصول امداد وتجزئ وترزيع عن موضعين .

(١) الجناح الايمن   في (١٢٢٧١٢٤٢) الطريق الرئيسي السودى الى محمد راجو فوه .

(٢) الجناح الايسر   في (١١٦٢٣١٢٤٢) سلم الثل الواقي بالجمه الترله من مستعمرة موتها والمشرف على طريق الله س/ كالوليا

(٢) الواجب

(أ) منع وصول اي نجدات او تجزئرة ثك بلغ بارسالها الحدوعلى هذه الداسرق .

(ب) الاحتباء من ثوات العدو وابها اذا نادمت لنجدة هذه المستعمره .

(ج) تدمير الناص المؤدى والى المستعمر عندها يتطلب الموقف ذلك .

(د) تتحرك من نقطة التزويح كل اوم الى مكانها المخصص لها بانشاء (ج) العراني .

(٤) قاعدة التنفير

(أ) الجناح الايمن • بعد التربة الواجب وبندا يحماى له الامر بالانسحاب يسلك الطريق من قرب مركــز التحمي عبدالا نزدحفي انه بيث سوية . ثم الى نقطة التحمي ولا ركب مع بقية الكتيبه .

(ب) الجناح الايسر • بعد التربة الواجب وبندا يحماى له الامر بالانسحاب يبث الطريق الجزاى المتجهه الى حمة الشيخ عبدالعزيز بالحمه الترله حتى حمة النوزع • بيث سوية • فنقطة التحمع عندكـ المكك الركوب بالسيارات .

تكم جداً

- 3 -

b) Supporting the Assault Force in its retreat until it is beyond the range of the enemy's fire.

c) The Company will move from the dispersal point to the place of the base - see Draught A', at 16441353.

d) The Company will retire after all the other forces complete their retreat. The C.O. of the Force will make sure that all the forces of the mission have retired.

2) Attached: A.A.O.

        M.F.S. (Mobile Fire Spatter)

3) Reorganization:

a) The Company will retire in full at the end of the operation when ordered by the Battalion Commander and will move by the track from SHEIH ABD EL AZIZ to BEIT SORIK, from there to the assembly point and from there by vehicles.

b) The Company will travel in vehicles with the Battalion to the Battalion's base at BITUNYA by way of EL GIB--BEIT AWAR Crossroads - BITUNYA.

D. Company plus pioneer platoon - Blocking-off reinforcements will establish two Road Blocks:

1) Right position; at (16371342) on the main road leading to ABU GOSH Camp.

2) Left position: (16631342) On the slope of the TEL situated on the East side of the MOTZA Colony and overlooking the JERUSALEM - KOLORYA Road.

3) The task:

a) To prevent the arrival of any reinforcements or forwarding succour which the enemy might send by their routes.

b) To engage the enemy in combat if he comes to the colony's aid.

c) Cut-off the road leading to the Colony, if the conditions require it, and that before the passage of the enemy.

d) Every force will move from the dispersal point to its position as seen on draught "A" which is attached.

4) Reorganization:

a) The right position: When the task is accomplished and when it receives the code word for the order to retire, will move by the route west of SHEIH ABD EL AZIZ up to BEIT SORIK Village and will then proceed to the assembly area, embarkation point with the rest of the battalion.

b) The Left position: When the task is accomplished and when it receives the code word for the order to retire, will move by the route leading in the direction of SHEIH ABD EL AZIZ from the East up to HIRBET LOZA, BEIT SORIK, assembly area and embarkation point.

../4

‏- ٤ -

‏مكتم جدا

‏• هـ‏ ‏فئة الزرير

‏(١) الموقع في (٣١٤٧١٣٥٦) شمال غرب الشيخ عبدالعزيز.

‏(٢) الواجب كما في خطة النار الملحق (أ) البول.

‏(٣) مبادئ التنفيذ. بعد انتهاء الواجب تنسحب من مواقعها لعبتك الطريق الترابي من الشيخ عبدالعزيز الى منسوبيك منطقة التجمع وتتحرك مع الكتيبه الى منطقة الركوب بالسيارات.

‏• و‏ ‏فئة التعميه _ تلتحق حسب مو. مع لواء منع التجداء.

‏(١) الواجب تقم بوضع النظم عند الآلية على الطرق الوؤديه الى مصد محورة مؤتسا ويأمر من قائد لواء منع التجداء.

‏(٢) مبادئ التقدم. تنسحب مع لواء منع التجداء حتى الوصول الى منطقة التجمع والركوب بالسيارات.

‏• ز‏ ‏التدليه.

‏(١) الواجب كما في خطة النار الملحق (أ) البول.

‏(٢) تلحق بنقاط ملاحظته لمكان القاعده وقوة منع التجداء.

‏• م‏ ‏فئة المتقدمه

‏(١) الواجب

‏(أ) فتم ثغرات بالأسلاك الشائكه معدل لكل لغم ثغره.

‏(ج) تدمير مستمره (موتسا) تدميرا كاملا بالتفجيرسواء بعد خروج قوة الاقتحام من تطهير البنايات.

‏(جـ) تلتحق بعد مباشرة الى قوة منع التجداء.

‏(٢) مبادئ التقدم. تنسحب مع قوة الاقتحام الى منطقة الركوب بالسيارات ثم تتحرك مع بقية الكتيبه الى موقعها.

‏• ط‏ ‏تعليمات التنسيق

‏(١) ساعة الصفر تعين في حينها من قائد الكتيبه
‏(٢) خطة النزول من السيارات ومنطقة الركوب بالعوده
‏(٣) خطة التجمع
‏(٤) نقطة التوزيع‏ ‏}‏ ‏الثبات
‏(٥) محور التقدم
‏(٦) توقيت اللواء ٥ الاقتحام ٥ القاعده ٥ منع التجداء.
‏(٧) خط البدء
‏(٨) الهدف
‏(٩) منطقة الركوب بالسيارات
‏(١٠) سرعة التقدم ١٠٠ يارد لكل ثلاث دقائق.

‏مكتم جدا

- 4 -

E. <u>Mortar Platoon:</u>
  1) Will take up position at 16471356 North-West of SHEIH ABD EL AZIZ.
  2) <u>The task:</u> According to annexed plan of fire (A).
  3) <u>Reorganization:</u> When the task is accomplished will retire from its position by way of SHEIH ABD EL AZIZ Village to BEIT SORIK - assembly area - and will move with the Battalion to the embarkation point.

F. <u>Pioneer platoon:</u> Will detach a reinforced section to the Blocking-off forces.
  1) <u>The task:</u> Will lay anti-vehicle and anti-personel mines on the road leading to MOTZA Colony when ordered by the C.O. Blocking-off force.
  2) <u>Reorganization:</u> The section will retire with the Blocking-off force to the assembly area and to the embarkation point.

G. <u>Artillery:</u>
  1) <u>Task:</u> According to annexed plan of fire (A).
  2) A.A.O.s will be attached to the firm base and to the Blocking-off force.

H. <u>Engineer platoon:</u>
  1) <u>Task:</u>
     a) Breaching the wire fences on an average of one breach per platoon.
     b) Will completely destroy the colony with explosives, after the breaching through force finishes mopping-up the Houses.
     c) The platoon will attach elements to the Blocking-off force.
  2) <u>Reorganization:</u> The platoon will retire with the breaching force to the embarkation area and from there will travel in vehicles with the Battalion to BITUNYA.

I. <u>Co-ordination:</u>
  1) "H" hour will be decided upon in due time by the Battalion Commander
  2) Disembarkation and embarkation points.
  3) Deployment area.
  4) Dispersal point.
  5) Route of advance.
  6) Dispersal of forces, breaching, firm base, cutting-off.
  7) Starting line.
  8) The target.
  9) Embarkation area.
  10) Rate of advance 100 yards every three minutes.

  — See draught "A"

سري - ٥ -

مكتم - ٥ا.

٤. الشؤون الادارية

أ • الفئات — نقل الفئات العالقة في منطقة التجمع شمال بيه سوريا (١٦٤١٣٧)

ب • الارزاق — تعطى وجبة العشاء في منطقة التجمع ولا تحصل الارزاق •

ج • الذخيره — تحمل الذخيره والمتفجرات الطرو لهذه العملية

د • الذخايه — تخلى الاصابات الى مولج اسعاف الكتيبه بواسطة العجلات الموجوده في قرية (بيه سوريا)

هـ • اللباس — لها المعركة كامل ويستحسن ان تكون الالبسه خفيفه قدر المستطاع •

٥. القياده والمواصلات

أ • قياده اللواء — تكون بمركزها الحالي •

ب • قياده الكتيبه • في كافة مراحل العملية تكون خلف قوة القتحام

ج • المواصلات •

(١) لا تغيير على شبكة الاتصالات السلكيه واللاسلكيه •

(٢) يفرض الصمت اللاسلكي حتى لحم المجم بحيث تبدأ خطة الرمي للمدفعيه والهوتر •

د • الكلمات الرمزيه

الكلمة	المعنى	تعطى من قبل
(مدهد)	بدأ الحمله من قبل الكتيبه الاحتياطيه	قائد اللواء
(عمان)	تدمير الهدف	قائد الكتيبه
(سلمان)	مغادرة منطقة التجمع	قائد الكتيبه
(كعك)	مغادرة منطقة الركوب بالسيارات	قائد الكتيبه
(اريد)	عودة الكتيبه الى مولعها الاحتياطي	قائد الكتيبه

صـــــــدرلوا

التوقيع
قائد لواء الامام علي بن ابي طالب
((احمد حماده الحوازشكيه))

كالمة التوزيع • المراقبه

الملاحق

الملحق (أ) خطة النار

الشلاف (ع) منطقة النزيل • التجمع • توزيع اللواء نقطة التوزيع • خط البدء • الهدف •

مكتم حدا

- 5 -

4. **Administration:**

A) **Transport:** Combat echelon vehicles will remain in assembly area North of BEIT SORIK (164137).

B) **Food:** Supper will be served in the assembly area, and no rations will be carried.

C) **Ammunition:** Ammunition and explosives as will be decided for this Operation.

D) **Medical:** The casualties will be evacuated to the Battalion Advanced Dressing station by stretcher Bearers which are in the village (BEIT SORIK).

E) **Clothing:** Full battle dress. Light clothing is recommended.

5. **Communication and Control:**

A) **Brigade H.Q.:** At its present place.

B) **Battalion H.Q.:** In all the phases of the operation behin the Assault force.

C) **Communications:**

1) No change in wireless or telephone nets.

2) Wireless silence will be observed up to discovery of the attack, when the artillery and mortar shelling will begin.

D) **Codes:**

Word	Meaning	Ordered by
"HADHAD"	Reserve Battalion starts Operation	Brigadier
"MA'AN"	Destruction of target	Battalion C.O.
"SALMAN"	Leaving Assemby area	Battalion C.O.
"MOHAMED"	Leaving Embarkation area	Battalion C.O.
"ARBED"	Battalion back to reserve positions	Battalion C.O.

Zaim

Brigadier IMAM ALI BEN ABI TALEB Brig.

(AHMED SHEHADA EL HUARTA)

Information:

Distribution List: Annexed.

Annexes:

"A" Annex - Plan of fire.

"A'" draught: disembarking area, assembly, division of forces, dispersal point, starting line, target.

../6

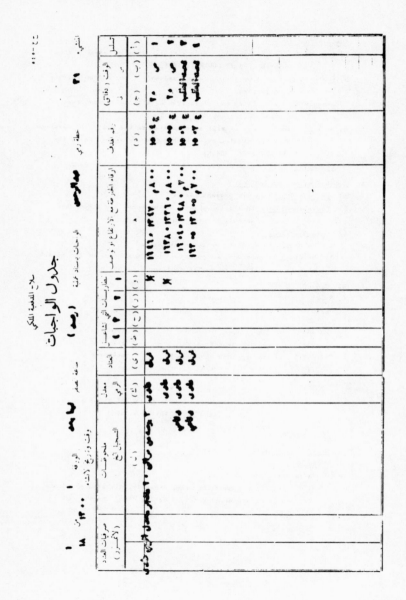

ROYAL ARTILLERY CORPS

FIRE MISSIONS PLAN

Prepared by: 39   Fire plan: Abd El Rahman   Missions "RA'AD"   "H" Hour:Later   Page: 1 of 1
Time and Date: 181300

SERIAL No.	Time in Minutes From	to	Target No.	Number on Map. Elevation. Description.	Batteries in action 1	2	3	4	Ammunition	Rate of Fire	Remarks	Ammunition Expanded	
A	B	C	D	E	F	G	H	I	J	K	L	M	N
1	H	20	G 1504	800m.; 1347; 1646.	½				High Explosive	Normal	3" Mortar from 'H' to 20	Explosive	Normal rate
2	H	20	G 1505	800m.; 1336; 1638.	½				High Explosive	Normal			
3	On Demand		G 1506	700m.; 1348; 1604.					High Explosive	Normal	Defensive fire.		
4	On Demand		G 1507	700m.; 1345; 1635.					High Explosive	Normal	Defensive fire.		

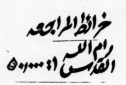

خارطة المراجعة
القدس ١:٥٠٠٠٠

الشفاف ، ع ، مطلق من سوا

لأمر عمليات رقم ع/١/١
تاريخ ٧ حزيران ١٩٦٦

١
١٦٥

١٤٠

منطقة النزول ⊙

منطقة التجمع ⊙

نقطة التوزيع ⊙

محور التقدم

أ،ب القاعدة

خط السير

الهدف

كمين أيسر ⊙   ⊙ كمين أيمن   + ⊙

مرتفع بنطل ٥

٢/١٦٥
١٣٤

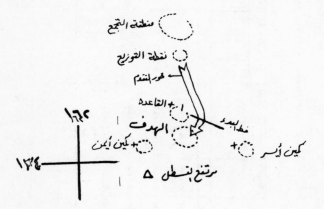

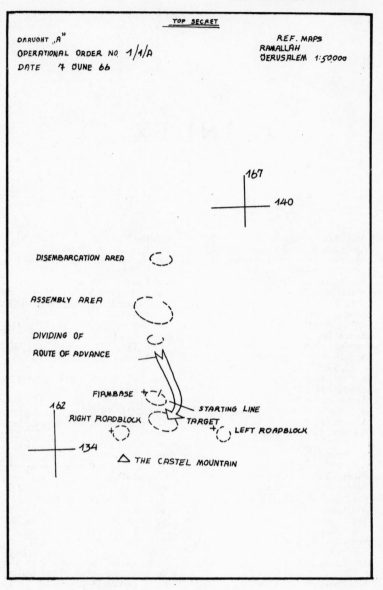

TOP SECRET

DRAUGHT „A"
OPERATIONAL ORDER NO. 1/1/A
DATE   7 JUNE 66

REF. MAPS
RAMALLAH
JERUSALEM 1:50000

167

140

DISEMBARCATION AREA

ASSEMBLY AREA

DIVIDING OF
ROUTE OF ADVANCE

FIRMBASE

STARTING LINE

162

RIGHT ROADBLOCK   TARGET   LEFT ROADBLOCK

134

△ THE CASTEL MOUNTAIN

INDEX

General Tire and Rubber Company,
133
Genocide, 40, 58, 105
Geopolitics, 15
Germany, 23, 26, 51, 53, 63, 81, 133
Ghettoes, 22, 55
Giado, 119-20
Glubb, John Bagot, 93, 95
Golan Heights, 173
Gonen, 174
Great Britain: and the Arabs, 28, 52,
54, 99, 159; authoritarianism of,
40, 42, 49, 89, 119; colonialism of,
4, 63; and Mandate of Palestine,
18, 27, 29, 33, 43, 45, 47, 51, 53,
55, 71, 76-78, 81, 83-84, 86, 88-
92, 94; Middle East affairs of, 3,
34, 68, 81, 138, 140; politics in,
67, 70, 153; and Canal Zone, 147-
148, 151, 154; and World War I,
23, 25, 27, 81; and World War II,
4, 7; sympathy for Zionism, 24
Great Dispersion, 14-15
Great Powers, 32, 85
Great Temple, 13-14
Greece, 11-12, 14-15, 21, 50, 60-61,
105, 107
Gromyko, Andrei, 160-61
Guerrilla warfare, 3, 5, 52, 60, 62-63,
85, 89, 114, 128, 138, 140, 143,
163
Gulf of Aqaba, 6, 27, 135, 156, 174
Gulf of Oman, 65

Hadassah, 44
Hadassah Medical Center, 87
Hadi, Awni Abdul, 130
Haganah, 48, 52, 62-63, 69-71, 83-
84, 86-87, 89, 91, 96-98, 109
Hagar, 9
Haifa, port of, 43, 47, 63, 69, 71-72,
83, 89-91, 96, 102, 109, 130, 133,
137, 150, 171, 176
Hammarskjöld, Dag, 101, 143, 156-
157
Haram Ramet el Kalil, 9
Hashemite: Bedouins, 28; Emir of
Mecca, 26; Jordan, 13, 103
Hawari, Nimr Al, 110
Hebrew University, 51, 54
Hebrews: origin of name, 8; yearning
for God, 9; in Palestine, 10; pray
for Jerusalem, 13
Hebron, 9, 23, 48-49, 82, 95
Hedera, 40
Hejaz, 27-29

Herzl, Theodor, 17-20, 22, 92
Hess, Moses, 20
Hilton Hotel Corporation, 133
Holy Alliance, 20
Holy City, 13, 16, 27, 89. *See also*
Jerusalem
Holy Land, 14, 34, 36, 61, 70
Hospitals, 2, 6, 35, 44, 54, 56, 118,
120, 160
Hourani, Akham, 116
Housing, 6, 111, 121, 160
Hovevei Zion, 19
Husein ibn-Ali, Sherif, 26, 28-29
Husein-McMahon agreement, 27, 29,
33
Hussein, King of Jordan, 115, 174,
176
Hyksos Dynasty, 10

Idolatry, 9
Illiteracy, 3, 64, 160
Immigration, 22, 32, 37, 39, 44, 50,
53, 55, 70, 73, 76, 81, 131, 161
Imperialism, 4, 7, 58, 67, 139, 154,
166, 179
India, 26, 63, 70, 105, 107
Indian Ocean, 3
Industrialization, 41, 54, 176-77
International Air Service Transit
Agreement, 132
International Telephone and Tele-
graph, 133
Iran, 140, 178
Iraq, 8, 23, 26, 28-29, 33-34, 38, 62,
65-66, 70, 74, 87, 89, 91, 93, 95-
97, 99, 107, 116, 118-19, 134,
140, 162, 178
Irgun Zvai Leumi, 52, 87
Irredentism, 110
Irrigation, 23, 35, 44, 56, 117, 139,
143
Isaac, 8
Ishmael, 9
Islam, 3, 26, 29, 32, 34, 119-20, 159
Island of Crete, 12
Island of Rhodes, 100, 106, 128
Ismailia, 151
Israel, State of: aid from France,
147; Arab hatred of, 5, 107, 110,
135, 141; and Armistice Agreement, 101, 103; attacked, 60, 92,
94, 96, 98, 101, 120, 143, 168;
blockade of, 99, 111, 137-40; boycott of, 129, 132, 134, 136; created, 1, 7, 20, 77, 92, 118;
development plans of, 117-18,